Introduction to Latin America

Introduction to Latin America

Twenty-First Century Challenges

Peadar Kirby

SAGE Publications
London • Thousand Oaks • New Delhi

The author and publishers gratefully acknowledge the permission of Serpost, Servicios Postales del Peru, S.A., to reproduce the Peruvian stamps used in the cover design.

SAGE Publications Ltd
6 Bonhill Street
London EC2A 4PU

SAGE Publications Inc.
2455 Teller Road
Thousand Oaks, California 91320

SAGE Publications India Pvt Ltd
B-42, Panchsheel Enclave
Post Box 4109
New Delhi - 100 017

British Library Cataloguing in Publication data

A catalogue record for this book is avaiable from the British Library

ISBN 0 7619 7372 9
ISBN 0 7619 7373 7 (pbk)

Library of Congress Control Number 2002112350

Typeset by Keyword Typesetting Services Ltd
Printed in Great Britain by The Cromwell Press, Trowbridge, Wiltshire

For Judy Ress and David Molineaux,
dearest friends, who live so generously the values that
continue to make Latin America a place of hope

Contents

Section I   Legacies

Section II   Neoliberal Reformation

Interlude

Section III   Popular Responses

Section IV   Prospects

List of Tables

List of Boxes

Preface

For much of the 1990s Latin America and the Caribbean all but disappeared from the horizon of interest of the world's news media. After two decades during which brutal military dictatorships, revolution first in Chile and then in Nicaragua, and guerrilla struggles in El Salvador and Guatemala had captured the world's attention, the casual observer could be forgiven for thinking that the embrace of the free market had magically resolved the region's problems. Indeed, sections of the media explicitly reported that this was so, like the World Bank confusing wishful thinking for fact. Therefore, when Sage Publications' commissioning editor for politics and international studies, Lucy Robinson, suggested to me in late 1999 that the time was ripe for a new introductory textbook on Latin America, she found a ready response. After a decade (and in some countries more) of thorough liberalizing reforms in the economies of virtually all the countries of the region, and at a time when the region's states were, for the first time in its history, ruled by elected civilian governments (with the exception of Cuba), the time did seem ripe for a new introductory overview that would take stock of these sweeping reforms, assess their impact on the lives and livelihoods of Latin Americans, and offer some diagnosis of the region's prospects as it entered the new millennium.

This daunting undertaking would not have been possible without the support and practical help of a large number of people. Facilitated by being granted a year's sabbatical leave from my academic duties in Dublin City University, I was able to make this book my principal undertaking over that period. Moving with my family to Santiago, Chile, the staff of the Political Science Institute at the Catholic University of Chile provided me with an ideal academic setting in which to undertake my research and begin my writing. While I am grateful to all my colleagues there, both academic and administrative, my special thanks go to Dr Alfredo Rehren, the Institute's director, for his warm welcome to me, to Professor Patricio Valdivieso who could not have been kinder or more helpful in everything from academic contacts to satisfying my need for an occasional drinking partner, and to Ms Adriana Sanchez, the Institute's secretary, who with the greatest efficiency and endless patience provided much needed administrative support. I also wish to thank the students who took my courses and coped with my less than perfect Spanish with good humour. I learnt a lot about Latin America from their contributions to my classes and I was impressed by their high academic standards. As a family, our immense gratitude goes to our dear friends David

Molineaux and Judy Ress, whose encouragement and practical support from the moment we first suggested we might move to Chile for a year made sure it happened. Indeed, without David and Judy's hard work we would not have had an ideal house awaiting us when we arrived and our daughters booked into a school that made all the difference in helping them settle in. To Judy and David I dedicate this book. My very special thanks go to the National Committee for Development Education, which gave me a very generous grant to help defray my research costs, allowing me to travel more widely in Latin America to find out at first hand the situation in various countries. The many people who gave me most willingly their time and shared their intimate knowledge of their countries with me are far too numerous to mention by name. Suffice it to say that in Chile, in Mexico, in Argentina, in Venezuela, in Bolivia, in Peru and in Ecuador, I was truly astonished by such people's generosity with their time and their expert knowledge. Many of them gave me books and reports, all of which proved immensely valuable to me in writing this book.[1] I only hope that they think it does some justice to the complexity and diversity of each and every national situation throughout Latin America.

I wish to say a very special word of thanks to Lucy Robinson of Sage, without whose initial suggestion I would never have begun thinking of writing a book like this. From our first meeting she has been constantly supportive and encouraging, as was her assistant, Claire Roberts, with whom I was dealing regularly during the writing of the book. Claire left Sage somewhere between Chapter 7 and Chapter 9 and I wish her well in her new job. Though her replacement, David Mainwaring, arrived late in the life of this project, he took it on with an enthusiasm and commitment for which I am very grateful. I thank all those who read the chapters as they were being produced and whose comments helped me a lot – the two readers whom Sage used as referees and the following friends and acquaintances: Ann Boran of Chester College, Benedicte Bull of the Centre for Environment and Development at the University of Oslo, Cris Kay of the Institute of Social Studies in The Hague, Fernando Leiva of the State University of New York at Albany, and Paddy Reilly of the Development Studies Centre, Kimmage Manor, Dublin. Finally, and of course not least, my heartfelt thanks go to my long-suffering family who always seem to have a distracted and preoccupied partner and father to put up with. I marvel at the positive way both Bríd and Caoimhe embraced the unknown in moving to Chile, to a strange language and far from their friends. I know it wasn't always easy for them but I hope its memories will long remain with them as a positive and enriching experience. And to Toni, who, following initial hesitation and caution, took it all in her stride, both learning a huge amount and giving a huge amount to those with whom she worked in Chile, all I can say is that none of this would have been possible without her.

Peadar Kirby
Dublin

[1] All translations of Spanish texts for this book were done by the author.

South America

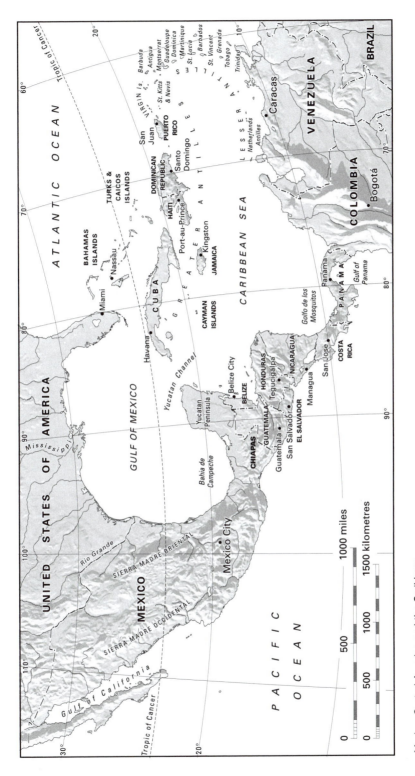

Mexico, Central America and the Caribbean

1

Introduction: Understanding Latin America

E ver since Europeans first stumbled upon its shores on 12 October 1492, the region we now call Latin America has been seen by outsiders as containing something of the exotic, whether in its native peoples, its fruits and vegetables, its Inca, Aztec and Mayan civilizations or its daunting geography. This continued in the twentieth century as Latin America became identified with heroic guerrilla bands, brutal military dictators and the seemingly interminable struggles of its many poor people for greater equality and justice. During the second half of that century, a number of Latin Americans achieved international recognition as personifying these elements of the region's make-up – Che Guevara, the Argentine adventurer who joined Fidel Castro and his companions in overthrowing the Batista dictatorship in Cuba in 1959 and who died in the highlands of Bolivia in 1967 during a futile effort to repeat the achievement; General Augusto Pinochet, the chief-of-staff of the Chilean armed forces who overthrew the democratically elected government of Salvador Allende on 11 September 1973 to usher in a 16-year-long repressive dictatorship which changed the face of Chilean society; or the Quiche indigenous woman from Guatemala, Rigoberta Menchú, who survived the grim poverty of her upbringing and the ferocious brutality of the Guatemalan army, which savagely murdered most of her family, to win the Nobel Peace Prize in 1992 (for her own account, see Burgos-Debray, 1984).

While these examples help illustrate aspects of Latin America and its historical development, they also run the risk of oversimplifying the variety and complexity of the region. In other words, by highlighting some dimensions and neglecting others, they embody an interpretation. So, for example, the heroic figure of Che Guevara and the romantic interpretation of the Cuban revolution neglect the harassment of dissidents and of minority groups like gays which took place. Highlighting the repressive nature of the Chilean military regime may serve to minimize the regime's economic successes which, in the 1990s, made Chile the economic showcase of the region. And appreciating the remarkable life history of Rigoberta Menchú must not avoid the responsibility of the US administration which organized a coup in 1954, overthrowing the elected government of Jacobo Arbenz and thereby helping unleash the grim terror which gripped Guatemala for the next 40 years. As can be seen from these examples, all accounts of any social phenomenon constitute an interpretation even where the basis for the interpretation is not made clear. In offering an account of the prospects for Latin America in a globalized world, therefore, this book devotes its first chapter to making clear the interpretative framework to be employed. The chapter firstly looks at the need for such interpretative or theoretical frameworks, and it then goes on to outline the principal frameworks which have been used for interpreting Latin America over the past half century. The following section highlights some of the main changes in the nature of the global order at the beginning of the twenty-first century that pose challenges for the theoretical frameworks previously used, before outlining in the final section the approach to be used in this book.

Need for Frameworks

In learning about distant parts of the world, most people rely on media accounts, whether newspaper and magazine articles or radio and television news reports and documentaries. The objective of such journalistic accounts is to communicate something of the reality of life in these countries, whether the subject is a particular news story or a more wide-ranging examination of, for example, the impact of the international debt crisis or drug production and trafficking. Often the story is told through reporting the lives of individual people who help to personalize and therefore communicate to a distant audience what can be a highly complicated and many-dimensional reality. At their best, journalists are masters of the art of storytelling, though the stories they tell can touch the great traumas of our times. However, the account offered by a journalist does not aspire to give the whole picture; instead, it selects some aspects because they are newsworthy and easily understandable to those not personally involved. Within the very limited length and time constraints of most media products, what can be offered is a snapshot or a series of snapshots of a situation.

The academic aspires to offer a more rounded and analytical account, probing the subject to discover causes and consequences in a more thorough way than does the journalist. After all, the academic is expected to have a more specialist knowledge of her subject to an extent rarely true of the journalist. In probing the subject, the academic will usually move away from the personal focus often employed by the journalist, devoting attention instead to categories of analysis that help to order a highly complex reality into an intelligible framework which distinguishes causes and context from effects and outcomes. In doing this, the intention is to offer an explanation of the phenomenon or situation that is incisive and enduring, moving beyond the surface impressions to the deeper reality beneath. Many academics are also concerned with the practical consequences of their analyses which they see as offering guidelines for action, whether through the policies of governments or organizations (such as the World Bank, for example) or through movements and groups that might challenge and contest such policies. As such, the academic account can be likened to an X-ray, often not as colourful or engaging as a snapshot, but uncovering far more that lies behind what is immediately observable.

Furthermore, many different types of academic account are possible. The historian offers an account that interprets the past, including at times the very recent past, often using a more narrative form of writing to describe and explain the forces that have shaped history. In contrast the social scientist is often more selective, focusing on particular aspects of society and developing analytical categories through which to examine them. The social scientist also works within particular disciplinary traditions, each of which have their particular focus of attention and analytical approaches. The economist is concerned with the production of goods and services and how they are distributed and exchanged and, if working within mainstream neoclassical economics, regularly uses mathematical models to understand the workings of the economy. Issues of power are what interest the political scientist, especially as it is institutionalized in forms of government, in political parties, and in other groups. The sociologist examines a wide range of social phenomena, such as social structure, poverty, the family, crime, religion, social movements, the media and many more. These divisions grew up in the nineteenth century as the economy, the political system and social problems began to be seen as discrete spheres requiring specialist approaches to understand them. Apart from these divisions, the twentieth century has seen the further fragmentation of the social sciences and the emergence of separate disciplines such as anthropology, psychology, cultural studies, feminist studies and development studies. Therefore, in looking at the same social phenomenon, such as Latin America in the second half of the twentieth century, each of these approaches has something distinctive to offer. The historian will offer an account of the main developments that have shaped the region over the period, with the economic or the political historian looking at developments in the economy or in politics. The economist or the political scientist, by contrast, while necessarily having to fill in some of the same general background, will focus in a more analytical way on the nature of the productive economy and how it has changed over the period, or on the political systems and such issues as the reasons for military interventions or the weaknesses of democracy.

This description of the work of the academic raises further questions, however – questions that do not apply to the work of the journalist. For any social situation is far too complex and multifaceted to be amenable to direct, personal knowledge of its many elements by any analyst. The journalist makes sense of it by selecting those elements which are considered newsworthy or which allow her to construct a good story that illustrates a wider social situation. But for the academic, the need to offer a more probing and analytical account raises particular challenges: what is the basis for selecting those elements of reality which are seen as significant and for discarding those many elements which are not? And, having selected elements, how are they linked together: what is cause and what is effect? So, for example, an academic analysis of the social conflicts in Guatemala, El Salvador and Nicaragua in the 1980s might concentrate on the situation of gross rural poverty and inequality which has long characterized these countries, showing how population growth exacerbated the difficulties for the rural poor in accessing a livelihood, thereby creating the conditions for the insurrections (as does Brockett, 1998), or it might concentrate on the failure of the political elites in these countries to introduce political reforms that would open the way for more peaceful forms of social change (as does Biekart, 2001). And what, for example, of the role of the United States on the one hand in offering support to the existing political elites, and that of Cuba on the other in giving at least moral backing, and at times more direct support, to their opponents? What weight is to be attached to such outside influences? It would, of course, be impossible to offer a full account of this bloody period without referring to all these elements, but there is no pregiven yardstick by which one can determine what weight is to be attached to each of the elements or to distinguish which are the more fundamental causes of the social conflicts and which are reactions to those causes. Obviously, one yardstick that can be applied (and sometimes is by academics) is a political one with the result that analysts with left-wing sympathies will tend to attribute greater responsibility to the United States as at least a contributory cause of the conflicts, whereas more conservative observers may be inclined to blame Cuba.

Such a resort to predetermined political positions is, however, something of a cop-out since it introduces elements extraneous to the study of society; in other words it imports its yardsticks from the outside.[1] Instead, the challenge and excitement of the social sciences is to elaborate yardsticks that derive from the field of study itself so as to deepen and develop our knowledge of how social phenomena operate and change, and of the nature of the challenges confronting them. This is the role of theory, since theory is the distillation of existing knowledge in the form of general frameworks of explanation which then act as a guide to exploring the nature of social reality. We will see in the next section some examples of the principal theoretical frameworks that have guided interpretation of Latin America at various times in the past. The general frameworks of explanation that constitute theory arise from the interaction of two fundamental elements – on the one hand those basic philosophical and value orientations which constitute the lens through which we view the world (these are sometimes called metatheory or grand theory) and, on the other, the actual empirical study of concrete situations. Two broad philosophical and value orientations have guided the development of Western social sciences since the nineteenth century – liberalism and Marxism. Liberalism is distinguished by its interest in issues of individual freedom which leads it to favour a free-market capitalist economic system and liberal democracy. It is the dominant influence within economics. Marxism emerged as the main critique of liberalism, placing emphasis on collectivities (especially social classes such as the bourgeoisie and the working class) and on their unequal access to material resources and power. It therefore places greater emphasis on issues of inequality and the struggles for emancipation by oppressed groups, and has been very influential within sociology. These differing concerns and value orientations have guided the empirical study of social scientists, influencing in great measure the frameworks of theoretical explanation that they have developed. Before giving examples of these theories, it is important to remember that there always exists what we can call a dialectical relationship between theory and empirical data – theory always guides empirical study in that it acts as the yardstick for choosing some elements over others, but theory is also changed as evidence emerges which seems to challenge or contradict generalizations expressed in the theory; if strong enough evidence emerges over time then it can give rise to a new generalization or theory. This process is rarely smooth and it often generates fierce debates among social scientists. Through such debates a new consensus can emerge.

Differing Understandings

Theory helps explain how different social scientists, looking at the same set of social phenomena, can arrive at very different or even contradictory conclusions. This is evident in examining interpretations of Latin America going back to the nineteenth century. Following the independence of most of the region's countries in the 1810s and 1820s, a generation of Latin American writers sought to turn their backs on the past and find a new future for their countries by imitating what they saw as the progress of the United States and the great European powers. This was expressed as follows in reference to a famous book *Facundo* (1845) by the Argentine writer, educator and statesman Domingo Faustino Sarmiento (1811–88):

> Thus there is posed a sort of choice between a past, characterized by the presence of the Indian, by the Spanish Catholic colonial theology and culture, and by the oscillation between anarchy and despotism on the one hand, and on the other a future that is thought of as the triumph of liberty within order, of democracy, of lay education, of science and general welfare, and of the civilized city confronting a retrograde and barbarous countryside. (Quoted in Davis, 1972: 98)

Sarmiento, as with many leading writers and statesmen of his time in Latin America, was influenced by positivism which identified progress with social order and institutions; these saw the main obstacles to such progress as being Latin America's colonial and Catholic inheritance and its rural and native peoples. Positivism was the guiding philosophy of the long and, to many, tyrannical presidency of Porfirio Díaz in Mexico that began in 1876 and was only ended by the outbreak of the Mexican revolution in 1910–11. It was also the guiding light for many of the leaders of the Brazilian republican movement that toppled the monarchy in 1889 and it finds expression in the words 'Ordem e Progresso' on the Brazilian flag. Inevitably such a negative evaluation of what was distinctively Latin American and such a positive evaluation of the United States led to a reaction by a younger group of Latin Americans such as the Cuban, José Martí (1853–95). These were highly critical of US imperialism towards Latin America and sought in the region's own culture a way to develop a distinctive society.

Some elements of these nineteenth century interpretations of Latin America find echo in the two principal theories through which the region has been interpreted by social scientists in the second half of the twentieth century – modernization theory heavily influenced by liberalism, and dependency theory, largely a variant of Marxism. Modernization theory emerged in the early

1950s within US universities as a way of understanding the path to be taken by developing countries (many of them in Asia, Africa and the Caribbean emerging into independence) to achieve development. Sociologist Talcott Parsons presented development as a move from a traditional society, in which individual achievement and initiative were constrained by community ties (such as the extended family), to a modern society characterized by individual achievement and mass consumption (Parsons, 1951). Economist Walt Rostow saw development as coming through imitating the example of the developed countries of the West: led by entrepreneurial elites, with the guidance of US advisors and the help of foreign investment, developing countries would move through the various stages of economic growth to industrialization and development (Rostow, 1960). Initially the theory saw democracy as coming hand in hand with this process of modernization; following military coups in Latin America, however (particularly the Brazilian military takeover of 1964), Samuel Huntington argued that democratization would have to be delayed until economic modernization had developed a strong enough middle class with an interest in defending a democratic system (Huntington, 1968). For many Latin Americans, therefore, modernization theory offered the goal of developing their own consumer societies in imitation of the United States through following US guidance and accepting US investment. It was presented with an air of inevitability and eagerly grasped by the region's elites.

Modernization theory, however, was based on abstract theoretical models which bore little relationship to the complex realities of Latin American societies where, since colonial times, power had been concentrated in the hands of small elites. One expression of this is the gross inequality in income and wealth that characterizes the region. In this situation, modernization theory seemed to offer a way by which these elites could justify their continued reluctance to share their power and wealth with the majority of their compatriots. These realities led to the emergence of a counter-theory, called dependency theory, developed in Latin America to offer an entirely different view of how the region might develop (for an overview of Latin American theories of development, see Kay, 1989). As its name suggests, dependency theory identified the dependence of the region on the 'core' countries of North America and western Europe as being the main cause of its underdevelopment. This dependence led to a relationship of exploitation through which the region's wealth was extracted for the benefit of local elites and the 'core' countries while the majority of Latin Americans benefited little from it. Meanwhile, the 'core' countries sought to prevent a local process of industrialization through which Latin American countries might break out of their situation of dependency and begin to develop their own resources for their own benefit. One way in which this happened was through foreign multinationals that set up in Latin American countries and which extracted more wealth than they invested in the region (Frank, 1967). Instead of following the advice of foreign advisors as recommended by modernization theorists, therefore, Latin America according to dependency theorists should, through state investment and guidance and through the struggles of its dominated groups and classes, develop its own industrial base by protecting its economies. Alongside this, as a means of developing a larger market for the goods produced by its new industries, social struggle holds the possibility of wresting the state from its capture by dominant classes so that it helps share the benefits of development with the poor major- ity, drawing them into the new industrial jobs being created and establishing the basis for a mass industrial society (Cardoso and Faletto, 1979). From the late 1960s, dependency theory emerged as an influential theory to challenge the dominance of modernization theory. Box 1.1 shows the influence these two theoretical currents continue to exercise on interpretations of the region.

Box 1.1 Differing interpretations of Latin America

Modernization theory and dependency theory still influence interpretations of Latin America, as illustrated by these quotes from two widely used textbooks on the region. Notice the optimistic conclusions of the former as against the pessimistic conclusions of the latter:

> Throughout Latin America's history, its people have debated their heritage and their future, whether Western or non-Western, First World or Third, capitalist or socialist, and the absence of consensus on these large issues has delayed its development.
>
> Now at last there seems to be hope of such consensus. The answers are not definitive or inevitable in all countries, but the general direction seems clear. Leaders in Latin America think of it as part of the Western world. It has non-Western, indigenous and black elements within its borders whose customs merit respect, but its basic institutions are and will continue to be Western, patterned after those of Europe and the United States. It has Third World pockets (more important in some countries than in others), but clearly most leaders want to cast their lot with the modern, industrial, democratic nations. Finally, with the collapse of the Soviet Union and the failure of socialism in Eastern Europe, Asia, Africa, Cuba, and Nicaragua, Latin America is determined to belong to the capitalist camp – although its economies may take different shapes and some of its statist and mercantilist traditions will probably be preserved. The resolution or near-resolution of these momentous issues in nearly all the countries of the area provides it a clear direction that will undoubtedly help stimulate further economic growth. (Wiarda and Kline, 1996: 3–4)

The second objective of this edition has been to set Latin American history within a broad interpretive framework. This framework is the 'dependency theory', the most influential theoretical model for social scientists concerned with understanding Latin America. ...

Writers of the dependency school employ some standard terms that we use in this text: *neocolonialism*, *neoliberalism*, and *center* and *periphery*. *Neocolonialism* refers to the dependent condition of countries that enjoy formal political independence. *Neoliberalism* refers to the policies of privatization, austerity, and trade liberalization accepted willingly or unwillingly

by the governments of dependent countries as a condition of approval of
investment, loans, and debt relief by the International Monetary Fund and the
World Bank. . . . The term *center* is applied to the dominant group of
developed capitalist countries, and *periphery* to the underdeveloped or
dependent countries. . . .

[A] rapid glance at the results of over a decade of application of neoliberal
therapy to Latin America's problems suggests that in all essential respects the
economic and social crisis of the area has worsened and its dependency vis-à-
vis the core capitalist powers has deepened. Our text documents these
conclusions in detail. (Keen and Haynes, 2000: x (emphases in original))

An Era of Major Change

As is clear from an outline of modernization theory and dependency theory,
they were developed to provide a general framework of interpretation for
particular challenges that presented themselves – the challenge of development
in the post-war world in the first case and the challenge of the failure of
modernization in the second. Furthermore, in the context of the Cold War
from the early 1950s to the late 1980s, these two theories mirrored the great
divide of that time, the divide between capitalism (championed by modernization theory) and socialism (which dependency theory saw as the way forward).
The end of the Cold War in the early 1990s, therefore, changes dramatically
the context in which these theories developed. For dependency theory, the
collapse of Eastern European socialism undermines at least for the foreseeable
future the viability of a road to development other than a capitalist one of some
kind. Even though some might see this as a vindication of modernization
theory, the continuing (and indeed growing) problems of poverty and inequality that plague Latin America continue to raise disturbing questions about the
adequacy of a capitalist route. By the mid 1980s it was being recognized that
neither of these two theories had proved to be useful guides to a fast-changing
world order, though both continued to provide useful insights.[2]

The end of the Cold War and of a feasible socialist alternative links to a
series of technological changes that have dramatically accelerated transnational flows of production, trade and finance, in which multinational companies play a crucial role. The new technologies of instant worldwide
communication that made these changes possible are now facilitated by
an ideological consensus in favour of the free market from which few states
dissent. Taken together, these technological and ideological changes have
produced a phenomenon that, since the late 1980s, has been called 'globalization' and which is widely seen as ushering in major qualitative changes,
not only in the world economy, but also in politics, society and culture.
These are the major 'twenty-first century challenges' referred to in this
book's subtitle. While the fact of globalization is now widely accepted, its
significance is vigorously debated between those who see it as producing a
largely positive era of intensified economic growth through the freeing up of

market forces (sometimes called the 'hyperglobalists') and those who question just how new it all is since trade and finance flows, as a percentage of gross domestic product (GDP), were at the end of the nineteenth century equivalent to or even greater than they are now. These 'sceptics', as they are called, argue that globalization is more an ideological position, hostile to the interference of the state in the economy, whose aura of inevitability should be challenged. A third position, however, influences the approach taken in this book. This can be called the 'transformationalist' position, as it accepts that major transformations are taking place in economics, politics, society and culture with the advent of globalization but that these are very uneven, impacting in different ways on different countries, regions and sectors, and that we have little clear idea yet of the sort of world that may emerge (for a fuller outline of these different positions, see Held et al., 1999: 2–10). Through examining the nature of the changes taking place in Latin America at the dawn of the twenty-first century, and the prospects for the region in this transforming world, this book is therefore a contribution to understanding how globalization is affecting more peripheral regions of the world.

If globalization is a major guiding theme for the book, what yardsticks or signposts does the social science literature on globalization give us to guide our examination of Latin America? The first concerns the changing role of peripheral regions in the world economy. Latin America's role since colonial times has been to supply raw materials to the industrialized countries, both foodstuffs like sugar, bananas, coffee or meat and industrial inputs like tin, copper and cotton. As we shall see in Chapter 3, the region made valiant efforts between the 1930s and the 1970s to change this situation through a process of industrialization directed by its various states, which met with some success. However, globalization is changing the world economy in ways that seem at one level to have returned Latin America to its traditional role as a supplier of unprocessed raw materials but on the other hand have opened up through the information economy new possibilities for economic growth that do not depend on such production. But, as Fernando Henrique Cardoso (a former dependency theorist and President of Brazil from 1995 to 2002) has put it, depending on the former products condemns the region to ever greater marginalization as these are of less and less importance to the industrialized countries (and by and large fetch ever lower prices); in this situation Latin America faces a stark choice: either it 'enters the democratic-technological-scientific race, invests heavily in R&D [research and development], and endures the "information economy" metamorphosis, or it becomes unimportant, unexploited, and unexploitable' (quoted in Nederveen Pieterse, 2001: 47). In a very real sense, then, this marks the end of seeing the countries of the South as a 'Third World' with a specific role in the world economy. Now, all countries need to try to avail themselves of the possibilities opened by the information economy or else they will have virtually no role left to them. Chapter 4 will examine how Latin America is faring in this regard.

Furthermore, these economic challenges pose major political challenges to Latin America's states. On the one hand globalization has closed off the option recommended by dependency theory – that states direct their own process of industrialization through protecting their markets from outside forces. But this does not mean that the state has become redundant as the market becomes the driving force; indeed, the challenges it now faces are even greater as each state seeks to find a role for itself amid intense worldwide competition in the new information economy. Chapter 5 will examine how the Latin American state is changing to meet these challenges. This new situation is also changing the nature of politics, as states seem to be devoting more attention to the demands of international competitiveness than to the welfare needs of their own citizens (the new financial orthodoxy requires moderation in spending and states that run up big deficits are punished). This is fuelling a disillusion with politics since the latter seems to be reduced to a marketing exercise between candidates who have little different to offer the electorate; Chapter 9 will look at how Latin American political leaders and parties are responding. As formal politics loses its ability to channel the demands and aspirations of citizens (despite the wave of democratization that has swept Latin America since the 1980s), social movements of many different kinds are filling the gap. The literature on globalization recognizes in this phenomenon the emergence of civil society as a political actor, though, as Manuel Castells argues in his influential trilogy on the information age, such movements can promote positive social changes or negative reactions against it (Castells, 1997: 68–72). He devotes attention to the Zapatistas in Mexico as an example of the former. Some of these movements mobilize on the basis of identity (such as feminist, gay, ethnic or religious identities) which can indicate a disillusion with the secularist national identities promoted by the nation state throughout most of the twentieth century and the promotion of alternative bases for communal bonding. Chapter 10 analyses the nature and significance of these movements in Latin America, devoting attention to the emergence of identity politics (through indigenous movements).

What often fuels these movements is the perception that globalization is having a divisive impact on national societies, favouring some groups who benefit from the liberalized economy, and disadvantaging others. Castells calls these losers the 'Fourth World'; unlike the Third World it is no longer limited to certain geographical areas of the world but is found in all countries (Castells, 1998: 70–165). Evidence of increasing inequality worldwide is therefore causing growing concern (for details, see UNDP, 1999). One of the causes of this inequality has been identified by Cox in the emerging occupational structure of the globalized economy. He identifies three groups:

> 1 the highly skilled workers whose skills are needed by the new economy and who therefore are fully *integrated* into it and benefit from good work conditions and high wages;
> 2 the large group of workers whose levels of skills make them more easily disposable and replaceable. These have a *precarious* relationship to the economy since they have no security and they face poor working conditions and low wages as firms cut costs in response to intensified competition;

3 those people with few skills to offer and who end up *excluded* from the new
economy. (1999: 9; emphasis in original)

Since Latin America has long been characterized by high levels of poverty and
socio-economic inequality, these concerns are of major importance for the
region. They are examined in Chapter 7, 'The Human Impact'.

This differentiation between winners and losers within countries is also
identified in the globalization literature as happening at the level of regions
(both groupings of countries and areas within countries). The global economy
is seen as being divided into three principal regions: North America, the
European Union and Japan. Each of these have their hinterlands into which
they subcontract labour-intensive operations and extend the markets for their
products – Latin America for the first, Eastern Europe for the second and the
emerging economies of East Asia such as Malaysia and Thailand for the third.
New regional groupings are emerging to give institutional form to these relationships, such as the North American Free Trade Agreement (NAFTA) which
includes Mexico in a free trade agreement with the USA and Canada, or
Mercosur, a common market between Brazil, Argentina, Uruguay and
Paraguay in South America (see Gwynne and Kay, 1999: 8–12). Chapter 6
describes this emerging regional architecture in the Americas.

This Book's Approach

Having outlined the explanatory framework or theory that guides the examination of Latin America in this book, what remains is to address the issue of
methodology. By methodology, social scientists mean the particular methods
they use to examine social reality. These can be highly quantitative, as is often
the case in economics, using complex mathematical equations to draw conclusions from statistical data. Or, they can be more qualitative, examining the
reality from a greater variety of angles, which can include statistical evidence,
but also include evidence taken from empirical studies, from interviews, from
opinion polls, and from other academic analysts. Furthermore, the focus of
attention can be limited to a particular aspect of the social reality; thus, economists concentrate on issues of production; political scientists on political systems; and sociologists on social processes and impacts. The benefit of these
approaches is that they offer the ability to dissect in a very focused way a
particular issue or problem such as, for example, inflation, unemployment or
voting systems. For this reason, they have been called 'problem-solving theory'
(Cox, 1995: 32). However, they solve problems by narrowing their focus with
the result that the wider system is accepted as a given and not subjected to
critical scrutiny.

The nature of the subject being analysed in this book requires a broader
focus since it is looking at economic, political, social and cultural issues, and
how they interact with one another. Furthermore, unlike much social scientific
work that focuses on problems or issues in a national context (the Chilean
voting system, inflation in Brazil, or Mexican unemployment), globalization

requires that attention be devoted also to the impact of global processes on national, regional and even local levels; otherwise the forces driving social change today, as well as the constraints or possibilities they produce, will not be fully appreciated. Finally, a subject like the present one requires a wider theoretical approach than that offered by problem-solving theory since its objective is not to solve problems but to contribute to an understanding of the prospects facing Latin America in a globalized world. For these reasons, an international political economy approach is adopted for this book. Its objective is well described by Cox:

> Political economy, by contrast [with economics or political science], is concerned with the historically constituted frameworks or structures within which political and economic activity takes place. It stands back from the apparent fixity of the present to ask how the existing structures came into being and how they may be changing, or how they may be induced to change. In this sense, political economy is critical theory. (1995: 32)

In addition, the approach adopted here favours a form of social change that develops the societies of Latin America. Since 'development' is often given very different meanings, and can be used simply to mean high rates of economic growth, it is important to define it more precisely (for a discussion of the different meanings of development over time, see Nederveen Pieterse, 2001: 1–17). As used in this book, development refers to a form of social change that improves the material conditions of life of the majority in an enduring way and that expands their opportunities for a satisfying life. It can therefore be defined as 'a process characterized primarily by growing social inclusion through rising living standards, meaningful employment, active political and social participation and a satisfying cultural life extending to all sectors of society and thus widening the life choices and possibilities for the great majority' (Kirby, 1997: 41). Since Latin America is examined in this book in the light of its possibilities for achieving this sort of development in a globalized world, we can call the approach used here the international political economy of development (IPED) (see Hettne, 1995 for a fuller discussion of this approach).

Examining the prospects for Latin America in a globalized world using this approach yields no easy conclusions. It requires a careful empirical examination, drawing on a broad range of sources, and a refusal to see the future as predetermined in either a positive or a negative way. For this reason, the structure of the book reflects the need to hold in balance both structure and agency. Structure in this sense refers to what we can call the 'objective' given realities (such as the nature of the global economy and financial system) that constrain the room for manoeuvre of actors, be they states, organizations, movements, parties or individuals (such as charismatic political or social leaders). While structure constrains, it does not predetermine; one of the major themes of the literature on globalization is that agency can affect outcomes, namely that what states, organizations, movements, parties or individuals do can change, for better or worse, how things turn out. For this reason, the book begins with a section on 'Legacies', in which Chapter 2 profiles the variety of societies constituting the region and Chapter 3 outlines the various attempts of the region to overcome its marginalization and inequality on the world stage since the 1870s. This deals with one form of structure, namely the legacies of history. Section II deals with a different form of structure, though this time influenced by agency. Entitled 'Neoliberal Reformation', its four chapters deal with the transformations through which the region has been passing since the early 1980s. Chapter 4 examines the economic transformation, Chapter 5 the political transformation, Chapter 6 the transformation in regional structures, and Chapter 7 the transformation in people's lives as a result. An Interlude follows as Chapter 8 examines Cuba and the prospects facing it; Cuba is given a chapter on its own because, since its revolution in 1959, it has followed a completely different development path to that of the rest of the region and therefore faces challenges that are distinctive and unlike those of any other country in the region. Section III places more emphasis on agency, since its two chapters look at how Latin Americans are responding to the new globalized situation in which they find themselves. Chapter 9 looks at the political actors, movements and currents of thought that characterize the current period, while Chapter 10 looks at the emergence of new social actors, usually referred to as social movements. The final section, entitled 'Prospects', has one chapter that assesses how Latin America and its constituent parts are faring in a more globalized world and the prospects for the region in the twenty-first century.

Notes

[1] This is not to say, however, that political biases do not exercise some influence, even subconsciously, on the choices exercised by academics. Inevitably they do, and it would be impossible for them not to since living as human beings involves negotiating power and therefore developing attitudes and values towards it. Sometimes it is those academics who most aspire to a value-free social science (especially evident in mainstream economics) whose work embodies clear (and usually conservative) political biases. A more realistic stance is to acknowledge the value orientation that influences our scholarship while endeavouring to exercise as much rigour as possible in the scholarly methods we use.

[2] It is often argued that the emergence of neoliberalism in the early 1980s and the immense influence it has exercised over developing and developed countries shows a return to the tenets of modernization theory. There is some truth to this claim, though neoliberalism has never been elaborated into a broad-ranging theory of social change as was modernization theory and remains a set of practical propositions related to economic and political restructuring. For this reason, it fails to provide a general explanatory framework for social change.

Section I

Legacies

2

Diversity amid Unity

To the outside observer, Latin America appears much more homogeneous than does any other region of the world. It is neatly divided into extensive areas speaking the same language, whether they be the Spanish-speaking republics stretching from the US–Mexican border all the way to the southern tip of Chile and Argentina, Portuguese-speaking Brazil, which is the world's fifth largest country occupying nearly half of South America, or the numerous small English-speaking states of the Caribbean. Yet, while culture may unite, the region's geographical diversity has placed obstacles that impeded regular interaction throughout history. The Andes mountains, running from present-day Venezuela down the west coast of South America until they form the border between Chile and Argentina for 2,500 miles, are the world's second highest mountain range. Mexico, too, is divided by the three ranges of the Sierra Madre, while even the small republics of Central America are divided by volcanic ranges. East of the Andes lies the world's largest extension of tropical forests and the three extensive river systems – the Amazon which covers more than one-third of Brazil, the Orinoco in Venezuela, and the River Plate running from southern Brazil down to Argentina forming the borders of Paraguay and Uruguay. These geographical features have played no small role in the constitution of the various states into which Latin America was divided following the end of colonial rule.

Adding to these divisions is the racial make-up of the population. Though it is estimated that the native population of the region at the time of the European conquest was between 50 and 90 million (at a time when the population of Europe was fewer than 60 million), this was quickly reduced through both the brutality of the conquerors and the diseases they brought with them. In 50 years, the native population of the island of Hispaniola (today's Haiti and Dominican Republic), where the first European settlements were established, was reduced from 1 million to 500, while the population of Mexico fell from 20 million to 1 million in the first century after the conquest (Guimaraes, 1997: 183). As a result, the new European ruling elite was obliged to import African slaves for use in plantation agriculture, particularly on the sugar cane plantations in northeastern Brazil and on the islands of the Caribbean. By the time of independence some 8.5 million African slaves had been brought to the Americas (Keen and Haynes, 2000: 115); slavery was not finally abolished in Brazil until 1888. Waves of immigration from Europe increased following independence when many of the new states, most particularly Brazil, Argentina and Uruguay (sometimes called 'empty' countries since their population density was so low), established schemes to encourage such immigration. Between 1857 and 1926, Argentina had a net immigration of 3 million people and Uruguay 350,000, mostly from Italy and Spain (de Ramón et al., 2001b: 24). In the twentieth century, immigrants came from further afield, such as Lebanon and Syria. About 200,000 Japanese emigrated to Brazil in the first half of the twentieth century and a further 30,000 went to Peru (Yelvington, 1997: 231), among them the parents of Alberto Fujimori, president of Peru from 1990 to 2000. The result of this racial diversity finds expression in such terms as *mestizo* (those of Spanish and indigenous parentage), and *mulatto* (of Spanish and black parentage). As Brazilian writer Darcy Ribeiro has written:

> So we came to be, New Peoples, born of the de-Indianization, de-Europeanization and de-Africanization of our origins. But this took place as part of a process dominated by assimilationism instead of apartheid. Here racial mixing has never been seen as a sin or a crime. Quite the reverse, our prejudice has always lain precisely in the general expectation that blacks, Indians and whites would not keep themselves apart, but blend one with another to produce a brown society, a mixed-race civilization ... (1990: 18)

Unity and diversity therefore intermingle in sometimes surprising ways in this 'mixed-race civilization'. This chapter offers a profile of the unity and the diversity of Latin America at the beginning of the twenty-first century. The first section builds up a picture of the region as a whole, before going on in the second section to compare its achievements with those of other regions of the world. The final section breaks Latin America down into its component parts, looking in more detail at the various regional identities that constitute it.

A Region Apart

At the beginning of the twenty-first century, Latin America has a population of 495 million; with an annual growth rate of 1.3 per cent, this is expected to reach 611 million by 2015. The rate of population growth in most of the region peaked at 2.7 per cent in the 1950–70 period and, with the exception of some Central American and Caribbean countries, has been declining since. Brazil is Latin America's largest country, with 170 million people, followed by Mexico with 100 million, Colombia with 41 million and Argentina with 37 million. Brazil, Mexico and Argentina have been the region's major powers throughout the twentieth century; only since the 1980s has Colombia's population surpassed that of Argentina. Colombia can be regarded as a leading power among a second tier of countries that also includes Chile (15 million), Venezuela (24 million), Peru (25 million) and Cuba (11 million). Cuba is included not just because it is the region's only communist country, but even before the 1959 revolution its levels of social and economic development placed it among this second group. Next come the smaller countries, whose importance cannot always be correlated with their size. Ecuador with 13 million people and Bolivia with 8 million people are of less regional importance, due to their less developed economies. Uruguay, though it has a population of only 3.3 million, has been one of the region's most developed countries, while Paraguay (5.5 million) has a history of isolationism, perpetuated by the regime of General Alfredo Stroessner (1954–89). In Central America, Guatemala (11 million) is the largest country, but El Salvador (6.5 million) and Costa Rica (3.9 million) rival it in importance due to their economic development, while Honduras (6.5 million) and Nicaragua (5 million) are of less importance.[1] Panama (2.8 million) has traditionally had a rather anomalous position, not being seen as part of Central America (since it was a province of Colombia up to 1903). The Caribbean has been divided by language, with the Spanish-speaking countries of Cuba and the Dominican Republic (8.2 million) looking to Latin America, while mainland English-speaking countries, such as Belize (200,000) and Guyana (800,000), and Dutch-speaking Surinam (400,000) identify with the small island states. Among these, Jamaica (2.6 million) and Trinidad and Tobago (1.3 million) are the more important countries; most of the other island states have populations of less than 200,000 people, Martinique, Guadeloupe and Guyane are *départéments* of France (fully integrated into the French Republic) and the islands of the Netherlands Antilles are not fully independent states. Finally Haiti (8 million), the poorest country in the hemisphere, has had a turbulent history all its own. While the microstates of the Caribbean have, since independence in the 1960s, tended to look to London and Washington, they are now forging closer links and a regional identity. More and more they see their future in association with Latin America.

Far more important than their size is the quality of life that these populations enjoy. Table 2.1 provides a range of data on quality of life for the principal countries of Latin America and the Caribbean. These include the following:

1 average annual incomes (in US dollars),
2 life expectancy and infant mortality, which allow a judgement on standards of health among the population,
3 literacy levels and, where available, the percentage of the relevant age-group attending secondary school, which allow a judgement on levels of education,
4 the percentage of the population living in urban areas, and
5 the number of telephones and television sets for each 1,000 of the population. Both of these latter sets of data allow a judgement on access to more modern conditions of life.

This reveals two major characteristics of the region. On the one hand, many of these indicators reveal that most Latin American and Caribbean countries have achieved relatively high standards of human development at the end of the

TABLE 2.1 QUALITY OF LIFE INDICATORS FOR LATIN AMERICA AND THE CARIBBEAN

Countries	Annual income (US$)[a]	Life expectancy	Infant mortality per 1,000 live births	Adult literacy[b]	Secondary school enrolment[c]	Urban dwellers[d]	TVs per 1,000	Phones per 1,000
Argentina	12,277	72.9	19	96.7	77	90	289	203
Bolivia	2,355	61.4	64	85	40	62	116	69
Brazil	7,037	67.2	34	84.9	66	81	316	121
Chile	8,652	74.9	11	95.6	85	85	232	205
Colombia	5,749	70.4	26	91.5	76	73	217	173
Costa Rica	8,860	76	13	95.5	40	48	387	172
Cuba	N/a	75.7	8	97	N/a	N/a	N/a	N/a
Dominican Republic	5,507	67.3	43	83.2	79	64	95	93
Ecuador	2,994	69.5	27	91	51	64	293	78
El Salvador	4,344	69.1	35	78.3	36	46	675	80
Guatemala	3,674	64	45	68.1	35	39	126	41
Haiti	1,464	52	83	48.8	N/a	35	5	8
Honduras	2,340	65.6	33	74	36	52	90	38
Mexico	8,297	72.2	27	91.1	66	74	261	104
Nicaragua	2,279	67.7	38	68.2	51	56	190	31
Panama	5,875	73.6	21	91.7	71	56	187	151
Paraguay	4,384	69.6	27	93	61	55	101	55
Peru	4,622	68	42	89.6	84	72	144	67
Uruguay	8,879	73.9	15	97.7	84	91	241	250
Venezuela	5,495	72.4	20	92.3	49	87	185	117

Antigua and Barbuda	10,225	75	20	N/a	N/a	N/a	N/a	N/a
Barbados	14,353	76.4	14	N/a	N/a	N/a	N/a	N/a
Belize	4,959	73.6	35	93.1	N/a	N/a	N/a	N/a
Dominica	5,425	76	16	N/a	N/a	N/a	N/a	N/a
Granada	6,817	72	22	N/a	N/a	N/a	N/a	N/a
Guyana	3,640	63.7	56	98.4	N/a	N/a	N/a	N/a
Jamaica	3,561	74.8	10	86.4	70	56	182	166
St Kitts and Nevis	11,596	70	24	N/a	N/a	N/a	N/a	N/a
St Lucia	5,509	73	17	N/a	N/a	N/a	N/a	N/a
St Vincent	5,309	73	21	N/a	N/a	N/a	N/a	N/a
Surinam	4,178	70.1	27	N/a	N/a	N/a	N/a	N/a
Trinidad and Tobago	8,176	73.8	17	93.5	N/a	N/a	N/a	N/a
Latin America and Caribbean	6,880	69.3	32	87.8	66	75	255	123

[a] Calculated on the basis of GDP per capita adjusted to take into account its purchasing power in each country – what is known as Purchasing Power Parity (PPP).

[b] Calculated as the percentage of the population aged 15 years and over.

[c] Calculated as the percentage of the relevant school-going age group.

[d] The share of the population living in areas defined as urban by each country.

Sources: UNDP, 2001: Tables 8, 10, 11; World Bank, 2000: Tables 2, 19. Data are for the closest year to 2000 available; most are for 1999 or 1998

twentieth century, particularly in their levels of education and health. On the other, however, the data reveal major differences among the region's countries. Annual per capita income goes from a high of US$14,353 for Barbados, better than the Czech Republic or Hungary, to a low of $1,464 for Haiti, lower than Bangladesh or The Gambia. Similar differences can be found on many of the indicators, revealing a group of countries that includes Haiti, Honduras, Nicaragua and Bolivia as lagging badly in human development compared to the other countries of the region. It must also be borne in mind that while these are indicators of human development, not all of them indicate an improvement in the quality of people's lives. The high rates of urbanization that characterize the region are worthy of particular mention in this regard since Latin America now contains some of the world's largest cities. Mexico City and Sao Paulo, with populations estimated to be about 20 million, are the largest, but Buenos Aires (11 million), Lima (8 million), Bogota (7 million), Rio de Janeiro (6 million), Caracas (5 million) and Santiago (5 million) have all expanded rapidly, particularly in the second half of the twentieth century, with urban services struggling to keep pace. In their physical layout, they reflect the marked socio-economic inequality of the region – their elegant and ultra-modern suburbs and shopping areas contrast with the large shanty towns on their outskirts, where flimsy dwellings are usually built of cardboard, wooden boards, corrugated iron or, in Lima, panels of matting. Life is dangerous in these cities – 61 per cent of Buenos Aires residents report being victims of crime, 55 per cent in Bogota and 44 per cent in Rio de Janeiro, higher than in any other major city on a list compiled by the UNDP (2001: 208–9). While people continue to migrate in large numbers to these cities in search of a better life, for many it must involve harsh living conditions.

The high levels of poverty and socio-economic inequality that characterize the region, therefore, cast a shadow over its achievements in the twentieth century. Though we associate images of extreme poverty with Sub-Saharan Africa and some Asian countries (like Bangladesh, India or Afghanistan), poverty remains pervasive in Latin America at the start of the twenty-first century and little improvement was seen over the twentieth century's final decade, as shown in Table 2.2. This uses three different measures of poverty, the first one a measure of extreme poverty, those living on an income of less than US$1.08 a day (revised to keep it in line with what such an income would have bought in 1993), the second based on an income of $2.15 a day (similarly revised) and the third one a measure of relative poverty. This last measures poverty in relation to living standards throughout society – as these rise, so too does the poverty line.[2] Estimates of poverty levels according to these measures are given for 1987 and 1998, both as percentages of the population and as numbers of poor.

Inequality is somewhat different than poverty, since it relates to the gap between the rich and the poor, not to the numbers who are poor. One could therefore have high levels of poverty but low levels of inequality, if most of the population were poor but there were few rich. In Latin America, however, the opposite is the case as a rich elite has dominated the region's societies since colonial times. Inequality is often measured by comparing the share of income

TABLE 2.2 POVERTY IN LATIN AMERICA AND THE CARIBBEAN, 1987 AND 1998

Measures	1987	1998[a]
$1.08 a day %	15.33%	15.57%
Number	63.6m	78.16m
$2.15 a day %	35.54%	36.44%
Number	146.5m	182.8m
Relative %	50.2%	51.35%
Number	208.4m	357.7m

[a]Data for 1998 are preliminary.

Source: Chen and Ravallion, 2000: Tables 2, 3, 5

received by the top 10 per cent of income earners with the share received by the bottom 10 per cent. This gives us a measure of the gap between rich and poor. In developed societies, the richest 10 per cent are estimated to receive somewhere between five and ten times what the poorest 10 per cent receive (though in the United States it was 16.6 times in 1997). In Latin American countries, however, the gap is far wider, reaching 119.8 in Honduras, 91.4 in Bolivia, 48.7 in Brazil, 42.7 in Colombia, and 33.7 in Chile (UNDP, 2001: Table 12). Thorp reports that inequality in Colombia, Mexico and Argentina tended to decline from the mid 1960s onwards, whereas in Brazil, Peru and Chile inequality has tended to increase since the 1960s (Thorp, 1998: 27–9). However, even where a decline had been evident, inequality tended to worsen again over the 1990s (IADB, 1998: 13–32).

Contrasts

To evaluate more fully the achievements of Latin America over the twentieth century, we need to compare them to what was happening in other regions of the world. If we make such comparisons over a longer time period, for example over the second half of the twentieth century, this gives us a better basis for seeing just how well Latin America has done. Referring to per capita income, the Inter-American Development Bank 2000 annual report calculated that while in the 1950s Latin America's per capita income was higher than that of any other developing region of the world and reached 50 per cent of that in the developed world, 50 years later the region's per capita income had fallen behind that of Southeast Asia, the Middle East and Eastern Europe and was less than 30 per cent of the per capita income of the developed countries (IADB, 2000). To explain this poor performance, it points out that while Latin American countries' economic growth in the 1950s to the 1970s was between 2 and 3 per cent annually, growth in Southeast Asia surpassed 5 per cent, in the Middle East it was 4 per cent and in Eastern Europe it was around 6 per cent. In the 1980s, Latin America's growth turned negative while it remained positive in the other regions. Taking a longer time horizon, the report states that in 1800 the average income of six leading Latin American economies was only one-third less than that of the United States, whereas a hundred years later, it was four times less.

In terms of health indicators, Latin America has made notable advances in life expectancy over the past half century, but is still behind the countries of Southeast Asia and the Middle East, while, on infant mortality, Latin America has reached a level virtually equal to that of the developed countries.

In education, Latin America's progress is a lot slower than in other regions of the world. For example, almost every other region of the world made swifter progress on increasing literacy rates. Taking average years of education of the adult population (over 25), Latin America increased this from an average of 3.2 years in the 1960s to 5 in the 1990s whereas over the same period Southeast Asia increased from 4.3 years to 7.2, the Middle East from less than 2 years to 4.6 and Eastern Europe from 6 to 8.7 years. Only in Africa was progress slower (IADB, 2000: 1–13). Comparing Latin America's advance in literacy to that of the United States, Thorp points out that despite a century-long effort to expand literacy, by the mid 1990s Latin America still had an illiteracy rate of 13.5 per cent, higher than the 11.2 per cent reached by the United States in 1900 (Thorp: 36).

Diversity

Within Latin America and the Caribbean, six distinct countries or groups of countries can be identified, characterized by features such as geography, shared history and culture, racial make-up and levels of development. From north to south, these are as follows.

Mexico

Officially known as the Estados Unidos Mexicanos (the Mexican United States), it is Latin America's second largest in population and third largest in size (it was double its present size up to the Mexican–American War of 1846–48 when it lost Texas, California and New Mexico to the US). Its history over the course of the last century has been deeply influenced by the Mexican Revolution (1910–20), the twentieth century's first social revolution. This led to the emergence of a one-party state under the control of the Institutional Revolutionary Party (PRI) which ran the country for 71 years (with new presidents chosen every six years by the party and endorsed by the electorate) until its dramatic loss of power to the opposition candidate, Vicente Fox of the right-wing National Action Party (PAN), in the 2000 presidential elections. Under the PRI and with active state intervention in the economy, Mexico was transformed from a backward producer of primary raw materials (minerals, coffee, henequen, rubber, cotton) to one of Latin America's leading industrial powers. As part of this development strategy, a distinctive Mexican identity was promoted, drawing on Aztec themes from the country's precolonial past but pri-

Box 2.1 Measuring human development

The Human Development Index (HDI) offers a way of measuring progress in human development that allows one to arrive at a more comprehensive measure of how well Latin America has fared over the last quarter of the twentieth century. The HDI has been elaborated by the United Nations Development Programme (UNDP) since 1990 and published each year in the UNDP's Human Development Report. It is arrived at through combining measures of three basic components of human development – longevity, knowledge and a decent standard of living. Longevity is measured through life expectancy at birth, knowledge through a combination of the adult literacy rate and the rate of enrolment in primary, secondary and tertiary education, and a decent standard of living by GDP per capita adjusted for purchasing power parity. These are then combined to arrive at a Human Development Index with every country lying somewhere between 0 and 1. The higher the index, the more successful a country has been in those basic aspects of human development that constitute the measure. The HDI is the most widely used measure of development available and offers an alternative to the World Bank's measure which is based solely on rates of economic growth.

Table 2.3 summarizes the HDI for the main regions of the world and how they have changed since 1975. Based on this composite measure, it can be seen that Latin America fares well compared to other regions of the world over the last 25 years.

The Human Development Reports also contain a Human Poverty Index (HPI) reflecting how well the progress achieved is distributed within each country and the backlog of deprivation that still exists, and a Gender-related Development Index (GDI) that measures how equitably women share in the country's development. Finally, a Gender Empowerment Measure (GEM) reveals whether women take an active part in economic and political life. Readers are recommended to acquaint themselves with how the countries of Latin America and the Caribbean fare on these measures, and how they compare with countries in other regions of the world.

TABLE 2.3   HUMAN DEVELOPMENT INDEX FOR REGIONS, 1975 AND 1999

Regions	Developed OECD	Eastern Europe	Latin America, Caribbean	East Asia and Pacific	Arab states	South Asia	Sub-Saharan Africa
1975	0.839	0.764	0.652	0.609	0.503	0.423	0.380
1999	0.928	0.777	0.760	0.719	0.648	0.564	0.467

The 1999 measures are based on HDIs for 162 countries, whereas the 1975 measures are based on HDIs for 97 countries. The results, therefore, are more indicative than definitive.

Sources: UNDP, 2001: data for 1999 from Table 1; data for 1975 calculated from Table 2

vileging the mixed-blood *mestizos* over that of the 10 per cent indigenous
population who continued to be legally and economically marginalized. The
rights of the indigenous are now being actively championed by the Zapatista
guerrilla group. Though a major oil exporter and therefore a beneficiary of the
international oil price rises in the 1970s, Mexico squandered a lot of its
income; in 1982 it sparked the beginning of the international debt crisis by
announcing it could not meet payments on its huge foreign debt. Since then,
Mexico has liberalized its economy and come to identify its interests more and
more with those of its northern neighbour, signing the North American Free
Trade Agreement (NAFTA) with the United States and Canada which entered
into force in 1994.

Central America and Panama

The five countries of Central America emerged into independence as a single
state but the United Provinces of Central America lasted only from 1823 until
1839. The subsequent history of the independent republics is, with the exception of Costa Rica, one of political repression and the economic marginalization of the majority as the region's elites promoted export-led agriculture, in
the process pushing the small peasant farmers off good land. In Costa Rica, by
contrast, due to its tiny population in colonial times and the absence of indigenous people who could be used as a cheap labour force, a more egalitarian
system of family farming developed; this history has allowed it to achieve much
higher levels of development in the late twentieth century. In Guatemala, the
largest state, the majority of the population belong to Quiche indigenous
groups, who have been subjected to brutal subjugation culminating in the
30-year-long genocidal war from the 1960s to the 1990s as, in their counterinsurgency strategy against guerrilla groups, the military targeted the indigenous population. The other republics have much smaller indigenous populations
and Costa Rica is largely European in its racial make-up. Growing social unrest
in tiny El Salvador (Latin America's most densely populated country) and
Nicaragua in the 1960s and 1970s, coupled with fierce political repression
by governments, led to the emergence of armed guerrilla groups there. The
victory of the Sandinista National Liberation Front (FSLN) in Nicaragua in
July 1979 brought the region to the centre of international attention and the
1980s was dominated by US-backed campaigns of terror in an attempt to
defeat the Guatemalan and Salvadorean guerrillas and the Sandinista government. As civil conflict abated in the 1990s with peace processes in Guatemala
and El Salvador, and with the defeat of the Sandinistas in the 1990 elections,
the region faces the challenge of finding an economic niche for itself amid the
pressures of economic liberalization and of avoiding being marginalized (particularly from the crucial US market) by the growing integration between
Mexico and the United States. The Panama Canal has dominated the history
of Panama and was the cause of its declaration of independence from
Colombia in 1903. The United States, which actively promoted Panama's
independence, maintained control over a 10-mile-wide canal zone until 2000
and used it to invade the country in 1989, capturing its leader, General Manuel

Antonio Noriega, and taking him to the USA where he was imprisoned for drugs trafficking offences.

The Caribbean

Divided by language (there are Spanish, English, French and Dutch-speaking countries), by geography, by politics (17 independent states, British colonies, French and Dutch dependencies and Puerto Rico, a 'commonwealth' of the United States) and by colonial history, only in the 1990s did the region's countries begin to find common cause. This was where Columbus first landed in 1492 and where Europeans first established settlements. As a result the original Arawak and Carib peoples were almost entirely wiped out and African slaves were imported in large numbers during colonial times to work the sugar plantations on which much of the region's economies depended. The descendants of these slaves led Haiti to independence in 1804, the first independent state in Latin America and the Caribbean, and give the region much of its racial diversity today. Most of the region's countries only achieved independence in the 1960s and maintained close economic ties with their former colonial masters. Thus, the English-speaking Caribbean countries form part of the ACP (African, Caribbean and Pacific) countries that benefited from the Lomé Convention, a series of development agreements with the European Union from 1975 to 2000 (this was succeeded by the Cotonou Agreement in 2000, due to last for 20 years). Cuba, the region's largest country, has until the mid 1990s identified more with Latin America, though it has suffered a certain isolation since its socialist revolution in 1959. Still highly dependent economically on the export of a few primary commodities (sugar, bananas and bauxite-alumina), the region faced particular vulnerability under the new orthodoxy of the 1990s. This was illustrated by the so-called 'banana war' under which the United States took and won a case at the World Trade Organization forcing the EU to change the preferential access to its lucrative markets given to Caribbean bananas under the Lomé Convention, thus opening its markets to the bananas produced by US multinationals in Central America and Ecuador. This threatens the economic viability of some small Caribbean states. In response to such threats, the Caribbean is deepening its regional integration both among its own countries (through Caricom) and with the Latin American countries surrounding it (through the Association of Caribbean States, ACS). Cuba, Haiti and the Dominican Republic are increasingly part of this process.

The Andean countries

This region stretches from the relatively developed and oil-dependent Venezuela on the Caribbean coast, through Colombia, Ecuador and Peru, to land-locked Bolivia, the poorest country in South America. This grouping is also very racially diverse – to the north the racial mix is more European, whereas the populations of Ecuador, Peru and Bolivia, which were the heartlands of the Inca Empire, are largely *mestizo* or, in Bolivia, indigenous (Quiche and Aymara). Though Venezuela and Colombia maintained formal democratic systems since the 1950s, by the 1990s they had become increasingly unable to channel the growing social discontent in both countries. This has led to an experiment in populism in Venezuela under Hugo Chavez that sidelined the country's traditional parties, and to growing social conflict in Colombia between guerrillas, the military and right-wing paramilitary squads, with the United States becoming increasingly involved. Ecuador, Peru and Bolivia each had their periods of military dictatorship in the late 1960s and 1970s, though they were largely socially progressive in the first two countries. United in the Andean Pact since 1969, each of these countries faces major economic problems at the beginning of the twenty-first century. Venezuela's arises from its extreme dependence on the export of oil and on the stop–go nature of its attempts at economic reform since the 1980s. In Colombia, economic development was more carefully managed and the country largely avoided the devastating impact of the international debt crisis in the 1980s; however, the growth of illegal cocaine production and trading has led to growing problems of corruption and violence that are undermining political and social stability. Despite decisive economic liberalization in the late 1980s and 1990s, Peru and Bolivia have yet to show sustainable economic growth and social development. Bolivia was badly hit by the collapse of the international tin market in 1986 on which its economy had long depended. Ecuador has lurched from crisis to crisis, deposing presidents under popular pressure in 1997 and 2000 and adopting the US dollar as its currency in an attempt to stabilize its financial system. None of these three countries has as yet found a way of capturing greater benefits from economic liberalization.

Brazil (and Paraguay)

Brazil ended the twentieth century as Latin America's dominant economic and political power, transformed from a largely traditional coffee-producing country at the beginning of the century to a major world industrial power at its end. However, the benefits of this economic development remain so unequally divided that some commentators refer to it as 'Belindia', namely a combination of Belgium and India. The more prosperous parts are in the south while the poorer parts are in the north-east. Brazil also displays a wide racial mix in its population, a combination of immigration from Europe and Asia, of the descendants of the African slaves brought in great numbers during colonial times, and the small indigenous population, largely tribal groups living in the vast interior of the country. It has proved a successful example of racial integration, though the country's wealthy elite is still largely white. Its spectacular growth and development from the 1960s to the late 1970s was regarded as an economic miracle, and was symbolized by its ultra-modern new capital city, Brasilia, built in record time on a semi-arid highland plain, an attempt to move the axis of development inland from the Atlantic coast. Governed by a military dictatorship between 1964 and 1985, Brazilian politics has been characterized by volatile alliances between weak political parties, often little more than electoral machines for dominant political personalities. The one exception is the Partido dos Trabalhadores (PT: Workers Party) which grew out of trade union and social movement activism in the mobilization against the dictatorship at the end of the 1970s and whose candidates have won election as mayors of some major Brazilian cities, including Sao Paulo. Plagued by high and persistent inflation from the mid 1980s to the early 1990s, Brazil ended the century under the reforming and liberalizing presidency of former dependency theorist Fernando Henrique Cardoso, whose actions in tackling the country's acute social problems failed to match his promises.

Paraguay is grouped here since its recent economic history has been heavily influenced by Brazilian immigration along the countries' borders and the joint construction of the giant Itaipú dam. However, for most of its existence Paraguay has remained largely isolated from its neighbours. After independence in 1813, it followed a policy of isolation and self-sufficiency under its early leaders, a fascinating and apparently successful experiment which was brought to an abrupt end by the War of the Triple Alliance against Brazil, Argentina and Uruguay (1865–70) in which the country lost most of its male population. It is the only Latin American country in which an indigenous language is the vernacular: Guaraní is widely spoken though most people also speak Spanish. Despite some economic liberalization since the end of the Stroessner dictatorship in 1989, contraband still constituted some one-third to one-half of the country's imports at the end of the twentieth century.

The Southern Cone

Argentina, Uruguay and Chile make up the Southern Cone, so-called because of the geographical shape of these countries. These are among the most European countries of Latin America since both Argentina and Uruguay virtually eliminated their indigenous populations following independence. While Chile prides itself on being largely European in its racial make-up, its Mapuche people, who were not finally conquered until the 1880s, constitute a small but increasingly vocal minority, whose size is disputed. Each of these countries is highly fertile in its combination of geography and climate and, by the early twentieth century, Argentina and Uruguay showed indices of social development better than many developed countries. Under President José Batlle y Ordóñez (1903–7; 1911–15) Uruguay became the world's first welfare state. Argentina became a significant industrial power and the incorporation of its working class owed a lot to the distributive measures of the governments of Juan Domingo Perón (1946–55; 1973–4), whose shadow has hung over the turbulent political life of the country since. While Chile and Uruguay were stable democracies for much of the twentieth century, Argentina was plagued by persistent military intervention in politics from 1930 to the mid 1980s. All three countries suffered brutal military dictatorships (Chile and Uruguay from 1973, Argentina from 1976) that sought to purge the left and to consolidate elite rule. With the return to civilian rule in the 1980s (the Chilean handover was in 1990), all three countries have had to deal with the traumatic legacies of the 'disappeared' and whether to hold the military accountable for their crimes. The arrest of former Chilean dictator Augusto Pinochet in London in 1998 helped open the floodgates in Chile to a large number of court cases against military officers of the former regime. The implementation of neoliberal economic policies by the Chilean military saw that country achieve some of Latin America's highest rates of economic growth from the late 1980s to the late 1990s, though doubts remain about the sustainability of that growth and its environmental impact. Argentina, on the other hand, ended the century with profound economic problems: maintaining a one-to-one link between its currency and the US dollar attracted capital inflows, much of it speculative, but hit the country's exports hard; meanwhile swift liberalization in the 1990s undermined much of the country's industrial base. Thus the country which began the twentieth century with some of the highest living standards in the world ended it with unprecedented levels of poverty and unemployment.

Latin America and the Caribbean enter the twenty-first century, therefore, with a solid base of achievement but still facing enormous challenges, particularly the challenges of economic development and of social inclusion. Before examining in more detail how it is responding to these challenges, the next chapter outlines the two principal strategies it has used to develop itself over the period since the middle of the nineteenth century.

Notes

[1] During the Sandinista Revolution (1979–90) Nicaragua took on far greater importance, but this has changed since the Sandinistas left power.

[2] The measure of relative poverty used here is arrived at by calculating those in the population whose income is over $1 a day *and* whose daily consumption is higher than one-third of the average consumption in their country. All those who fail to meet this standard are deemed to be in relative poverty (see Chen and Ravallion, 2000: 16).

3

Towards Development

T he pervasive practice of labelling regions and countries as 'developed', 'developing' or 'underdeveloped' can have the effect of distracting attention from the complex process of producing and distributing goods and services, whether for the consumption of the producer's family as in subsistence economies, for sale in local markets as in regional economies, or for sale in other countries, as is common in today's more globalized world economy. Looking backwards through the development categories that only came into general use in the second half of the twentieth century runs the risk of seeing a region like Latin America, or the varied countries that constitute it, as being predetermined to something we call 'underdevelopment'. This tendency is common in both the dominant forms of understanding the region outlined in Chapter 1: modernization theory situates Latin America as being a 'developing' region which will become in time a mirror image of the mass consumer societies of North America and western Europe, whereas dependency theory sees the region as being condemned to underdevelopment as long as it remains part of the capitalist world economy. Both of these accounts miss the variety and complexity of the many ways in which Latin Americans and their governments have created wealth, distributed its benefits, and taken advantage of opportunities presented to them by trade, financial flows and technology. In accounting for how Latin America has become the sort of region described in Chapter 2, we need therefore to examine empirically the interaction of these various elements.

This involves keeping a balance between structure and agency. Due to its geography, climate, population and history, Latin America was predisposed to supplying certain types of products to the world economy. In looking at what it produced, how it traded these products, where it found investments to expand and change production, and how new technologies were adopted, we can outline these structural features of its development efforts. Yet these features never predetermined the outcomes achieved; the most they did was to create opportunities. How these opportunities were availed of depended on the agency of different groups in society. Foremost among these were the dominant classes, for example the land-owning class and the state administrators in colonial times and in the early independence period. These could work in conjunction or, where different interests were involved, one might seek to dominate the other, leading at times to social unrest. But such elite groups, though they hold a lot of economic and political power in their hands, always depend on larger groups in society such as the workers and peasants who provide most of the labour, or middle class groups such as shopkeepers, bureaucrats, lawyers, teachers and priests who help to ensure in many different ways the smooth functioning of society. Where the interests of such groups are satisfied through, for example, decent wages and working conditions for labourers, or a share in power for the middle classes, goods can be produced and traded more success-fully. To help achieve such successful outcomes, the role of the state can be crucial if it tries to serve a wider national interest rather than simply the inter-ests of particular powerful groups.

This chapter traces these interactions and their outcomes up to the major economic and political transformations of the 1980s. The first section exam-ines the way the region was integrated into the world economy in the colonial period before going on, in the second section, to look at the first major effort to develop Latin America through primary commodity exporting, a phase that lasted from around 1870 to the Great Depression in 1929. The final section covers the major change in the 1930s to a development strategy based on import-substitution industrialization that was only finally and decisively jet-tisoned in the early 1980s.

Latin America in the World Order

The European conquest of Latin America in the late fifteenth and early six-teenth centuries is seen by some authors as marking the emergence of 'early modern globalization' (Held et al., 1999: 418), the first stage in the develop-ment of global European empires. To this extent, Latin America played an early role in globalization, supplying Europe with raw materials such as silver and gold that were crucial to its emergence as the dominant global power in the nineteenth and early twentieth centuries.[1] Before the arrival of Europeans, the region's peoples had developed some complex civilizations such as the Aztecs of the Valley of Mexico (around present-day Mexico City), the Mayans of Central America (south-eastern Mexico down to Honduras) and the Incas of the Andean region (centred on Peru but stretching from Ecuador down to central Chile). In these regions, foodstuffs were developed which afterwards became part of Europeans' staple diet, such as maize, beans, tomatoes, choco-late, potatoes and turkeys. The coca leaf, from which cocaine is made, is another product of the Andean region which in its processed form is now widely consumed in North America and western Europe. However, in pre-colonial times, trade in foodstuffs, textiles and the elaborate silver and gold ornamentation produced by these civilizations was largely limited to areas under the political control of the then dominant regional powers.

The sudden arrival of Europeans and the swift control they achieved over the heartlands of the great native civilizations transformed Latin America into a region where production was now reoriented to serve the needs of the colonial power. More interested in precious metals than in such goods as sugar,

tobacco, cocoa, dyes and spices, the Spanish Crown organized its new posses-
sions so as to ensure a stable supply of native labour to work the silver mines of
Mexico and Peru, at the heart of the two viceroyalties into which the region
was initially divided. To avoid the emergence of a class of land-owners that
might develop interests contrary to those of the Crown, individual Spaniards
were given the right to collect tributes from native villages that could take the
form of goods or labour. The decline of the native population and the need to
feed urban centres such as Mexico City and Lima led to the emergence of
extensive European-style agricultural production by the end of the sixteenth
century, particularly wheat and pasture (sheep and cattle). However, little
interest was shown in developing the productive capacity of such regions of
fertile land as Argentina, Chile, southern Venezuela or northern Mexico, on the
outer reaches of the new viceroyalties (Weaver, 2000: 13–20). By contrast, the
Portuguese Crown developed in Brazil sugar plantations to supply the growing
European market for what was becoming an essential food ingredient. When
the supply of native labour was exhausted, slaves began to be imported from
west Africa where the Portuguese had an established foothold since the early
fifteenth century. 'By 1580, the Portuguese were importing more than 2,000
African slaves a year to work the sugar plantations of northeastern Brazil. ...
Brazil received more African slaves (at least 3.65 million, and some estimates
are considerably higher) in total than any other region of the Americas'
(Skidmore, 1999: 17). In this system, therefore, the productive economy served
the needs of the colonial power that established forms of rule, under the watch-
ful eye of colonial administrators sent from the mother country, to ensure a
labour supply for the mines and plantations as well as for the local colonial
elite. Seething unrest regularly erupted and was fiercely repressed. Referring to
New Spain (present-day Mexico), Suchlicki writes: 'Mutinies against taxes and
ill-treatment were common. In 1598, Tepic miners rebelled; in 1680, Indians of
Tehuantepec rose in arms and controlled the Isthmus for several years; in 1692,
roaming mobs of Indians set fire to large sections of Mexico City; in 1761,
Mayan descendants rebelled in Yucatán. All of these ended in defeat for the
native populations' (2001: 40).

The accession of the Bourbons to the Spanish throne in 1700 opened a
period of reform that marked the first major change in the economic and social
relations between Spain and its Latin American colonies. Imbued with the zeal
of the Enlightenment, the new Bourbon kings turned their attention to fostering
a productive agriculture and industry, both at home and in their colonies. The
monopoly under which all trade was to pass through the Spanish port of Cadiz
was gradually lifted, stimulating a big increase in trade both within the Spanish
American colonies and between them and Spain, though trade with countries
other than Spain was still prohibited (except in time of war). This stimulated
the production of goods such as sugar, hides and tobacco, sought after in
European markets. For example, the opening of Buenos Aires port to trade
in 1735 helped stimulate development in the Rio de la Plata area (present-day
Argentina). In this period, there developed 'a marked trend toward regional
specialization and monoculture in the production of cash crops' (Keen and
Haynes, 2000: 138) which was to become accentuated in the century that

followed. The Bourbon reforms also had negative consequences as greater trade led to more imports that damaged such local manufacturing industries as cloth, wares and wines. After a long period of growth, these began to decline in the latter half of the eighteenth century. The reforms also stimulated opposition as they involved extensive administrative reorganization and the imposition of new taxes that were often resisted not just by workers and peasants but also by the American-born *criollo* elite who were excluded from the highest positions in church and state. For example, in May 1791 a tax revolt of between 15,000 and 20,000 Comuneros who marched on Bogota, the capital of New Granada (a viceroyalty covering present-day Colombia, Venezuela and Ecuador), included among its demands that 'in government positions of the first, second and third level the nationals of this America are to be preferred and privileged above the Europeans, since the latter daily show the antipathy which they maintain against the people here' (quoted in Safford and Palacios, 2002: 67). In Brazil also, the reforming policies of the Marquis of Pombal, who became de facto prime minister of Portugal and its colonies from 1750 to 1777, reorganized the colony and greatly increased trade in sugar, wheat, rice and indigo. By the end of the eighteenth century, Brazil was furnishing some 60 per cent of Portugal's exports.

In these developments, historians see early signs of the sentiment that led to the independence movements of the first two decades of the nineteenth century. Taking advantage of Napoleon's invasion of the Iberian Peninsula in 1807, local *criollo* elites took power in a number of Spain's American colonies, while the Portuguese Court moved to Rio de Janeiro. By the 1820s, after protracted struggles, most had become independent republics; in 1822, following the Portuguese king's return to Lisbon, his son proclaimed Brazilian independence with himself as its first emperor, Dom Pedro I. The vacuum left by the colonial powers was quickly filled by the British, whose principal interest was to expand the markets for the products of its Industrial Revolution. However, the new states were weak and rent by deep political divisions between conservatives who sought strong central authority and liberals who espoused more federalist systems with devolved power. In this situation, rather than spurring trade, British investment served to fuel the civil unrest which convulsed many of the Spanish-speaking states until mid-century. The countries which fared best were those able to specialize in products for which there was an export market – Chile in copper, Cuba in sugar, Costa Rica and Brazil in coffee. Meanwhile local manufacturing of products like textiles and clothing remained weak, due to the lack of access to capital and technologies, and under threat from European imports. In these ways, the foundations were being laid for the emergence in the 1870s of a model of development in which countries specialized in the export of a small number of largely unprocessed raw materials.

Primary Commodity Exporting, 1870–1930

It was conditions in the industrializing countries of western Europe that laid the foundations for the emergence of primary commodity exporting. Firstly, industrialization created needs for two different kinds of goods that could be supplied by Latin American countries – raw materials for industry such as tin, copper or cotton, and foodstuffs such as coffee, beef, wheat, bananas and sugar for the growing urban masses in the industrializing countries. The second major condition was the ability provided by new technologies to cut dramatically the costs and time of getting these products to the European markets, particularly the railway and the steamship. Railways in Latin America were primarily constructed to get goods to ports; the first railway was built in Cuba in 1837 to facilitate sugar exports to the United States. But particularly from the 1870s onwards rail networks extended rapidly – in Brazil from a mere 745 kilometres in 1870 to 32,478 km in 1930 and in Mexico from 638 km in 1876 to 19,280 km in 1910. It is estimated that the time taken for overland journeys was reduced 30 times and that freight costs dropped to one-twelfth of alternative means. From around the 1870s also, steamships came into more general use with greatly increased services to and from Latin American ports, doubling vessels' carrying capacity and their speeds. The opening of the Panama Canal in 1914 further reduced transport costs and time, especially for trade from ports on the west coast of Latin America to Europe and to the east coast of the United States. The third major condition facilitating the emergence of primary commodity exporting was growing European and US investment in Latin America. Led by Britain, such investment spurred not only the production (and in the case of mining, the extraction) of export commodities, but also the infrastructure (machines and railways), the import and export businesses, and the banking and insurance sector that offered credit to Latin American governments. British investment rose from £80 million sterling in 1865 to £1,179 million in 1913, the single largest amount being loans to governments followed closely by railway construction. While most British investment went to Argentina and Brazil, most US investment was in countries close to it, particularly mining and railways in Mexico and sugar plantations in Cuba. France and Germany were also major investors in Latin America over this period. The US share of investment was gradually growing; the First World War (1914–18) marked a decisive shift and made it the principal source of capital and credit for the region. A final condition came from within the region itself as the civil unrest which marked the first half-century of independence began to resolve itself around the 1870s. Argentina's struggles between federalists and unitarians were finally settled in the 1860s, in Mexico the Porfiriato (the rule of Porfirio Diaz, 1876–1911) ended 50 years of violence and bloodshed, and in Brazil, the overthrow of the monarchy in 1889 resulted in the interests of the powerful coffee producers dominating the First Republic (1891–1930). All of these conditions provided the basis for Latin America to play a significant role in the huge increase in world trade from around 1870 up to the Great Depression. In 1913, the region provided 62 per cent of world exports of coffee, tea and cocoa, 25 per cent of rubber, hides and leather, 18 per cent of cereals, 14 per cent of fruit and vegetables, and 12 per cent of livestock products.

To play this role in the world economy, Latin American countries transformed themselves into what are often called monocrop economies. By this is meant that many countries came to depend on the export of one or two products for most of their export earnings. The extent of this dependence is illustrated in Table 3.1.

Of the 21 countries listed, 13 depended on one export product for over half of their export earnings and 16 depended on two products for two-thirds or more of export earnings. The dependence of Bolivia on tin, of Chile on nitrates, of Cuba on sugar, and of Guatemala and El Salvador on coffee is particularly striking. This made them very vulnerable to fluctuations in the prices these commodities fetched on the world market. For example, during the First World War the prices of strategic minerals required for the war effort boomed, whereas those for foodstuffs like coffee, cocoa and bananas slumped. This is why this model of development is sometimes called a 'commodity lottery' (Bulmer-Thomas, 1994: 43), since the fate of countries is largely dependent on factors beyond their control. Neither has such vulnerability ended at the beginning of the twenty-first century, as shown by the newspaper headline in Box 3.1.

Countries that depended for their economic growth on the export of primary commodities faced major obstacles to industrialization. Firstly, since the production of export commodities was often in the hands of foreign companies (banana plantations or mining companies) or landlords (many foodstuffs), there was little incentive to reinvest profits in industry. Secondly, such industry would have depended on a local consumer market to sell its products, and the low wages received by many workers in the export economy, or the fact that they constituted a relatively small proportion of the national population, worked against the development of a significant consumer market.[2] Thirdly, it was in many cases cheaper to import goods than to manufacture them in Latin America, given the lack of an industrial tradition, of necessary raw materials, and of suitable sources of credit. For these reasons, the development of industries during this period tended to be limited to goods for which there was a large consumer market (breweries, flour, clothing, shoes) or which served the needs of the export economy (mechanical repair workshops for the railways). Foreign immigrants were the driving force in many countries: in Argentina in 1895, 80 per cent of industrial proprietors had been born outside the country, while in Uruguay in 1908 the figure was 60 per cent. It was similar in Chile, Peru and Mexico. In Brazil, however, due to the nature of coffee production which did not require much reinvestment of surplus for continued profitability, profits were invested in industry, the output of which increased almost five-fold between 1900 and 1930. Despite this, industry remained a tiny sector of even these countries' economies: in 1910, industrial workers constituted only 0.3 per cent of Mexico's population, and in 1920, only 1 per cent of Brazil's. In this situation, countries were highly dependent on importing many of the goods needed both for consumption and as economic inputs (machines, spare parts). And, as Bulmer-Thomas relates, the leading industrial powers were only too keen to provide:

> Throughout the period up to the First World War, British exports to Latin America remained concentrated in textiles and clothing. Rival industrial powers were unable

TABLE 3.1 DEPENDENCE ON COMMODITY EXPORTS, CIRCA 1913

Country	First product	Export share (%)	Second product	Export share (%)	Share of two principal exports (%)
Argentina	Maize	22.5	Wheat	20.7	43.2
Bolivia	Tin	72.3	Silver	4.3	76.6
Brazil	Coffee	62.3	Rubber	15.9	78.2
Chile	Nitrates	71.3	Copper	7.0	78.3
Colombia	Coffee	37.2	Gold	20.4	57.6
Costa Rica	Bananas	50.9	Coffee	35.2	86.1
Cuba	Sugar	72.0	Tobacco	19.5	91.5
Dominican Republic	Cocoa	39.2	Sugar	34.8	74.0
Ecuador	Cocoa	64.1	Coffee	5.4	69.5
El Salvador	Coffee	79.6	Precious metals	15.9	95.5
Guatemala	Coffee	84.8	Bananas	5.7	90.5
Haiti	Coffee	64.0	Cocoa	6.8	70.8
Honduras	Bananas	50.1	Precious metals	25.9	76.0
Mexico	Silver	30.3	Copper	10.3	40.6
Nicaragua	Coffee	64.9	Precious metals	13.8	78.7
Panama	Bananas	65.0	Coconuts	7.0	72.0
Paraguay	Yerba maté[a]	32.1	Tobacco	15.8	47.9
Peru	Copper	22.0	Sugar	15.4	37.4
Puerto Rico	Sugar	47.0	Coffee	19.0	66.0
Uruguay	Wool	42.0	Meat	24.0	66.0
Venezuela	Coffee	52.0	Cocoa	21.4	73.4

[a]Yerba maté is a herbal drink, imbibed through a short pipe, widely drunk in Paraguay and Argentina.

Source: Bulmer-Thomas, 1994: Table 3.2, p. 59

Box 3.1 Illustration of dependence

The following was the main story on the front page of a leading Chilean newspaper, *La Tercera*, in its edition of 23 October 2001:

LOWER PRICE THAN DURING THE ASIAN CRISIS: US$0.608
Copper falls to its lowest level in 14 years

The metal accounts for 49% of Chilean exports and the country loses US$100 million for every cent the price drops. The price trend is reflected in the fact that in 1990 Chilean copper exports fetched US$1 billion^3 compared to US$700 million now.

to mount a serious challenge to Great Britain in this field, but they did succeed in outperforming Great Britain in other areas. Thus by the end of the century US agricultural and mining machinery was much in demand, German 'fancy' goods were highly prized, and France was considered the best source for luxury consumer goods. (1994: 77)

For virtually all Latin American countries, taxes on these imports constituted the state's principal revenue source. By the First World War no country received less than 50 per cent of public revenue from customs duties and in many cases the share was more than 70 per cent. Mostly these were on imports, though given the virtual world monopoly that Chile possessed in nitrate production, it could tax its exports with little fear of losing market share and these provided nearly 50 per cent of the country's public revenue between 1890 and 1914.

Primary commodity exporting offered Latin America a dynamic role in the world economy for about 60 years, allowing the region to achieve significant growth in exports and in GDP over the period. For example, between 1900 and 1929 average annual growth rates in Venezuela were 5 per cent, in Colombia and Peru 4.5 per cent, in Brazil 4.2 per cent, in Cuba 4.1 per cent, in Argentina 3.8 per cent and in Chile 2.9 per cent (Thorp, 1998: Table 3.1, p. 52). Yet, as Bulmer-Thomas put it, 'Latin America's place in the world economy depended on the export of primary products and the import of manufactured goods' (1994: 78). This was an inherently unstable development model, subject to the vagaries of international demand over which the producing country had virtually no control.[4] Not only did prices for these products fluctuate, but markets simply disappeared for some of them. This was the case with Peruvian guano (bird droppings collected from coastal rocks), a natural fertilizer, which constituted the country's principal export between the 1840s and the 1870s; revenue from this trade constituted 80 per cent of the state's income in the 1860s. But by the 1870s guano stocks were exhausted. Another example is Amazonian rubber: from its first development as an export product in the 1860s up until 1910 it became one of Brazil's main export items. However, with the development of rubber plantations in the British colony of Malaysia in the early years of the century, demand for Brazilian rubber disappeared almost overnight. Today, its main legacy is the beautiful opera house in the Amazonian city of Manaus where Europe's top singers were brought to entertain the rubber barons. A final example is Chilean nitrates, for decades the basis of the country's economic growth. However, the development of synthetic nitrates following the First World War led to the industry's sudden collapse in the late 1920s.

In terms of social development, therefore, the key question is to identify the extent to which these export booms stimulated economic activity and social progress. This can be done through looking at linkages between the dynamic sectors and the rest of the economy and society. Three kinds of linkages are often identified – forward linkages which stimulate economic activity through, for example, the processing of raw materials; backward linkages which stimulate such activity through making inputs for the dynamic sector such as machinery or tools; and what are called income-multiplier linkages which relate to the incomes received and how these might stimulate economic and social development. All three forms of linkages were extremely weak in Latin America's primary commodity export phase. Most inputs such as machinery were imported rather than being manufactured in the region and most exports were loaded in unprocessed form on to ships for export. Only in a small number of cases can one identify robust forward linkages such as the refrigerator plants in Buenos Aires where beef was slaughtered and packed for export. Much of the mining or plantation agriculture constituted what are called 'enclaves', namely virtually self-contained units that contributed little to the national economy. An exception were the nitrate mines in the north of Chile, as the government, aware that it had an exhaustible resource, taxed its exports in order to promote industry, education and social development (Thorp, 1998: 70–71). The third linkage was also weak as wages tended to be low and work conditions unstable in many primary commodity sectors. An exception were the coffee-growing areas of Colombia and Costa Rica, as here, unlike coffee production in Brazil and El Salvador, production took place on small family farms. This helped to reinforce a strong sector of prosperous family farms that endures to the present day. Thus, as Weaver concludes, 'in good part because of the lack of backward-linked production, Latin American manufacturing neither generated a self-sustaining dynamic of its own nor stimulated other sectors of the economy even where its level of output was most impressive. Manufacturing production rose and fell with the fortunes of the principal exports' (2000: 83).

A focus on economic production, however, fails to notice some of the most important changes brought by primary commodity exporting. Even though the region's oligarchies were the ones who principally benefited from the export booms, these booms also created new social forces. For the growth of a middle class, and of a small, but in places militant, working class, led to pressures for political and social change that began to challenge the oligarchic states in the region. The most dramatic expression of this was the Mexican Revolution which led to 'remarkable institutional development, as both the state and civil society were fundamentally changed' (Thorp, 1998: 68). Meanwhile the First World War showed the vulnerability of the primary commodity export model, as demand for some exports fell and as the banking system was suspended, causing financial panic in Latin America. However, as Thorp put it:

> Despite the incipient tensions and weaknesses which we have shown to be appearing in the export model it was to require more time and louder signals before the major economic groups could perceive their interests as significantly distinct from those of foreigners. In a sense also, the changes that did occur during the war were premature, lacking the necessary base in the prior extension of the industrial sector and the growth of a middle class or other groups prepared to see their interests as lying with the growth of industry. For both kinds of reasons, Latin America had to await the depression before the forces for change could coalesce in a manner which made a real alternative policy possible. (1986: 80–1)

Import-Substitution Industrialization, 1930–80

The Great Depression of 1929 delivered the blow that was to force a decisive move to industrialization. Most Latin American countries faced a sudden and sharp decline in the prices for their products, with the value of the region's exports falling from $2.6 billion in 1929, to $1.7 billion in 1930 and to a low of $945 million in 1932 before recovery began. Mineral exporters Bolivia and Chile and sugar exporter Cuba were particularly badly hit. Alongside this, most of the region's countries faced debt repayments that did not decline; as a result, spending on imports had to be drastically cut back. As governments depended on customs duties for most of their revenues, the effect was particularly severe. At the height of the crisis, it is estimated that about half the region's workforce was unemployed (de Ramón et al., 2001b: 392). The crisis therefore hit at the heart of the primary commodity exporting model of development and forced governments to take a much more active role in the economies of their countries – initially through immediate efforts to manage the crisis which, over the longer term, developed into a new model of development, not based on exporting primary products but on manufacturing at home goods which had previously been imported. For this reason, it is known as import-substitution industrialization (often referred to simply as ISI).

Governments reacted to the initial crisis by instituting public works programmes and other forms of spending to generate demand within their economies. For example, Thorp mentions Uruguay's hosting of the 1930 World Cup and military spending by Paraguay and Bolivia on the Chaco War (1932–5) as examples (1998: 112). Debt defaults by Latin American countries between 1931 and 1934 were condoned by international financial markets (unlike what was to happen in the next great international debt crisis of the early 1980s), easing greatly the pressures on national budgets. Added to public spending was the use of import quotas and tariffs as a way of stimulating industrial production by protecting the domestic market from competitive imports. This turning inwards, as it can be called, was given impetus by the protectionist measures taken by many developed countries, most notably the famous Smoot–Hawley tariff introduced by the US Congress in 1930 which raised the import barriers faced by Latin American primary commodity producers in their most important market. As recovery picked up in many countries from the early 1930s, governments took steps to consolidate these early moves towards industrialization. The most important example was the rise to power of Getúlio Vargas in Brazil in 1930 (he was president of Brazil from 1930 to 1945 and from 1950 to 1954); defeating an uprising in 1932 by the Sao Paulo coffee growing elite which had dominated political power over previous decades, he went on to institute a vigorous policy of industrialization ensuring, through corporatist measures inspired by Italian fascism, that trade unions and their members gained substantial benefits in return for industrial peace. Similarly the legendary presidency of Lázaro Cárdenas in Mexico (1934–40) further stimulated industrialization, nationalized the oil industry in 1938, and institutionalized the trade union movement as one of the props of the ruling Institutional Revolutionary Party (PRI). In 1939 Chile established a state development agency, Corfo, that was to play a major role in that country's industrialization. The Second World War further deepened these initial moves since it provided buoyant markets for many of Latin America's exports but further restricted the region's imports. Many countries therefore accumulated foreign reserves which some used to pay back their debts, while the needs of the US war-time economy led it to foster strategic industry in some Latin American countries, most notably the Volta Redonda steel mills in Brazil. These helped to further develop state capacity and to lay the foundations for a more autonomous manufacturing sector, particularly in Mexico and Brazil.

The post-war years therefore saw the development of a coherent, state-led industrialization strategy, particularly in Brazil, Mexico, Argentina, Colombia, Chile and Uruguay. In countries whose primary commodities still found easy export markets such as Peru (mining), Bolivia (tin), Ecuador (bananas) and Venezuela (oil), domestic lobbies in favour of ISI did not develop to the same degree, though some efforts in that direction were made under certain governments. Cuba, too, remained highly dependent on sugar exports and, following the revolution in 1959 and early attempts at agricultural diversification, the communist government returned in the 1960s to emphasize sugar production, this time for the Soviet market (see Chapter 8). In smaller countries, such as the republics of Central America, markets were too small to facilitate full-blown ISI and primary commodity exporting continued to dominate (though the development of the Central American Common Market in the 1960s did stimulate regional industrialization). With the foundation in 1948 of the UN Economic Commission for Latin America (known as CEPAL for the initials of its Spanish name or, in English, as ECLAC),[5] a theoretical justification for ISI began to be developed, particularly in the writings of its first director, the Argentine economist Raul Prebisch (1901–86). His work emphasized that Latin America's terms of trade (the imports it could afford to buy with what its exports would earn) would continue to deteriorate if it maintained its dependence on the export of primary commodities, since he identified a long-term tendency for the prices of these to decrease relative to the prices of manufactured goods. Therefore Latin American governments should take a lead in fostering industrialization which would require initial protectionist measures to succeed (see Kay, 1989: 29–46). This view directly challenged the prevailing approach in neoclassical or mainstream economics that held that developing countries should concentrate on producing and exporting those goods in which it had a comparative advantage, namely primary commodity exports.

The 1950s to the 1970s marked the high-point of ISI. Its main components can be broken down as follows, though different countries applied these in different ways. Firstly, unlike primary commodity exporting in which market forces determined what goods would be produced and where they would be sold, the state played a key guiding role in the ISI strategy. It did this through creating a climate for the development of industry; among the principal means used were tariffs on consumer imports (those goods which might compete with domestically produced manufactured goods), import quotas or licences allowing the state to decide what could or could not be imported, multiple exchange rates making cheaper in the local currency those imports favoured by the state (for example, inputs or machinery needed for industry) and more expensive those not favoured (those competing with domestically produced goods), and politically determined interest rates to facilitate borrowing and industrial expansion. Secondly, in certain strategic sectors (such as steel, petroleum, electricity generation), the state took a direct role in production either through nationalizing existing industries or through establishing new ones. Thirdly, industrialization generally moved through four different stages:

1   Non-durable consumer goods, such as foodstuffs, beverages, pharmaceuticals and clothing which were the easiest to manufacture;
2   Durable consumer goods such as household electrical goods;
3   Intermediate goods such as inputs for cars or machinery;
4   Capital goods such as iron and steel production.

While most Latin American countries began with non-durable consumer goods (often called the 'easy stage' of industrialization) and moved into durable consumer goods, it was only the larger countries (with more state resources and larger markets) that moved successfully into the final two stages, particularly Brazil and Mexico and, with somewhat less success, Argentina. This process of necessity changed the composition of these countries' imports as, instead of importing the consumer goods now being manufactured at home, they required more sophisticated imports such as machinery. Fourthly, the attempt to deepen the industrialization process led countries to attract multinational companies (MNCs) to set up subsidiaries to manufacture for their domestic markets, sometimes with conditions that they use inputs manufactured nationally often by relatively small domestic firms (see Box 3.2 for the example of Brazil's automotive industry). While bringing new product designs, new technology and new forms of organization, these MNCs tended to absorb or displace many large domestic firms. Thus ISI involved privately owned national

Box 3.2 Brazil develops an automotive industry

The following quote is from Gordon (2001: 42–3):

[Brazil's automotive industry] was launched in 1956, with the announced aim of securing by 1960 domestic production of 90 to 95 per cent by weight of all components, as well as final assembly, of some 170,000 vehicles per year. The longer-range goal was an annual capacity of 300,000. European and American automobile companies were given highly favourable exchange rates for importing manufacturing equipment and key components during the short transition period of progressive 'Brazilianization'. In turn, they had to accept rigorous schedules for the production of components in Brazil and undertake specific measures to secure local suppliers. For the more complex parts, the assembly companies often persuaded their own home component manufacturers to invest in joint ventures with promising Brazilian firms.

Although the 1960 production target was not reached until 1962, the industry subsequently grew to major magnitudes, reaching 400,000 vehicles by 1970 and over 1 million by 1978. In 1994, it passed the 1.5 million mark, and in 1997 reached 2 million units, the world's eighth largest output that year.

At the beginning, passenger car costs were well above those of hypothetical imports (actual imports were forbidden), but jeeps and commercial vehicles were competitive from an early stage. Exports became possible by the mid-1970s and in the 1980s accounted for almost one-quarter of total sales. By then, Brazil's automotive industry ranked tenth [in the world], close in size to Britain's. The 'ABC' suburbs of Sao Paulo (Santo André, Sao Bernardo do Campo, and Sao Caetano do Sul) had become a little Detroit. At the industry's start there were too many producers and far too many individual car and truck models, which later had to be shaken down. Yet the experience as a whole was a remarkable demonstration of successful infant-industry promotion.

industries, state-owned industries and foreign-owned industries in what has been called a Triple Alliance (Evans, 1979). As a result, business success often depended more on being able to play politics than on conventional productive strategies. The final component of ISI was the benefits it brought to the workers in the new industries, as labour codes and social security benefits were developed which favoured in particular those in the formal sector. This reflected the power of unions and the symbiotic relationship they developed with the state. The symbolic exemplar of this relationship is offered by the governments of Juan Domingo Perón in Argentina (1946–55; 1973–4) which used the profits of the agro-export industry to raise workers' wages, improve their work conditions and develop for them extensive welfare provisions such as low-cost housing, and health, educational and recreational facilities. However, in doing this Perón effectively took control of the Argentine labour movement, the General Confederation of Work (CGT), making it the key support base for the Peronist Party. These populist tactics can also be observed under Vargas in Brazil, under the PRI in Mexico and in different ways in other Latin American countries (for an account of the major manifestations of populism in Latin America throughout the twentieth century, see Conniff, 1999). Populism is seen by some as characterizing the politics of ISI.[6]

Among the major achievements of ISI was that it allowed Latin America to achieve higher GDP growth rates over the periods 1945–72 and 1972–81 than it has achieved before or since. Taking the annual average of the six leading countries (Brazil, Argentina, Mexico, Chile, Colombia and Venezuela), this shows growth rates of 5.6 per cent and 5.2 per cent respectively during these two periods of ISI, while growth reached 4.3 per cent between 1900–13 and 3.3 per cent between 1913–29. Similarly, GDP per capita, which shows the growth in living standards, grew faster than over the previous period. For the same six countries, average annual incomes grew from $413 to $973 over the 30-year-period 1950–80, whereas they had grown from $185 to $277 over the period 1900–30. The increase for Brazil and Mexico was greater, around threefold. However, even more significant is that manufacturing had now become the engine of growth; the average annual rate of manufacturing growth between 1950 and the mid 1970s was 6.9 per cent in Latin America, 6.4 per cent in the then European Economic Community (EEC), 5.4 per cent in Canada, Australia and New Zealand, and 4.8 per cent in the United States (Weaver, 2000: 129). To achieve this, many of the leading Latin American states had significantly increased their capacity for action and their aspiration as to what they wanted to achieve, constructing transport and communications infrastructure and developing energy supplies but also creating specialist agencies for the development of industrial, mining and agricultural sectors and of scientific and technological skills. For example, Argentina's development of a nuclear power industry was based to a significant extent on indigenous skills and components, while in the 1970s and 1980s Brazilian state agencies acted 'as midwife in the creation of a new set of entrepreneurs and corporate organizations with vested interests in the development of local computer production' (Evans, 1995: 124), even having the goal early on of developing its own Brazilian-designed minicomputers. As Box 3.3 shows, the Allende government in Chile sought to become a world leader in using technology for economic planning.

For all its successes, however, ISI began to display some deep-rooted structural problems from the 1960s onwards. Three principal problems can be identified. The first one derived from the conditions for manufacturing success, namely manufacturing behind protective barriers for a relatively small home market. This resulted in inefficient, high-cost industries, often having a monopoly in their own market and lacking the competition that might spur greater efficiency. As early as 1959, Raul Prebisch was arguing vigorously for the need 'to restore the spirit of competition' (quoted in Thorp, 1998: 150, footnote 60), and attempts were made through regional integration (for an account, see Chapter 6) and industrial export schemes to address these problems but with limited success. The second problem derived from the bias against industrial exports that characterized ISI. As a result, countries remained highly dependent on earning foreign exchange from their traditional primary commodity exports

Box 3.3 Harnessing technology for socialist planning

When Socialist candidate Salvador Allende won the Chilean presidency in September 1970 there were fewer than fifty computers in the country, less than in Brazil, Colombia and Venezuela. However, this did not deter his government from the ambitious task of constructing a unique computer system capable of networking all factories in the nationalized sector of the economy to a central computer in Santiago and monitoring their activities in real time. This system, known as Sistema Synco (or, in English, Project Cybersyn), sought to provide technical solutions to Chile's economic problems in a manner consistent with the socialist principles of Allende's government. Engineers from Chile and Britain contributed to the system's construction, using computer technology imported from the United States.

In his speech inaugurating Sistema Synco, President Allende said that in the advanced countries the power of science had not been used wisely. He went on: 'We have begun valiantly to construct *our* system in *our* way. What you will hear today is revolutionary – not only because it is the first time that this has been done anywhere in the world. It is revolutionary because we are deliberately giving the power of science to the prople, in a form that they themselves can use.' Whether this would have happened we will never know since the government was overthrown in the military coup of 11 September 1973 before the system became operational (Miller, 2002).

in order to import the inputs needed by their manufacturing sector. Yet these traditional sectors were often neglected or even discriminated against in the drive to industrialize, giving rise increasingly to the third problem. This was a growing balance of payments deficit as countries faced reduced foreign exchange earnings but increased costs for imports (including food imports to feed their expanding urban populations), for the capital investment needed by the growing state industrial sector and for the social investment required by the process of modernization (in education, health, and social security). The failure to reform taxation systems exacerbated this problem, leading countries to resort increasingly to foreign borrowing to cover the gap between income and expenditure. Dependence on these loans rose dramatically in the 1970s as western banks, awash with 'petrodollars' from the four-fold oil price increase in 1973, lent irresponsibly. Colombia was the only country that resisted this trend, introducing instead an unpopular tax reform and measures to increase savings. The availability of such easy sources of finance at negative interest rates meant that Latin American governments faced few pressures to deal with the growing problems with ISI; they also faced high levels of capital flight and growing inflation that was to rise to dizzying heights in the 1980s. With the increase in US interest rates in 1980–1, Latin American governments suddenly found their debts unpayable, since they were mostly denominated in US dollars. Mexico's announcement of a moratorium on debt repayments in August 1982 marked the beginning of the international debt crisis and the end of ISI.

The structural problems of ISI had also found increasing expression in social and political problems throughout the region. The expansion of industry and the neglect of agriculture had drawn people in large numbers to cities but the modern economic sector failed to keep pace with fast population growth, with the result that many of those migrating to the cities ended up living in shanty towns and eking out a meagre living in the fast-growing informal sector (such activities as street trading, unlicensed service provision, small workshops). In this situation, government attempts to address the region's huge legacy of poverty and inequality met with only limited success. These economic and social problems fuelled growing political unrest. On the one hand, governments made periodic attempts to address the problems of ISI through austerity measures, economic rationalization or institutional reforms, but these often met with the determined resistance of vested interests, whether of national industrialists or the strong trade unions organized in the industrial sector. On the other, a wave of guerrilla groups emerged in most Latin American countries, inspired by the success of the Cuban revolution in 1959; their activities, particularly in the case of the urban guerrillas in Uruguay and Argentina, heightened the sense of threat to the status quo felt by privileged groups. In Chile, the threat came from the electoral success in the left-wing Unidad Popular in the 1970 presidential election. In this situation of 'political contestation and stalemate' (Weaver: 139), the military took power in many countries, beginning in Brazil in 1964. While some of these military governments, most notably that of General Juan Velasco Alvarado in Peru (1968–75), tried to solve the problem of social unrest through essentially left-wing programmes of economic, social and political transformation, most implemented severe repression, torturing and making disappear those perceived as political opponents. The Chilean (1973–90), Uruguayan (1973–83) and Argentine (1976–83) national security regimes, as they were called, took this approach while also seeking to reorganize in a radical way the economic and political system in an attempt to liberalize the market and eliminate permanently the influence of the left. This right-wing revolution was most successful in Chile.

By the early 1980s, therefore, the potential of ISI seemed exhausted. Most Latin American countries faced a major problem of indebtedness, and the free-market ideological climate ushered in by British prime minister Margaret Thatcher in 1979 and by US President Ronald Reagan in 1981 was hostile to the state-led experiments through which the region had industrialized. To avail of the opportunities being offered by the more globalized world economy that was fast emerging, Latin America embraced the free-market neoliberal creed with zeal. The next four chapters examine the nature and impact of this neoliberal reformation.

Notes

[1] Weaver reports estimates stating that between 1493 and 1800, 85 per cent of the world's supply of silver and 70 per cent of gold came from the Americas. He continues: 'The Spanish economy was unable to supply enough products for colonial and home markets. This together with the Crown's penchant for engaging in expensive European

adventures meant that large proportions of those precious metals almost immediately passed through Spain into the hands of other Europeans, or else directly to others by means of extensive smuggling throughout the colonial period' (2000: 20).

[2] Indeed, many workers during this period did not receive wages in money but tokens that could be exchanged for goods in shops owned by the employer. Payment in money was one objective of early trade union struggles in Latin America (de Ramón et al., 2001b: 38).

[3] One billion (US) = 1,000 million. The US billion is used throughout the book.

[4] The contrast with manufactured exports is worth recalling: if countries export sugar, beef or bananas, there is little they can do if demand for their products slump; if, however, they export manufactured products, a slump in demand for one product can prompt a change to another product line for which demand may be growing.

[5] Up to 1984 it was known as ECLA (Economic Commission for Latin America) but changed its name to ECLAC (adding Caribbean to the end) to reflect the growing number of member states from that area. In this book, the organization is referred to as CEPAL in cases where its publications in Spanish are being referred to and as ECLAC when its publications being referred to are in English. Thus, its publications in Spanish are listed in the Bibliography under CEPAL and in English under ECLAC.

[6] For example, de Ramón et al. entitle the period 1920–70 as 'the epoch of national populism' and the economic development of the period following the Great Depression as 'the political economy of populism' (2001: titles of chapters 2.4 and 2.5).

Section II

Neoliberal Reformation

4

Liberating the Market

The international debt crisis of the 1980s created the climate for a series of sweeping reforms which put an end to the state-led, inward-looking approach that characterized ISI and ushered in a new model of development, usually known as neoliberalism. These reforms therefore mark an historic turning point for Latin America and constitute a major effort by the region's governments to avail of the new opportunities opened by a more globalized world economy. Their introduction was accompanied by heightened expectations that they would put the region on the road to robust economic and social development. For example, in its 1993 Latin American survey the World Bank likened to Colombian writer Gabriel García Márquez's classic novel *One Hundred Years of Solitude* the 'irregular and magical cycles of sorrow and frustration' which have marked the region's economic history, and it confidently predicted: 'The recent reforms that have engulfed the region have broken this melancholic circularity. After decades of timid performance and spiralling inequalities, there are rays of hope' (World Bank, 1993: 143).

As Latin America moves into the twenty-first century, the neoliberal reforms introduced over the previous two decades are maturing and taking effect. Though introduced at a different pace and with distinctive features throughout the region, neoliberalism now constitutes the dominant means of developing Latin America over the coming decades.[1] For this reason it warrants sustained attention. Furthermore, enough time has elapsed to allow an evaluation of its impact. The four chapters of this section, therefore, devote attention to different aspects of the 'neoliberal reformation'. The title is chosen to capture the fact that neoliberalism constitutes a major change in development paradigm, equal to the major change from primary commodity exporting to import-substitution industrialization ushered in by the Great Depression of 1929. In this sense it is a reformation, in that it reforms the basis for the region's development. However, being more neutral, the term 'reformation' also avoids giving an implicit evaluation of these sweeping changes such as was done, for example, by the World Bank in its 1993 document in which it spoke of most Latin American countries having gone through 'a true economic revolution in the past decade' (p. 138). The term 'revolution' in this context implies a highly positive evaluation of what has happened. The account in the following chapters seeks to avoid such a rush to judgement and instead examines with care the evidence as to what actual impact this reformation is having. This chapter examines the economic impact of the reforms, while the next chapter looks at the ways in which the state has been reformed under the influence of neo-liberal ideas. Chapter 6 describes the fast-changing forms of regional integration throughout the Americas that have been spurred by the neoliberal reformation, while Chapter 7 asks what has been the impact of neoliberal reforms on Latin Americans' quality of life.

As its title indicates, this chapter focuses on the changing nature of the region's economies. It begins by describing firstly the context that gave rise to the reforms of the 1980s and early 1990s as well as the nature and pace of the reforms themselves. As part of this, it discusses the meaning of the term 'neoliberalism' (Box 4.1). It then goes on to examine how the productive base of Latin America's economies has changed, looking at industry, agriculture and services. The chapter's next section looks at how development is being funded, and in particular at the volatility of capital flows in the liberalized financial marketplace. Following that, the chapter examines the record of economic growth in this new era before finishing with a section on the criminal economy, a growing sector of many Latin American economies.

Structural Adjustment

The impact of the international debt crisis on Latin America has been likened to that of the 1929 Depression (Gwynne, 1999: 76; Thorp, 1998: 216). The region again found itself with large current account deficits as it faced declining prices for its commodity exports while the large rise in international interest rates increased its debt repayments substantially. Furthermore, at the first sign of repayment problems by Mexico in August 1982, the creditor banks took fright, ceasing new lending and taking a tougher position in renegotiating debt payments while investment virtually dried up. Soon, virtually all the Latin American countries, with the exception of Colombia which had avoided heavy borrowing, were squeezing imports, cutting consumption, and seeking to boost exports as a way of remaining solvent. This led to a deep recession, further deepening the debt problem. GDP per capita fell 8 per cent, while real wages fell 17 per cent in the first two years of the crisis (1982–3) and per capita social spending fell 10 per cent in real terms between 1982 and 1986. The result is often called 'the lost development decade'. Adding to the crisis in many countries was a surge of hyperinflation as governments were not immune to printing money in an attempt to balance budgets. Inflation reached 8,170.5 per cent in Bolivia in 1985, 7,649.6 per cent in Peru in 1990, 4,923.6 per cent in Argentina in 1989 and 2,500 per cent in Brazil in 1993. Capital flight also reached dizzying heights as individuals spirited their money abroad. Between 1979 and 1982 it reached US$26.5 billion in Mexico, $22 billion in Venezuela and $19.2 billion in Argentina. While some timid attempts were made to develop a common regional approach to the crisis, most notably the meeting of Latin American presidents in Cartagena, Colombia, in 1984, the creditor banks with the strong backing of the Reagan administration sought to avoid such a 'debtors' cartel' through offering terms of debt renegotiation to those countries which played by the rules of the game. Cutting off Peru from international credit following its declaration in 1985 that it would only repay one-tenth of its export earnings on its debt further ensured that other countries were not similarly tempted. The only way out of the problem therefore was for countries to turn to the International Monetary Fund (IMF) and the World Bank, whose funding came with strings attached, usually known as conditionality. The rationale of these Structural Adjustment Programmes (SAPs) was to pressure countries to introduce policies that might help them achieve higher growth, thereby earning the foreign exchange to repay their debts. The conditions related to three principal areas:

1 the need to achieve higher exports through trade liberalization and realistic exchange rates for their currencies;
2 the need to liberalize financial systems as a way of attracting foreign investment and to reform tax systems to raise more revenue;
3 the need to reduce government intervention in the economy through privatizing state enterprises (Gwynne, 1999: 78).

Not convinced of the validity of this free-market approach, Argentina, Brazil and Peru attempted so-called 'heterodox' packages to find a way of restarting growth through a combination of wage and price controls, restrictions on debt repayment, currency reforms and social spending. While all seemed to have initial success in the mid 1980s, this was short-lived and, certainly in Argentina and Peru, they served to deepen the recession.

By the late 1980s the depth of the crisis was clear and the lack of alternatives to the free-market approach of the multilateral agencies increasingly accepted throughout Latin America. The acceptance by the creditor banks of the need to write off some debt if the problem was ever to be solved opened the way for the Brady Plan, announced in 1989 by the US Treasury Secretary, Nicholas Brady. This resulted in direct debt reduction agreements between some banks and Latin American governments but also in more imaginative debt–equity swaps whereby debt was traded on secondary markets for new investment.[2] Though this by no means eradicated the debt problem, it did bring substantial investment back to Latin America, making service of the debt far easier. The region began to grow again from 1991 onwards, leaving behind it the lost development decade during which it had seen net outflows (that is, the amount of capital that left the region minus the amount that entered it) of nearly US$220 billion (Green, 1999: 17). While most Latin Americans' living standards were plummeting, they were in effect subsidizing the US economy.

With the debt problem becoming manageable, attention switched to the fact that the reforms being implemented were not just adjusting structures in order to overcome the debt crisis, but permanently reforming them. Influenced by such international events as the fall of eastern European communism and with it the hopes invested in the ability of the state to transform economies, the success of the East Asian economies of South Korea, Taiwan, Singapore and Hong Kong which were being favourably compared to the

Box 4.1 'Many and varied neoliberalisms'

The term 'neoliberalism' has come into wide use to describe the free-market turn in Latin America since the early 1980s and, by the mid 1990s, was also being applied to describe economic changes in the European Union and its member countries. However, it is less usual to find definitions of what precisely it refers to. For example, how is this new variety different from the classical economic liberalism of the nineteenth century?

This lack of definition reflects the fact that, as Draibe puts it, neoliberalism 'does not properly speaking constitute a body of theory which is original and coherent' (Draibe, 1994: 181). Instead it is composed of practical propositions, such as those formulated in the Washington Consensus, which contain two elements: firstly, a belief in the efficacy of the market as the best mechanism to ensure the efficient production of goods and services and their optimal distribution and, secondly, a belief that the role of the state is to ensure the free and effective operation of market forces, imposing these on society by force if necessary. It thus is a return to a nineteenth century belief in the market with the addition of a clear view of the role of state institutions in facilitating the market. In the political economy of each country, as Draibe reminds us, 'these "ingredients" are combined in different ways, thus producing many and varied neoliberalisms' (p. 181). This can be illustrated by examining the ways in which four Latin American countries have neoliberalized.

Chile, the first reformer, implemented a thoroughgoing trade liberalization, privatization and deregulation (of labour rights, for example) from 1975, privatizing even its pensions system and much of its higher education. Though lacking policy to promote industrialization, the state did facilitate private investment in non-traditional primary resource exports (such as fruit and wine, fish farming, wood and wood products) which with copper have formed the bulk of the country's booming exports. Moreover the state maintained an active role, stepping in to bail out financial institutions during the 1982–3 crisis, and imposing a strongly deregulated labour market very favourable to employers.

Mexico was also an early reformer, though it liberalized amid a severe economic crisis. It opted for a cooperative approach to labour and in 1987 representatives of the government, business and labour signed an Economic Solidarity Pact supporting neoliberal reforms. A cornerstone of the Mexican strategy was the signing of the North American Free Trade Agreement (NAFTA) with the United States and Canada which has opened the huge North American market to which some 85 per cent of its exports now go. Liberalization of its financial system fuelled short-term speculative investment that led to a deep crisis in 1994–5 when a necessary devaluation of the peso resulted in massive withdrawal of capital. While some industrial sectors have adjusted to the new environment, US and other foreign-owned assembly plants called *maquiladoras* (Box 4.2) make up a large part of Mexican industry.

Argentina was another early reformer, since it liberalized its financial system under the 1976–83 military dictatorship. However, this resulted in an overvalued currency which prompted speculative investment, damaging the competitiveness of the country's exports. It was not until Carlos Menem took over as president in 1989 that a more thorough liberalization was carried out, including widespread privatization, trade liberalization and the flexibilization of labour markets. Reform of the state has been less thorough and regulation of the new privatized sector is weak. A key element of the reform was pegging the peso to the dollar, a policy which again hit Argentine exports in the late 1990s as the dollar rose in value and Brazil, Argentina's leading export market, devalued its currency, the real. Much of traditional Argentine industry has found it difficult to adapt to these new conditions and investment has been concentrated in natural resource exports such as oil, natural gas, grain, wine and minerals.

Brazil, partly due to its huge size and the success of its ISI policies, felt under little pressure to liberalize – the state's role in the economy and restrictions on foreign investment in certain areas were even written into the 1988 constitution. On his inauguration in 1990, President Fernando Collor de Melo sought trade liberalization, privatization of state assets and the reduction of state intervention in the economy but his impeachment in 1992 on charges of corruption put paid to those plans. It was not until President Fernando Henrique Cardoso took power in early 1995 that liberalization began in earnest with the privatization of some major state companies and trade liberalization. Reform has been gradual, however, and protection from competition for domestic industries such as automobiles and computers still remains in place.

Key differences between the four counties relate to the speed of liberalization and to the role of the state in the newly liberalized situation. The swift pace of liberalization in Chile, Argentina and Mexico meant that much traditional industry built up under ISI was unable to adjust, while Brazil has been more careful in this regard. Brazil still keeps a relatively strong state with an active industrial policy, while the Chilean state is probably the best example of a neoliberalized state, facilitating the market but not trying to guide it. In Argentina and Mexico the state has emerged much weaker and Argentina's lack of flexibility in its exchange rate policy has proved economically and socially damaging.

failures then being experienced in Latin America, and the ability of neoliberal policies imposed by the Pinochet dictatorship to bring Chile to what seemed to be sustained high rates of economic growth following a deep recession in 1982–3, policy-makers throughout Latin America were converted to the free-market road to development. After the severe economic, political and social crises of the 1970s and the 1980s, economic liberalization seemed to offer a route to overcoming their problems. Following on from the conditions imposed by the IMF and the World Bank, these reforms sought to achieve three major objectives:

1 link Latin America more closely to the world economy through trade liberalization and easier foreign direct investment (FDI);
2 reduce direct government intervention in the economy through privatization as well as increasing the professional role of economic ministries through introducing fiscal discipline, balanced budgets and tax reform;

3 increase the significance of the market in the allocation of resources and
   make the private sector the main instrument of economic growth through
   deregulation, secure property rights and financial liberalization (Gwynne,
   1999: 83).

These reforms form the core of the neoliberal reformation and were summed
up in 1990 in a list of 10 policy items by John Williamson and labelled the
Washington Consensus, since they expressed the common sense of the multilateral agencies headquartered in Washington DC and of the US administration.[3]

   Despite the fact that the neoliberal recipe offered the same policy advice to all
countries, inevitably the political culture, the parties in power, vested interest
groups and the economic climate influenced greatly the pace and nature of
reforms (see Box 4.1). Chile under the Pinochet dictatorship was an early
reformer, because the so-called Chicago Boys, Chilean economists trained in
neoliberal economics in the University of Chicago under an exchange agreement with the Catholic University of Chile in Santiago since 1955, were given
control of the Chilean economy and were able to impose their reforms with the
backing of the military. Another early reformer was Bolivia, paradoxically
under the same man who had led the 1952 revolution, Jaime Paz Estenssoro,
who returned to power in 1985 amid runaway inflation to implement a radical
trade and financial liberalization coupled with a massive devaluation and an
incomes squeeze. Other countries were, however, far more reluctant converts
to the new creed. Colombia's traditional economic moderation also meant that
liberalization did not begin in earnest until the 1990s and the state has still
maintained much control. In Venezuela, the strength of public reaction to
President Carlos Andrés Pérez's proposed liberalization in 1989 effectively
reversed it, following military coup attempts in 1992 and the President's
impeachment in 1993. Buoyed by its oil revenues, Venezuela has resisted the
neoliberal trend, though it posted some of the lowest growth rates in Latin
America from 1990 to 2000.

   However, despite the different pace adopted by different countries, the market-led approach to development has now replaced the state-led approach of
ISI. As Weaver put it, 'the market, rather than the government, [has become]
the principal mechanism for regulating society, resolving conflicts, and determining directions of change' (2000: 181). States have grown smaller, having
divested themselves of much of their economic assets, both service companies
(electricity, telephones, airlines, railways) and productive firms (steel mills,
processing companies). Major companies that remain in state hands, such as
Mexico and Venezuela's giant oil companies or Chile's copper company, are
exceptions. Private companies, both owned by national capital and by foreign
capital, are now the key economic agents. After a period of 50 years in which
the region's governments sought carefully to regulate their international economic contacts, Latin America has now fully integrated itself into the global
economy as countries seek to boost their exports, attract foreign investment
and find new overseas markets. In this context, governments have far less room

for manoeuvre in economic policy-making as they seek to ensure a climate of macroeconomic and fiscal stability so as to keep the investment they have and attract more. 'In the course of ten years, the shape of the Latin American economy was profoundly changed' (Thorp, 1998: 227). The era of neoliberalism had arrived.

The Productive Economy

The expectation was that the opening of the Latin American economies to greater competition and trade would boost international demand for the products of those sectors in which the region had a comparative advantage. Unlike the more developed economies which suffer from labour shortages, Latin America's comparative advantage was seen to lie in its large reserve of unskilled labour. It was therefore expected that labour-intensive sectors, producing goods for export, would benefit most. Since small firms dominate in such sectors, the belief was that such firms would grow most rapidly and provide increased employment. Alongside this, it was expected that multinational companies, attracted to Latin America by the opportunities that liberalization opened up, would provide technological and managerial skills to improve efficiency (Stallings and Peres, 2000: 154). Is this, in fact, what happened?

Surveying the 1990s, ECLAC describes the impact on productive sectors as being more destructive than creative (2000a: 62). This refers to the fact that all processes of productive restructuring involve the death of some firms and even whole sectors that are no longer competitive but the creation of new firms and sectors better able to compete and achieve market success. ECLAC finds it paradoxical that the most successful sectors in Latin America have been ones that do not trade, such as transport, communications, energy and financial services, while manufacturing has suffered the most, especially in more traditional, labour-intensive sectors such as clothing, footwear, leather manufactures and furniture, due to the impact of imports. Instead, the emerging industrial strengths of what Katz and Stumpo call the 'new Latin American economic model' are centred on two 'great dominant models of productive and trade specialization' (Katz and Stumpo, 2001: 138, 141):

1   The first, centred on Brazil, the Southern Cone (Chile and Argentina) and some Andean countries (Colombia and Peru), is based on the processing of natural resources, producing industrial commodities such as vegetable oils, paper and cellulose, iron and steel, wine, and fish meal. These productive activities involve the intensive use of natural resources and are processed in capital-intensive automated plants using little labour. They are products for which international demand grows slowly and they involve mature technology with few opportunities for technological innovation.

2   The second, centred on Mexico and Central America, is based on assembling electrical goods, computers and clothes, principally for the US

market. Some of this assembly work is done in *maquiladoras*, the products of which constitute almost a half of Mexico's exports (see Box 4.2).

Of the national high-technology industries fostered by Latin American governments under ISI, only the automotive industries of Mexico, Argentina and Brazil, and the Brazilian aerospace industry, still occupy a significant place in their countries' export profile due to continuing programmes of government support. Many other sectors producing capital goods and machinery, and employing engineering knowhow, have declined. Katz and Stumpo sum up the impact of the neoliberal reforms on Latin America's productive sectors as follows: 'Not only were few countries of the region able to improve their international competitiveness during the 1990s, but they only managed to do it in a small number of productive activities' (p. 144). ECLAC speaks of the region's 'structural heterogeneity', namely the increased internal diversity of its productive sectors (2000a: 63).

Box 4.2 *Maquiladoras*: Industrialization by invitation

Maquila industry refers to assembly plants which began to be established by US multinationals in northern Mexico (close to the US border) and in some Caribbean and Central American countries, from the 1960s onwards. These took advantage of low-cost labour and government incentives to assemble tax-free imported inputs (mostly apparel and textiles, and electronic goods) for re-export to the US market. By the turn of the century, there were over 4,000 such plants in Mexico, employing over 1 million workers (more than a quarter of the industrial workforce), but they were also widely spread around the Caribbean and Central America. In the Dominican Republic they provide some 160,000 jobs, in Guatemala 120,000, in Honduras 60,000, in Costa Rica 50,000 and in Nicaragua and El Salvador 22,000.

Usually established in specially designated export-processing zones (EPZs), the *maquiladoras* use unskilled labour (much of the workforce is made up of young women) and are notorious for paying low wages, employing coercive labour practices and resisting the establishment of trade unions. They therefore have a record of high labour turnover. While providing jobs and badly needed foreign exchange, they have been criticized for their low level of linkages to the rest of the economy (and thus not stimulating the development of other productive enterprises) and for having little interest in developing the skills of their workforce.

Over the 1990s, however, the sector has been diversifying in a number of ways. Taiwanese and Korean firms have established plants but a significant percentage of *maquiladoras* are now locally owned. In Mexico they are moving into the production of more sophisticated goods, such as car parts and electrical and electronic machines and devices, and the employment of technologically skilled men has been growing faster than that of unskilled women.

It is possible to identify a number of the structural features of this new Latin American economic model. The first is that productive activities are concentrated in sectors that call for relatively little technological innovation. Thus Katz and Stumpo state that 'in the new pattern of productive specialization that derives from mergers or privatization, the local firm tends to concentrate on activities with less value added, closer to the stages of assembly and of the primary processing of natural resources than to subprocesses with high levels of local added value' (pp. 152–3). This may be linked to a second feature, namely the model's poor performance as regards raising productivity, except in some subsectors such as telecommunications, mining and energy. However, in most countries, even in sectors where productivity has risen, there has been a widening of the gap between levels of productivity in Latin America and those in industrialized countries (ECLAC, 2000a: 63). A third feature of the model is that it has reconfigured the economies of Latin America so that the primary links of the different subsectors are with sectors external to the region rather than to other sectors of the national economy. An example is the mining industry, which has received a lot of foreign investment, but which Stallings and Peres describe as tending to function as 'enclaves, with scant, albeit increasing, articulation to the rest of the national economy' (p. 186). As a result, there is a heavy reliance on imported inputs instead of those manufactured at home, destroying in the process many small and medium-sized industries which had grown up under ISI to supply such inputs. A fourth structural feature derives from this, since the exterior orientation and reliance on imported inputs have resulted in growing trade deficits, leading Katz and Stumpo to question whether the model is sustainable over the long run (p. 154). A final feature relates to ownership, since the neoliberal reforms have led to a rapid increase in the participation of foreign firms in production and sales: of the sales made by Latin America's 500 largest businesses, those of foreign companies increased from 26.6 per cent in 1990–2, to 29.5 per cent in 1995 and to 38.7 per cent in 1998 (ECLAC, 2000a: 61).

Both agriculture and services have also been changed under the impact of neoliberal reforms. The liberalization of land, labour and financial markets, and the drive to export, has led to an entrepreneurial agriculture, often known as agribusiness, in which different countries have sought to specialize in particular products. Chile, which led the way, saw its fresh fruit exports increase from US$30 million in 1977 to $1.1 billion by the mid 1990s, but others have followed suit with such 'non-traditional exports' as soyabeans from Argentina, Bolivia, Brazil and Paraguay, fresh flowers from Colombia, African palm from Costa Rica, Guatemala and Honduras and fresh fruits and vegetables from Argentina, Brazil, Costa Rica and Mexico. In the case of fruit, vegetables and flowers, many Latin American countries are able to offer products when they are out of season in the US and European markets. In some cases these non-traditional exports are replacing the more traditional agricultural exports from the region, such as coffee, sugar, wheat and cotton, the international prices of which have been declining. They have also been growing at much higher rates than have subsistence crops, usually grown by small farmers for local consumption. Furthermore food imports have increased considerably with liberalization. As a result, it is possible to identify a process of growing polarization in the agricultural workforce, which has declined in size over the 1990s. Many of the non-traditional export crops are grown on large estates and require little labour, or seasonal labour (at harvest time). Meanwhile, the labour-intensive small farmers are being marginalized and many are leaving the land altogether. To some extent this is due to the dismantling of the state supports (credit and advisory services) that had existed under ISI, to competition from imported foodstuffs and to the concentration of land ownership under the agro-export model. Spoor describes this exclusionary dynamic that seems a structural feature of Latin American agriculture under the new model:

> The dynamics of economic growth are largely to be found within the sectors of commercial farmers who have been able to establish linkages with foreign, mostly transnational, capital, thereby integrating themselves in domestic and international agribusiness complexes. The early optimism about the options for small farmers and peasants to modernize through contract farming for agribusiness has not been sufficiently justified in practice. Furthermore, there are indications that the gap (in levels of technology, productivity and income) between the commercial and entrepreneurial farmers and the 'non-viable peasants' has grown larger than ever. Economic policies directed toward modernizing the latter group are largely absent, as are social policies to mitigate the human costs of economic adjustment in view of continuing high levels of rural poverty. (2000: 7)

Services also present a picture of growing heterogeneity. It is the sector that saw the greatest expansion in employment over the 1990s, contributing more than 95 per cent of new net job creation over the period 1990–7 (Stallings and Peres, 2000: 198). Yet the category 'services' covers two very different groups: on the one hand there are the relatively well-paid jobs in the telecommunications, energy, transport and financial services subsectors. These are areas that benefited from high levels of inward investment due largely to their privatization by the state and, after initial lay-offs and restructuring following privatization, began to create new jobs as they modernized. However, other service sectors which saw the highest levels of job creation – namely commerce, restaurants and hotels; social, communal and personal services; and business services – include such activities as domestic service, retail trade, waitressing, and security and cleaning services. Many of these offer low-paid and insecure jobs, often in the informal economy, a term used to denote that large sector of all Latin American economies in which people work in poorly paid jobs such as domestic service or street traders and are usually not covered by labour laws or the social security system (see Box 7.2). On average, over 6 out of every 10 non-agricultural jobs were created in the informal economy during the period 1990–8 and this sector's share of non-agricultural employment grew from 43 per cent to 46.7 per cent (CEPAL, 2001e: 193).

The new Latin American economic model did not, therefore, meet the expectations held out for it. Instead of creating demand for the products of labour-intensive subsectors, these lost out to capital-intensive subsectors such as natural-resource-based commodities. Only in Mexico, with its strong *maquila* sector and its access to the US market under the North American Free Trade Agreement (NAFTA), did labour-intensive manufacturing subsectors increase their share of employment, though the wage levels and conditions of employment were relatively poor. Before evaluating the impact of these changes on the region's development prospects, the next section examines the nature and impact of investment over the 1990s.

Funding Development

Development of a country's productive economy requires investment, whether that comes from domestic savings (for example through the banking system or through pension funds) or from foreign investment. With the growth of multinational companies in the second half of the twentieth century, the latter source has become increasingly important and few countries in the world do not actively seek such investment. Liberalization of financial systems since the 1980s has opened another source of often short-term investment in the region's emerging stock markets. The nature and levels of investment, therefore, are an important dimension of development prospects and for that reason the topic is examined here.

The level of gross domestic savings in Latin America has traditionally been low, declining from 22 per cent of GDP in 1990 to under 20 per cent by the decade's end. By comparison, the East Asian and Pacific region saw its gross domestic savings increase from 35 to 37 per cent over the same period. Factors such as high income inequality and poverty mean that most Latin Americans can save little, while the rich elites have a tendency to move their capital outside the region, particularly in times of political and economic volatility. Furthermore, the wave of privatizations associated with neoliberal reforms has greatly reduced state investment in the economy, one of the reasons for the decline in the domestic savings rate. Neither have the hopes that the privatization of pension systems in Latin America would become a new source of domestic savings and investment been met: ECLAC points out that the gross contribution of pension reform to savings tends to be small, a little over 3 per cent of GDP during the 1990s in the case of Chile, the earliest reformer (ECLAC, 2000a: 224). In this context, foreign investment becomes even more crucial.

As has already been outlined, the lost development decade of the 1980s in Latin America was associated with a severe decline in foreign investment in the region and a net outflow of capital. On the other hand, growth resumed from 1990 onwards with a strong return of foreign capital. Thus, between 1983 and 1990 annual average capital flows equivalent to 2 per cent of GDP left the region, while between 1991 and 1999 flows equivalent to 3 per cent of GDP entered. However, apart from the amounts, the composition of these flows was also very important. For in the early 1990s Latin America relied heavily on portfolio investment, whereas by the late 1990s foreign direct investment (FDI) had come to constitute over three-quarters of total investment flows. Portfolio investment, namely investment by international fund managers in the bond issues and the stock markets of Latin America, tends to be very volatile, withdrawing at the first sign of economic or financial troubles. FDI, on the other hand, is invested in productive assets, whether manufacturing, services (like electricity or telecommunications) or agriculture, and therefore tends to be more stable. The large amounts of portfolio investment in the region resulted in a high level of volatility. As Griffith-Jones put it:

> Indeed, the pattern of surges and reversals not only has been repeated over time but has become more frequent in recent years. Two recent crises, the Mexican peso crisis of 1994–95 and the international financial crisis of 1997–99, brought violent swings in the levels of capital flows to Latin America. The peso crisis led to significant but fairly brief reversals of portfolio flows to the region in 1995, while the international financial crisis that began in Asia led to major declines in capital flows to Latin America and a currency crisis in Brazil. (2000: 7)

She finds that the economic and social impact of these crises is more severe in Latin America than in industrialized countries, and points to the case of Mexico, regarded by the international financial markets as a model reformer until the country's sudden devaluation in late 1994: 'The experience of Mexico during the peso crisis of 1994–95 showed how a financial crisis can result in serious disturbances to production and investment. Mexican GDP fell by 7 per cent in 1995, many firms had to close, investment and consumption levels fell dramatically, and the country's banking system was severely weakened' (p. 15). The impact was also severe on Argentina and Brazil, which suffered large capital outflows as a result. In wider terms, ECLAC concludes that the great instability of capital flows which began with the Mexican crisis resulted in lower GDP growth for the region as a whole in the second half of the 1990s (ECLAC, 2000a: 56). A common feature of the Mexican crisis in 1994–5 and the Argentine crisis in 1998–2002 was the overvaluation of the national currency due to high capital inflows and the governments' attempts to defend the value to reassure investors. Overvalued currencies, however, had a damaging effect on exports and production, since it made Mexican and Argentine goods more expensive abroad. Both governments had to devalue amid severe economic and social crises, amid calls from many quarters to adopt the US dollar as the national currency in a bid to achieve monetary stability (see Box 4.3).

Amid such volatility, the growing percentage of capital inflows coming in the form of FDI is seen as hopeful. While the larger and more developed countries (Argentina, Brazil, Chile, Colombia and Mexico) received most FDI at the beginning of the recovery, by the late 1990s it was diversifying to countries like Bolivia, Costa Rica, Ecuador, Peru, the Dominican Republic and Venezuela. Overall FDI increased from US$18 billion in 1990–4 to $103 billion in 1999, though it had declined to around $59 billion by 2001, reflecting a deepening international recession. Most FDI in Latin America comes from the USA and Europe, with Japan also showing a small but growing share. In 1998 for the first time, Europe overtook the USA as the main source of FDI, principally due to Spanish capital buying privatized industries in the region.

Box 4.3 Is dollarization an answer to volatile financial markets?

In 2000, Ecuador announced that it was adopting the US dollar as its national currency. El Salvador followed suit in 2001, while Guatemala was studying whether to do the same. These join Panama that, since independence in 1903, has used the US dollar (though calling it the balboa). Even in such large countries as Mexico and Argentina, the issue is actively debated and was proposed at the end of 2001 by former President Carlos Menem of Argentina as a solution to that country's crisis.

Dollarization is being seen as a response to the growing monetary instability associated with globalization as financial liberalization and technology allow huge sums of speculative capital to slosh around the world at the touch of a button. For a region like Latin America, these capital flows can result in overvaluing a national currency which is much in demand as international investors flock to that country, but dramatically undermining the currency if they lose confidence in it. In such a volatile situation, adopting the US dollar as the national currency seems to offer the prospect of monetary stability.

At first glance, Ecuador's experience with dollarization seems to be positive. With economic growth stagnant at 0.4 per cent in 1998 and declining by 7.3 per cent in 1999, the country's economy grew by 2.3 per cent in 2000 and 5.6 per cent in 2001, the highest in Latin America. Inflation also dropped from an annual rate of 97 per cent in 2000 to 12.9 per cent by 2002. However, for Ecuadorian economist Alberto Acosta, these mask deeper problems caused by dollarization, for adopting the US currency has steadily undermined the country's exports, making them more expensive in relation to the currencies of neighbouring countries, while imports become cheaper. The country is therefore facing a growing trade deficit, with exports declining from \$2.5bn in 2000 to \$2.3bn in 2002 while imports rose from \$1.4bn in 2000 to \$2.9bn in 2002. Furthermore, the country's private debt has doubled from \$2.2bn in 2000 to \$4.5bn in mid 2002. A major contribution to bridging the growing current account deficit, argues Acosta, are remittances from the half-million Ecuadorians who emigrated in 1999 and 2000, equal to 10 per cent of the country's economically active population. These remittances came to \$1.4bn in 2001, more than the value of Ecuador's traditional (agricultural) exports and of its industrial exports. By mid 2002, however, economic growth had turned negative, while remittances were declining, and Acosta was calling dollarization a 'time bomb' (2002: 10). Polls showed majority support for returning to a national currency (IESOP, 2002).

However, the picture is not entirely positive, for two principal reasons. Firstly, despite the large increase in absolute amounts of FDI to Latin America, the region's share of global FDI has declined significantly from 12.5 per cent in 1975–80 down to 9.6 per cent in 1990–6 (Dunning, 2000: 22). Secondly, not all the investment reaching Latin America results in increasing productive capacity, since it is estimated that about 40 per cent of it was used to acquire existing assets or to finance mergers. As Guillén Romo put it referring to

Mexico, this has led to the arrival of US chains Wal Mart and Taco Bell often displacing local producers of goods and services rather than supplementing them (Guillén Romo, 1997: 182).

Despite the high levels of capital flows to the region during the 1990s, the outlook for investment in Latin America's development is not bright. This is the conclusion of a study by Moguillansky and Bielschowsky that identifies an uncertain future for investment due to four principal reasons:

1 High levels of vulnerability due to the volatility of capital flows and the fragility of the region's financial systems. These do not encourage investment in capacity expansion due to the risks involved;
2 Lower profits and higher risks stemming from the more competitive environment caused by trade liberalization. As a result national firms tend to concentrate in safe sectors and neglect innovation, research and development;
3 Lower public investment in infrastructure resulting from the privatization of public utilities;
4 Business strategies of multinational corporations that have tended to concentrate on acquisitions and mergers, making it uncertain whether capital inflows will begin investing in new sectors and businesses.

They conclude that the new environment created by neoliberal reforms combines two types of uncertainty: macroeconomic uncertainty stemming from the globalization of financial markets and microeconomic uncertainty related to the behaviour of firms in the more competitive market now prevailing. 'These two types of uncertainty reinforce each other, affecting the "entrepreneurial spirit" and propensity to invest,' they write (Moguillansky and Bielschowsky, 2001: 143–4).

Towards Dynamic Growth?

The conventional way of evaluating a country's economic progress is by looking at GDP growth rates. These measure the increase from year to year in the goods and services produced in that economy. However, despite their widespread use, they tell us little about a country's development because they don't indicate what sectors of the economy have produced the increases,[4] nor do they tell us about how the benefits from them have been distributed. They could have made a tiny minority stunningly rich while the majority continued to live in poverty, or they could have been used to improve social services and the lives of the majority. Finally, looking at one country on its own fails to appreciate how it has fared compared to neighbouring countries or compared to its previous performance. In evaluating Latin America's new economic model, therefore, we need to examine these various aspects of the region's performance in the 1990s.

CEPAL evaluates the region's growth over the 1990s as being poor (CEPAL, 2001e: 85) and divides it into two phases – an early promising phase where it reached 4.2 per cent per annum between 1990 and 1994 and a second, more unstable phase following the Mexican crash at the end of 1994 when growth reached a disappointing 2.5 per cent per annum up to 2000. However, the growth of exports in a region that since the 1930s had shown a marked anti-export bias was more heartening. Between 1990 and 1999 exports grew by 8.9 per cent per annum, the fastest growth in the region's history. Examining the sectors from which these came, a number of trends can be identified. Firstly, commodities declined from 35.5 per cent of exports in 1988 to 22.9 per cent in 1998. Secondly, industrial goods grew from 63.9 per cent to 76.2 per cent over the same period. Thirdly, within industrial goods the exports of such goods as household electrical appliances, vehicles, machinery and instruments showed the largest growth. Similar trends are reflected in employment per sector – the numbers employed in agriculture fell quite markedly, industry showed a slight rise, while services provided the bulk of new jobs. In all these ways, therefore, Latin America appeared to be approximating more and more to the profile of a modern industrialized region.

However, a closer look at the evidence shows that such an evaluation is far from warranted. Table 4.1 compares the performance of Latin America over periods, taking the 1945–80 period as the height of ISI, the 1980–90 period as the lost development decade, and the 1990–2000 period as the advent of neoliberalism.

This shows what has been achieved in terms of stable macroeconomic management of the region's economies and the major success in reducing the hyperinflation of the 1980s. It also shows the region's export success. But, as Katz and Stumpo state, it gives grounds for great scepticism about the reforms of the 1990s in terms of the trade deficit, the sluggish growth rates and the persistence of poverty. Only a small number of countries managed to grow faster in the 1990s than they had during the ISI phase and most of these – Argentina, Bolivia and Peru – did so only because their growth rate under ISI was so low. While Chile also showed sluggish growth rates under ISI, it achieved an annual average rate of 6.1 per cent growth over the 1990s, the region's highest. Taking a wider focus and looking at Latin America's changing place in the world, the evidence is no more heartening. Despite the region's export drive, only eight countries out of 25 managed to increase their share of world exports; of these only Mexico showed a notable increase, from a 1.55

TABLE 4.1 LATIN AMERICA'S PERFORMANCE, 1945–2000

	1945–80	1980–90	1990–2000	2000
Annual inflation rate	20	400	170	9.2
Export growth rate	2.1	4.4	9.4	11.1
Import growth rate	5.9	−0.8	12.8	12.3
GDP growth rate	5.6	1.2	3.3	4.3
GDP per capita growth rate	3.1	−1.8	1.6	2.2
Percentage of poor households	35	41	38	38

Source: Katz and Stumpo, 2001: Cuadro 1, p. 140

per cent share in 1985 to a 2.24 per cent share in 1998. Even Chile, seen as the great success case of export-led growth, only increased its share from 0.23 per cent to 0.32 per cent over the same period (Katz and Stumpo, 2001: 141). In measuring the convergence of Latin American countries to the growth rates and living standards of the developed countries (something predicted by main-stream economic theory), Hofman found no such convergence had taken place in the 1990s (Hofman, 2000: 19). He concluded that the evidence from Latin America contradicts the strong consensus among neoclassical economists that macroeconomic stabilization and market-oriented structural reform are conducive to the acceleration of long-run growth (p. 17). Nobel economics laureate 2001 Joseph Stiglitz shares this sceptical evaluation (Box 4.4).

Finally, as outlined in Chapter 1, a political economy analysis prompts us to identify the winners and losers in Latin America's neoliberal restructuring in order to show that these are not impersonal processes but result from the actions of organized groups; that is, they are a question not primarily of economics but of power. Katz and Stumpo identify the winners as the subsi-diaries of multinational companies and large national economic groups, while the losers have been small and medium-sized family firms (p. 147). Widespread privatizations (often on terms very favourable to the transnational companies) and the liberalization of markets have contributed to 'the concentration of market power' in agriculture, industries and services throughout Latin America (Spoor, 2000: 25). Behind the seemingly impersonal and abstract

---

Box 4.4 Stiglitz's verdict on the 1990s in Latin America

Professor Joseph Stiglitz, former World Bank chief economist and 2001 Nobel economics laureate, summed up the impact of neoliberal reforms on Latin America as follows:

> In Latin America, the record since reforms is little if any better than before (by some calculations it is even worse), and even the good years can be thought of as little more than a partial catch-up from the lost decade of the '80s.
>
> What growth has occurred has largely benefited the already relatively well off – even in a country like Mexico that has seen growth, those at the bottom have not shared the gains.
>
> They were told that market reforms would bring them unprecedented prosperity. Instead, it has brought unprecedented instability. Why should they continue to believe in these reforms? Why should they not turn to other nostrums, as false as they might be? Time may be running out.
>
> The IMF and the international community can play either a positive or a negative role in how the story unfolds. Will there be a new generation of alienated young men, unable to find gainful employment, disgruntled with a system that has failed them, as it failed so many of their parents and grandparents? We have the knowledge to do better. We even have the institutions to implement it. The question is, will we have the will to do better? (Stiglitz, 2001)

notion of 'liberating the market', therefore, lie organized groups with very strong political influence. Thus, it would be more accurate to describe the reforms of the 1990s as 'liberating capital'; as we shall see in coming chapters, the state and organized social groups (such as trade unions, social movements, and political parties) have been changed, fragmented and, in many cases, greatly weakened by these reforms. This, then, illustrates some of the dynamics of globalization in its current form: it integrates national economies into the international marketplace in ways that respond to the needs of the large global economic players, rather than to the needs of development at national or local level. As a result, the possibility for states to promote national development, as was the guiding theme of policy throughout Latin America under ISI,[5] is greatly weakened or even lost entirely.

The Criminal Economy

Before turning to examine the changing nature and role of the state under neoliberalism in the next chapter, no account of Latin American economic restructuring would be complete without reference to the criminal economy. This is placed at the end, since it is largely a hidden economy, the turnover or exports of which do not feature on government accounts, though it has profound economic, social and political effects in a number of Latin American countries. For Manuel Castells, the criminal economy with its international criminal networks is 'an essential feature of the new global economy' (Castells, 1998: 167). Taking advantage of the lifting of government controls on trade and on financial flows, and offering a lucrative income to groups whose livelihoods and job prospects have been undermined by the economic restructuring of the 1980s and 1990s, the criminal economy has spread its influence to more and more Latin American countries over the 1990s. While the trafficking of young women for sex has become established as a major criminal activity in Europe, there is no evidence as yet that this activity has established itself in Latin America, though the emergence of a local sex trade for tourists (see Box 4.5) may indicate the beginnings of a trend in this direction. Instead, the criminal economy in Latin America is heavily centred on the production, processing and trafficking of drugs.

Latin America is the world's only supplier of cocaine, processed from the coca leaf, a traditional crop of the Andean highlands. Bolivia, Colombia and Peru supply virtually the entire world output of the coca leaf and produce an estimated 550 tons of cocaine a year. Though largely grown by small farmers and indigenous people as a means of increasing their income, powerful cartels control the processing and trafficking of the product. In Bolivia, the coca economy accounts for around 135,000 jobs, 6.4 per cent of the country's total employment. However, since the mid 1990s, production has been declining in both Peru and Bolivia due to more efficient control measures and a crackdown on trafficking. Meanwhile, despite increased spraying of crops to destroy them and higher levels of seizures, the area devoted to growing the coca leaf in Colombia has increased from 45,000 hectares in 1994 to 78,200 in 1998.

Box 4.5 Selling sex in the Dominican Republic

The following quote is from UNICEF (2001: 34–5):

> In the Dominican Republic, in massage parlours, clubs and the *casas de chicas*, as such places are called, 'business is booming', according to one tourist guidebook. The industry sells sex and has turned both boys and girls across the island into merchandise.
>
> A 1994 study on the commercial sexual exploitation of children, which looked at four areas (Boca Chica, Puerto Plata, Santo Domingo and Sosua), estimated that there were more than 25,000 children under 18 involved in sexual activities for money in the Dominican Republic. Both girls (64 per cent) and boys (36 per cent) were exploited.
>
> Although the study indicated that a significant number of adolescents were involved in traditional prostitution – in brothels and clubs where clients, mainly Dominican, purchased their services through an intermediary – it also documented a 'new' type of prostitution involving children engaged in sexual activities with adults whom they met on beaches, on streets and in restaurants. The children became involved in prostitution around age 12 on average; their exploiters were mainly foreigners. Ninety per cent of the clients were men, although women also preyed on young boys: about 55 per cent of the boys in the Puerto Plata sex trade had their last sexual encounter with a woman.
>
> Today, 1.5 million tourists visit the Dominican Republic each year. On the Internet, a number of sex guides with names like 'Dominican Delight Erotic Vacations' market 'hot blooded' women and an 'anything goes' attitude.
>
> (Reproduced with kind permission of UNICEF)

In Colombia, the only Andean country to produce and export three narcotic substances (cocaine, marihuana and heroin), illegal drugs had by the 1980s become the country's dominant export sector. Income to Colombia from the drugs trade is estimated at US$36 billion between 1980 and 1995, equivalent to 5.3 per cent of the country's GDP at the time. By comparison, Colombia's traditional export, coffee, accounted for 4.5 per cent of GDP over the same period. Income from the export of drugs over this period is estimated as being equivalent to more than 40 per cent of the income of all the country's legal exports (Safford and Palacios, 2002: 315). The huge incomes received by the drugs barons were spent on contraband imports, and on investments in land, real estate and construction, thus boosting land prices in many places. As an economically powerful group living a sumptuous lifestyle, the drugs barons developed close relations with the country's two main political parties, which included channelling them campaign funding. Meanwhile, workers who had lost their jobs due to economic restructuring and peasants migrated to the regions of drugs production. Since the 1970s, Mexico and Guatemala had been producing opium to make heroin for the

US market, from where it spread to Colombia and Peru. Marihuana is culti-vated in Mexico and the Caribbean.

While drug production is limited to these countries, trafficking has increas-ingly spread throughout the region. Roughly half of South American cocaine passes through the Caribbean, but it also reaches the United States through Mexico. Panama has been a major trans-shipment point, as evidenced by the US invasion of 1989 which seized the country's leader, General Manuel Noriega, and brought him to trial in Florida on drug trafficking charges. However, the attempt to find new secure trading channels has led to the emer-gence of Argentina, Brazil, Chile and Venezuela as important transit points for the smuggling of drugs destined for North America and Europe. In all these countries, a new phenomenon of 'microtrafficking' has been identified, as low-income sectors, including women and the elderly, become small-time dealers in illegal drugs. As ECLAC has noted: 'We are now in a situation where, just as large-scale trafficking poses a constant threat of corruption in public life and the financial system, given the large amounts of money involved, microtraffick-ing is a constant threat to the basic standards of community life in the areas where it is most prevalent' (ECLAC, 2000b: 200). In these ways, the criminal economy is taking an evermore firm hold throughout the region.

This chapter has shown that the expectations of the early 1990s about the positive impact neoliberal reforms would have on the economies and societies of Latin America have been far from met. While they benefited some, many have lost out and questions are being asked about the sustainability of the model. In this situation, a consensus is emerging that the economic reforms need to be complemented by a strengthening of the state. This is the subject of Chapter 5.

Notes

[1] As well as being the dominant approach, it could be said to be the unique approach being tried by governments. The only exceptions are Cuba and the Chavez regime in Venezuela in which the state still plays a leading role. However, neither constitutes a coherent alternative to the dominant neoliberalism nor, rhetoric notwithstanding, is either strikingly more successful.

[2] Under these debt–equity swaps, an investor could pay off part of a country's debt at a reduced rate and receive in return the full value in local currency from that country's government as a loan. Thus the bank could take the debt off its books, the investor had a loan for which they had paid only a fraction of the full cost, the national government saw its debt reduced, and it would in time get its loan repaid (see Gwynne, 1999: Box 4.1, p. 80 for a hypothetical example).

[3] Williamson's list includes: fiscal discipline; public expenditure to be switched from administration, defence and indiscriminate subsidies to primary health, education and infrastructure; tax reform; financial liberalization; competitive exchange rates; trade liberalization; allowing foreign and domestic firms to compete on equal terms; deregulation; and secure property rights (Williamson, 1993: 1332–3).

[4] For example, the increase could come from producing more high-tech products or from the export of unprocessed commodities. Or, it could have come because a major natural

disaster hit the country and the rescue and recovery operation added to GDP. Each of these examples would warrant a very different judgement on that country's development.

[5] Of course, the ways this was interpreted varied according to governments' ideological leanings and support base. But the state played a key role in seeking to promote national development, in some cases more efficiently than in others, through fostering national economic groups and imposing limitations on transnational capital.

5

Resituating the State

D iscussion of neoliberal reforms throughout Latin America in the 1980s
and 1990s has tended to devote most attention to economics. However,
their impact on the nature and role of the state has been just as important.
Indeed, as was explained in Box 4.1, what distinguishes neoliberalism from the
classic economic liberalism of the nineteenth century is its emphasis on the need
to reform the state so that it ensures the free and effective operation of market
forces. For this reason, the full extent of the neoliberal reformation cannot be
understood unless equal attention is devoted to the state as is devoted to the
market. This is the purpose of the present chapter.

Only as the reforms advanced did an understanding grow of the state's role
in ensuring the success of market liberalization. The emphasis of much of the
early reforms was on reducing the state's size and its role in the economy, as
this was seen as hampering the dynamism of the market. These are often called
'first-generation reforms' and the impact these had on greatly weakening the
state in most Latin American countries is described in the first section of this
chapter. The second section examines the wave of democratization that swept
through the region from the early 1980s as the military returned to barracks
and Latin America became, for the first time in its history, a region of democratic states.[1] Democratization is introduced here, since discussion of state
reform in Latin America by and large treats the state as a complex of organizations and institutions, somewhat akin to a large corporation. This is often
called a technocratic approach, since it reduces the reform of the state to the
plans and decisions of technical experts. However, it must always be remem-
bered that democratic states are run by politicians elected to implement policies, for which they should be accountable to the electorate. The second section
of this chapter will, therefore, examine the relationship between the democratization of the political system and reform of the state.

By the turn of the century a widespread consensus existed throughout Latin
America that a more effective and agile state was needed if the full promise of
the neoliberal reformation was to be delivered, both in terms of economic
development and of social provision. Section three deals with this second generation of state reforms, describing some of the major reforms being promoted
and assessing how the reform agenda has advanced in practice. The chapter's
final section places the discussion of the state and its relationship to the market

within the wider context of the World Bank's agenda, called 'Beyond the Washington Consensus', drawing attention to the rationale underlying state reform. This highlights the fact that, for proponents of the neoliberal reformation like the World Bank, the objective being sought is not the reduction or marginalization of the state, but, in Richard Falk's terms, 'resituating the state' which is being pushed 'by degrees and to varying extents into a subordinate relationship with global market forces' (Falk, 1999: 49, 50).

Slimming Down the State

For long the state in Latin America had been criticized for its inadequacies. During the phase of primary commodity exporting at the end of the nineteenth and the beginning of the twentieth centuries, an oligarchic state was dominant throughout the region representing the interests of the exporting elites, often a conservative land-owning class. This state excluded most of the population, since the vote was restricted to property-owning men. It saw its role as being to facilitate the smooth functioning of the exporting model through maintaining social order (not sparing the repressive use of the police and army when necessary), collecting taxes mostly through customs duties, and building the necessary infrastructure for the model's successful operation. Though similar in some ways to the state in Europe and North America at the time (also exclusionary and elitist), the state in Latin America displayed particular traits derived from its Spanish and Portuguese colonial past. A central aspect of this was the lack of a clear distinction between public and private interests, with the result that public office was often used to promote private interests. Thus the Latin American state failed in general to develop institutions that could define and safeguard a public interest such as a strong and independent judiciary and a professional bureaucracy. The tendency of the military in most Latin American countries to take control of the state at times of crisis was but one of the principal symptoms of this failure to develop an autonomous state.

With the emergence of import-substitution industrialization (ISI) from the 1930s onwards, the interests of the new social classes favoured by this development model (the national industrial bourgeoisie, state-dependent professionals and the industrial working class) came to dominate the state, which was called upon to play a much more active role in economic and social development. This 'interventionist and entrepreneurial state', as it has been called, intervened in six principal ways: assigning resources (trade and industrial policies), stimulating economic growth (policies for investment, credit and technological development), supporting production (developing public companies and support systems), regulating and controlling prices (the prices of goods and services, exchange and interest rates), regulating the labour market (labour legislation, salary negotiation, arbitrating labour conflicts), and providing social services (education, health care, housing, social security) (Muñoz Gomá, 2001: 73). To fulfil these many functions, the state grew in size and complexity, creating new agencies, recruiting large numbers of personnel and, from the 1960s onwards, nationalizing many industries.

Though this state successfully developed a national industrial base in most Latin American countries (see Chapter 3), by the 1980s it was in severe crisis. There were two principal dimensions to this crisis:

1 *Lack of efficiency*. The expansion in the size and role of the Latin American state often took place with little regard to issues of efficiency. In many cases, political criteria took precedence as state agencies and nationalized companies were expected to provide jobs for supporters of the governing party, social security funds were raided by governments to help balance budgets, and the prices of public services were kept so low that investment in modernizing and expanding these services was severely curtailed. These tendencies were particularly marked under populist governments. For example, the government of Alan Garcia in Peru (1985–90) increased the number of workers in the Peruvian Institute of Social Security from 25,000 to 45,000 during its time in office, while it reduced the minimum contributions required by beneficiaries and expanded their numbers. All of this it did without making sufficient provision for extra funding (Bonicelli, 2001: 28). In these ways, therefore, the state under ISI can be seen as succumbing to the long-standing tendency of the Latin American state to use state power and resources to favour private interests (including those of particular party leaders) rather than a wider public interest, what Bresser Pereira called the growing privatization of the state as political and bureaucratic elites enriched themselves through their control over state institutions (Bresser Pereira, 1998: 105).

2 *Excessive cost*. This led inevitably to the second problem, surely the most grave of the two, namely the increase in fiscal deficits as governments found costs mounting and income stagnating or even dropping. A growing population and high levels of migration to large cities from the 1960s onwards created ever-growing demands for infrastructure and services, while poorly designed taxation systems with high levels of tax evasion led governments to resort to foreign borrowing or printing money as a way of maintaining income. Both routes proved disastrous as they led to high levels of indebtedness and inflation. Again, the Peruvian case illustrates the vicious circle. In 1990, when Alan Garcia left office, the state's day-to-day spending was equivalent to 14.2 per cent of GDP, whereas its day-to-day income was equivalent to only 5.6 per cent of GDP. The annual inflation rate in the middle of that year was 4,778 per cent. In this situation, the real value of government salaries tended to fall, with the result that a pervasive culture of petty corruption took hold in many Latin American states as bureaucrats came to expect (private) payment for the services they provided.

As Bresser Pereira puts it, therefore, the crisis of the 1980s in Latin America was above all a crisis of the state and not a crisis of the market, as had been the case following the Great Depression of 1929 (1998: 105). Already, in the national security states of the southern cone of South America (Argentina, Chile and Uruguay), an authoritarian attempt was made under military governments from the mid 1970s to address this crisis through cutting state spending, liberalizing the economy and, in the case of Chile, privatizing state companies. When the 1982 debt crisis hit, most Latin American states sooner or later adopted the same formula.

This is what is known as the 'first generation of reforms' and, while designed to reduce the state's role in the economy, these reforms also fundamentally changed the nature and role of the Latin American state. Chapter 4 has outlined the main areas in which these reforms took place, constituting the core of this first stage of reform, though their pace and intensity varied from country to country. The first related to trade liberalization and realistic exchange rates in order to boost exports: the state eliminated and simplified a swathe of controls it had for decades exercised to protect the domestic market. The second area of reform related to financial and taxation systems in order to attract foreign investment and balance national budgets: the state eliminated controls over interest rates, credit provision and foreign investment, established the independence of central banks and divested itself of nationalized banks, and reduced or eliminated taxes on profits, wealth and international trade, substituting a more generalized tax on consumption, a value-added tax. The third area related to the privatization of state companies: this both helped to balance budgets through providing a stream of (once-off) income for the state and divested the state of often loss-making enterprises. Between 1982 and 1993, the Mexican state reduced the number of enterprises it owned from 1,155 to 213, selling in the process two state airlines, the state telephone company, banks, a television company, firms producing bicycles and cornmeal, and many others, generating an income of US$23.7 billion for the state between 1988 and 1994 (Guillén Romo, 1997: 120). However, as the lessons of the sweeping and swift process of privatization carried out by Argentina in the early 1990s show, the immediate benefits offered could mask deeper problems in the long run (Box 5.1).

This contraction of the state inevitably affected social spending, which fell in most countries during the 1980s (Stallings and Peres, 2000: 67). However, the recognition that the reforms were having a devastating effect on the poor led a number of countries to introduce novel programmes of social spending, often called 'social safety nets', using in part income received from the privatization of state companies. From the beginning of its reforms in 1985, Bolivia established a Social Emergency Fund. An early and influential example was the National Solidarity Programme, Pronasol, established in Mexico under the Salinas administration (1988–94). This fund, whose budget grew from $950 million during the first half of the Salinas presidency to $2.5 billion at its end, helped build infrastructure (water, electricity, paved streets) and provide services (education, nutrition, health) in poor areas, and allowed recipients to influence the design of projects. A similar approach was used in Peru by President Alberto Fujimori (1990–2000) who established a Ministry of the Presidency in 1992. Infrastructure and social spending, reaching some 25 to 30 per cent of the national budget, was channelled through this new ministry, bypassing the traditional social ministries. These social funds were to become a permanent feature in many countries (see Box 5.4). While hailed as a recognition that the state, despite its reduction in size and functions, needed to attend

Box 5.1 Privatization in Argentina

In a little more than three years, between 1990 and 1993, almost all the public enterprises producing goods and services in Argentina were sold by the government to the private sector. Together these generated nearly 8 per cent of the country's GDP and around 20 per cent of total investment in the country and included the national communications and airline companies, the national railway system, natural gas, electric power, water and sanitation, steelworks, oil refineries, defence industries, and even a racetrack. Up to the end of 1993, the state received over US$15 billion from the process.

While this income greatly helped the Menem government's economic stabilization plans and, in particular, its policy of maintaining a one-to-one parity between the Argentine peso and the US dollar, weaknesses in the privatization process also contributed to the severe economic crisis into which the country was plunged from 1998. Two main weaknesses have been identified:

1 Beyond the immediate short-term impact on the state's finances, privatization did not help overcome Argentina's chronic problem of budget deficits and mounting indebtedness. Indeed it may even have worsened it as many of the companies sold were undervalued, as the state assumed their debts before selling them, as tax exemptions and benefits given to the new private owners reduced the potential tax income the state could have received, and as the new owners (many of them joint ventures with foreign involvement) remitted growing amounts of profits and dividends out of the country.

2 The conditions under which the privatizations took place consolidated the market power of a small number of conglomerates. The failure to put in place adequate regulatory authorities, and the granting of effective monopolies to some of the privatized companies, strengthened the ability of the private sector to fix prices and to make relatively risk-free high profits. Teichman reveals that 'potential purchasers were directly involved in the privatization process, forming an integral part of the domestic policy networks developing privatization and, later, regulatory policy' (2002: 296). Thus, privatization has not developed an entrepreneurial business class that might invest in other sectors of the economy. Furthermore, as Azpiazu and Vispo put it, 'the growing bargaining power of the conglomerates weakens the state in its role of promoting better links and relations within society as a whole' (1994: 146).

to the needs of the poor, such programmes have been criticized as populist attempts to concentrate state funds under presidential discretion so as to consolidate popular support for ruling parties (Guillén Romo, 1997: 138–9; Crabtree, 1999: 117–18).

While some countries included elements such as political reform, decentralization or judicial reform at an early stage in the reform process, the elements outlined above are widely seen as defining the first generation of reforms. They were marked by an attempt to eliminate and cut back the powers and institutional remit of the state to interfere in the economy. What resulted was a slimmed-down state, with fewer personnel and entities (particularly companies) and less capacity to direct market activities; the development of the economy was seen as something best left to the market. These reforms were essentially a form of 'crisis management' amid severe problems of fiscal deficit and chronic inflation in many cases, and the objective was essentially one of macro-economic stabilization. As Tomassini reminds us, they lacked any vision of what role the state should play in seeking economic success, or how it should play it (Tomassini, 2002). They were also relatively easy, involving few costs or issues of appropriate institutional design. These are the issues that characterize the more difficult second generation of reforms through which, since the early to mid 1990s, Latin American states are seeking to build institutions more effectively to meet the challenges of economic development and social equality in a globalized world.

Before turning to these, however, the political economy focus of this book requires that we place the changes in the Latin American state in the context of the democratization of these states since the 1980s. For the slimming down of the state not only changes its nature and role but also what we can call its class composition, namely the social groups to whose needs and interests it gives priority. If the oligarchic state of the nineteenth century embodied the interests of the agro-export elite, and the populist state of the twentieth century those of the national bourgeoisie, state-dependent professionals and the industrial working class, the neoliberal state of the early twenty-first century gives priority to the interests of corporate capitalists, both national and foreign. As Teichman has written of Argentina and Mexico: 'Although institutionalized channels to policy makers were certainly present, personal access and personalized institutional relationships between businessmen and policy makers were a predominant feature of the process of market reform. ... Policy during the period inordinately benefited those with the closest contacts to senior policy makers: it was the companies of the big conglomerates who were able to take advantage of government programmes and move into export markets; these too were the purchasers of public companies. Close political alliances between the executives of conglomerates and government policy reformers were the order of the day' (2002: 507). These close business-political links also opened new opportunities for corruption, and allegations of corruption at the highest political levels abound throughout Latin America at the beginning of the twenty-first century, further undermining the credibility of politics. On Transparency International's 2002 Corruption Perceptions Index (CPI), which scores 102 countries from 10 for the least corrupt to 0 for the most corrupt, Chile (with 7.5) and Uruguay (with 5.1) are the only Latin American countries with a score above 5, while 10 of the region's countries have a score of 3 or below.[2] However, the fact that corporate interests became dominant during a period of widespread democratization raises a puzzling paradox, what Tedesco has called the paradox of a democratic system seeking the political inclusion of all and an economic system characterized by the economic exclusion of the majority (Tedesco, 1999: 138). How this happened is examined in the next section.

Democratization

Latin America has never been as democratic as it is at the beginning of the twenty-first century. Saved from the experiences of fascism and Stalinism that helped reinforce a general commitment to liberal democracy in Europe, many Latin Americans were equivocal in their attachment to democracy. The right, when it felt its interests threatened, was only too willing to see the military take power, while many on the left scorned the inability of what they called bourgeois democracy to transform society. However, the severe repression suffered under the military dictatorships of the 1970s convinced many of the values of a democratic system. This, coupled with a new-found commitment by the United States to support formal democratic systems in the region (linked to its policy of trying to overthrow the Sandinistas in Nicaragua in the 1980s and to the end of the Cold War), created a new climate. A wave of democratization swept the region from the early 1980s, not only sending the military back to barracks in countries in which there was a strong democratic tradition before the armed forces had taken power (such as in Chile, Uruguay and Brazil) but implanting formal democratic systems in countries whose citizens had rarely had a chance to elect their leaders (such as Paraguay, Guatemala and El Salvador). By the 1990s, elected civilian rulers were in power in all Latin American states (with the exception of Cuba) for the first time in the region's history. Attempts by sections of the military to regain power in Paraguay and in Haiti had been firmly repulsed by international action (the threat by the presidents of Brazil, Argentina and Uruguay to expel Paraguay from Mercosur in the first case, and UN action led by the United States in the second (see Box 10.1)). In four countries, Congress impeached the president, forcing his resignation: Fernando Collor de Mello in Brazil in 1992, Carlos Andrés Pérez in Venezuela and Jorge Serrano in Guatemala in 1993, and Assad Bucaram in Ecuador in 1997. Argentina, which since the 1920s had not seen one elected civilian president hand power to his successor without the military intervening first, not only consolidated civilian rule since 1983 but lived through an acute economic, social and political crisis at the turn of the century (during which the country had five presidents in less than two weeks at the end of December 2001 (see Box 11.4)) without any hint of military intervention. Democracy, in the sense of an electoral system under which citizens choose their presidents and parliaments at regular intervals in a secret ballot, looked firmly established throughout Latin America as the new century opened.

A large scholarly literature exists on the subject of Latin America's democratization. In the late 1980s, the transition from authoritarian rule dominated scholars' attention (see O'Donnell et al., 1986; Malloy and Seligson, 1987; Huntington, 1991) while, in the early 1990s, attention turned to the consolidation of the new democracies (see Mainwaring et al., 1992; Tulchin with Romero, 1995). However, by the late 1990s a new phase in the literature had opened as the quality of the democracy so widely established came under scrutiny (see Agüero and Stark, 1998). As Roberts put it, 'the dominant issue on the political agenda is no longer whether democracy can survive but whether it can become a meaningful way for diverse sectors of the populace to exercise collective control over the public decisions that affect their lives. . . . In much of the region, democratic form survives in the absence of democratic substance' (Roberts, 1998: 2). The impressive strength and regularity of formal democratic practice hides a wide variety of anti-democratic structures and practices in most Latin American countries, leading to the proliferation of terms like 'low-intensity democracy', 'exclusionary democracy', 'technocratic democracy' or 'protected democracy'. Six characteristics of the processes of democratization in Latin America in the 1980s can be identified that help explain this outcome:

1 *Political context.* In most countries democracy returned through a process of negotiation with the armed forces. Only in Argentina, where the military left power following defeat by Britain in the Falklands/Malvinas war of 1982, was their power significantly undermined. The new democracies, therefore, were sometimes called 'pacted democracies', since the military maintained substantial power, including in most cases an amnesty for crimes they had committed. In this situation, incoming civilian governments were reluctant to antagonize the armed forces, sought to maintain a climate of social stability and moved to control their political followers rather then mobilize them in a bid to achieve major social changes.

2 *Structural limitations.* In some cases, the military established legally protected privileges and a political role for themselves and their right-wing civilian allies. Chile is the most notorious case where the electoral system favours the political right; nominated senators make it effectively impossible for the government to change the constitution inherited from the military, since this would require a two-thirds majority in Congress, and the powers of the President over the military are circumscribed. But in other countries also, the military maintained significant power within the new democratic systems. Due to his reliance on the armed forces to defeat the Sendero Luminoso guerrillas and his restructuring of Congress, President Fujimori's period in office in Peru (1990–2000) was sometimes described as a co-government with the armed forces.

3 *Economic context.* Democratization coincided with the neoliberal reformation throughout the region. In some countries the military had implemented the reforms and the new civilian governments continued them (notably Chile), in others the new civilian rulers came to see they had no other options (Fujimori in Peru, Andrés Pérez in Venezuela and Menem in Argentina had all rejected neoliberalism in their electoral campaigns but once elected implemented them with zeal). The slimming down of the state and the new role allocated to the market in economic growth reduced greatly the ability of civilian governments to implement substantial social change, especially in favour of the poor. Instead, they sought to ensure that the market delivered economic growth since their political success depended on this.

4 *Technocratic decision-making.* Paradoxically, ensuring economic success meant handing more decision-making over to technocratic experts. These often had backgrounds in finance or business rather than in politics, and

were often graduates of elite US universities. Thus they shared the same worldview as the officials of the World Bank, the International Monetary Fund and international banks on which Latin American governments depended for advice and investment funds. As a result, decision-making in the new democratic governments was restricted to a small elite, with even senior members of ruling parties often feeling they had little influence.

5 *Cultural changes.* Democratization also coincided with some fundamental changes in Latin American political culture, as many people lost interest in collective projects of social transformation. To some extent this was due to the experience of military rule when extensive propaganda equated democracy with chaos, but even some of those who were staunch opponents of the military began to lose interest in politics. Some were exhausted by the long struggles they had waged while a disenchantment also set in as the high expectations that democracy would bring social change were not met. Furthermore, the new consumerism fostered by neoliberalism fuelled a culture of individualist consumption, replacing the previous attachment to collective social projects.

6 *Social fragmentation.* The severe undermining of collective social actors (like the trade union movement) has greatly diminished the social base of an alternative political project, whether of a socialist or a populist variety. As Roberts puts it: 'The heterogeneity and dispersion of popular sectors impede the organization of an effective counterweight to capital, which has the advantage of being less reliant on collective action to defend its interests' (1998: 275). In this situation, politics tends more and more to resemble marketing – selling candidates and their promises to a fragmented electorate on the basis of pandering to their self-interest.

As a result of these features, an elitist political system is being consolidated in Latin America that, if anything, limits popular influence on decision-making. As illustrated in Box 5.2 on the Chilean experience, this system has little to do with different projects of social transformation competing for popular support but has a lot to do with social control by wealthy elites. It is not surprising therefore that it is leading to high levels of disenchantment with politics throughout the region. As Silva puts it, 'political apathy has ... become generalized' (1999: 62). In these ways are the tensions between democracy and neoliberal reform being resolved.

Both the themes of the preceding two sections – the slimming down of the Latin American state and the new form of restricted democratization that is being consolidated – echo some of the concerns of the globalization literature as outlined in Chapter 1. For they show how Latin America is responding to the demands of international competitiveness. But it is being increasingly recognized that the reforms undertaken have not created a state and a political system able to capture more of the opportunities presented by globalization, such as more high-tech investment, more effective social services and a more transparent and accountable political system. The state has been slimmed down but not necessarily made more capable or effective. Furthermore, as

Box 5.2 Money and politics

The following is a commentary by Chilean political scientist Carlos Huneeus written at the end of the country's 2001 congressional election campaign:

> The present electoral campaign has certain similarities to that of 1997. The parties have avoided competing at the level of ideas, they have dodged offering their views about the country's major problems, they have hidden their names and emblems and even the differences between them, opting instead for the personalization of politics, with smiling and youthful candidates appearing on the posters which fill our streets and squares.
>
> This confirms something that was evident in the 1997 congressional elections and even more so in the 1999 presidential and 2000 municipal elections: the enormous amount of money available to the [right-wing] opposition. This has contributed to changing the nature of the campaigns as thousands of paid activists help the candidates, substituting for the volunteers who did it in times past when politics was attractive and the parties stood for ideas which gave a certain *mystique* to their adherents, especially the young.
>
> With the aim of getting votes, people are given gifts – spectacles, sewing machines, kitchen appliances, etc. This new style of politics is similar to clientelism, namely creating political loyalties through offering economic advantages. This is an anti-democratic practice since it destroys the nature of the electoral process and, in abusing the needs of the poor, corrupts democratic life. It constitutes a serious step backwards in political modernization as this practice was rejected at the end of the 1950s. (2001)

The right-wing UDI party which was the main objective of Huneeus's criticisms emerged from the 2001 elections as Chile's largest, gaining 25 per cent of the vote and increasing its seats in the Chamber of Deputies from 24 to 35. In the same election, some 40 per cent of the electorate did not register a valid vote, either because they had not registered to vote (2 million electors), abstained (1 million) or spoiled their vote (880,000). Of Chileans between the ages of 25 and 29, 44 per cent did not register to vote.

the neoliberal model fails to deliver tangible and sustained improvements in the living standards of the majority of Latin Americans (see Chapter 7), proponents of the new model fear its legitimacy being undermined. The president of the Inter-American Development Bank, Enrique Iglesias, has recognized that 'the economic reforms are politically legitimized through their social effectiveness' (quoted in Tomassini, 2002). For these reasons, there was a widespread consensus by the mid 1990s about the need for a second generation of reforms, this time designed to consolidate a lean but agile, participatory and effective state.

'Institutions Matter': Reforming the State

In 1998 the World Bank published a report on Latin America that carried the subtitle 'Institutions Matter' (Burki and Perry, 1998). This recognized that the first generation economic reforms had not delivered the benefits they promised and emphasized the importance of state institutions to bring the reforms to fruition. As Latin America entered the twenty-first century, modernizing and reforming the state had become the dominant agenda, often described simply as 'good governance' and attracting major funding from the international financial institutions. As described by Bresser Pereira, this would be a social liberal state, complementing rather than replacing the market, boosting the competitiveness of the economy, financing but not necessarily producing the many social services that the market cannot provide, and making decision-making more transparent and controlled by society rather than by bureau-cracies (1998: 108). Vellinga emphasizes the need for a 'new interventionism' by the state, guiding rather than replacing the market through expanding technological capacity, strengthening links with the international business community and providing a directional thrust to selected industries (Vellinga, 1998: 18–19). Tomassini (2002) identifies three elements to the reform agenda: creating a new quality-oriented administrative culture in the public service, a profound redesign of public institutions, and an opening to civil society so that the state responds to citizens' needs. The agenda is therefore a broad one, encompassing economic, political and social reforms. It includes, for example, reform of the judicial system, the professionalization of public employment, experimenting with new forms of social service delivery, reform of taxation, and various reforms to political systems. Unlike the first generation reforms, many of which were implemented through presidential decree, it is recognized that this new reform agenda is much more difficult, requiring the design of appropriate institutions and building a broad base of political support. Since this process is far from complete throughout Latin America, three examples are here examined to illustrate how the principles guiding the reform process are being implemented in practice.

Economic reforms: Regulation

When, in the 1980s and 1990s, the Latin American state withdrew from playing an active role in the market, it often paid little attention to the need to ensure that the market operated in a competitive manner. As Manzetti and dell'Aquila write: 'In the rapid sell-off process, Latin American governments usually disposed of assets with the criterion of maximizing profits. The result was often the creation of monopolistic or oligopolistic markets under private ownership at the expense of economic efficiency considerations and, in some cases, transparency of the process itself' (2000: 281). As a result, the issue of how to develop appropriate forms of regulation of the private sector is one of the principal economic reforms facing Latin American states. Regulation can cover many issues, such as ensuring minimal conditions of employment, safety standards or environmental protection. But at a more fundamental level,

regulation is required to ensure that private producers do not create monopolies that allow them to overcharge consumers or to protect producers against
interference from the state. State regulatory rules and mechanisms are particularly important in areas such as electricity, telecommunications or water supply
where competition may be lacking, or in financial services, where state oversight is vital to ensure standards are upheld.

By the 1990s many countries were experimenting with designing and implementing regulatory bodies. In the electricity, telecommunications and water
sectors, for example, countries have to decide how much competition to
allow, what pricing mechanism to put in place, how to attract new investment
and, in some cases, how to ensure social needs – such as the extension of
services to poor groups or isolated areas – are met. Regulation of the financial
sector raises other issues, such as accounting standards and reporting systems,
and how government guarantees may help foster market discipline or undermine it. Overall, such issues as the relationship of regulatory bodies to government, whether there should be separate regulators for each sector or one large
regulator, and how to ensure the independence of regulators from operators
arise in all sectors (for a detailed account of regulatory policy in various Latin
American countries, see Manzetti, 2000). However, putting in place effective
regulatory institutions requires more than institutional design, since it touches
on issues relating to the wider political and administrative system and to political culture. Thus effective regulation requires an independent judicial system,
efficient legislative oversight of regulatory bodies, high levels of administrative
competence, legal protection for producers and consumers, independent and
inquisitive media, and scrutiny by non-governmental organizations.

These final elements touch on the wider political context in which decisions
are made, moving the question of regulation beyond the technical issues that
have dominated the reform agenda. Studies by Bull (2000) and Snyder (1999)
draw attention to this wider political context. Comparing reform of the telecommunications sector in Guatemala and Costa Rica, Bull finds that the way
the reform proceeded depended on the nature of competing political elites and
the role the state telecommunications company had played. Thus, in Guatemala
where under military rule up to 1985 the company had been under military
control and used for surveillance of the civilian population, privatization saw it
being sold to a Guatemalan and Honduran consortium with no experience in
telecommunications despite bids by one international telecom company,
Telmex. Questions were raised about links between the consortium and the
ruling PAN party. In Costa Rica, on the other hand, the telecommunications
company was seen as a 'jewel in the crown' of the state and had high levels of
support among the population due to its efficiency in providing services over the
years. As a result, the government did not even propose privatization and failed
in its bid to win public support for opening the sector to competition. In neither
case has a well-regulated depoliticized company emerged, leading Bull to conclude that 'the political underpinnings of regulatory institutions is not yet well
understood, and neither is the possible political backlash that a withdrawal of
the state from the telecommunications sector can produce' (p. 29). Snyder's
account of the reregulation of the coffee industry in Mexico raises similar issues.

He shows how neoliberal deregulation by the state spurred politicians and organized social groups (such as small producers) to struggle over ways of reregulating the market. As a result, he finds that in some Mexican states new institutions reproduced top-down exclusionary decision-making that protects the interests of rural oligarchs, while in others they opened new channels for small farmers to compete in the international market. Snyder concludes: 'The varying strengths and strategies of politicians and societal groups ... determine the various types of new institutions for market governance that will result from these reregulation processes' (p. 174). The issues raised here show how a reform agenda based on technical criteria, usually derived from US experience, fails to understand some key determinants of regulatory outcomes, namely the balance of political forces in each particular context.

Political reforms: Decentralization

A central element of the political reforms undertaken in Latin America, especially in the 1990s, has been the decentralization of decision-making powers, including taxation, to subnational levels, either regional or local. A number of concerns motivated these reforms. Firstly, the fiscal crisis of the 1980s was associated with strongly centralized states and it was hoped that decentralization would help avoid such problems. Secondly, by moving government closer to the people, it was hoped that it would result in greater local participation in decision-making, especially by groups such as ethnic minorities or the poor. Thirdly, such participation would lead to greater accountability and transparence in governance. Fourthly, the design and delivery of programmes at local level should be more efficient and cost-effective. Finally, multilateral agencies like the World Bank and the Inter-American Development Bank were actively promoting such reforms. They have taken place in virtually all Latin American countries, though they have been taken further in the larger countries – Argentina, Brazil, Colombia, Mexico and Venezuela. Typically they have involved creating or strengthening municipal or provincial governments, electing mayors and devolving greater responsibility (for implementing programmes and for budgets) to subnational entities (see Box 5.3).

Decentralization has had a major impact on national politics in some countries. Opposition parties captured control of capital cities (such as the PRD in Mexico City or the Frepaso/Radical alliance in Buenos Aires, both in 1997) or used power at municipal level to offer an example of an alternative way of governing (the Frente Amplio in Montevideo or the PT in some Brazilian cities, notably Porto Alegre) (see Chapter 9). However, the early promise of such reforms has given way to a more sober assessment of their impact and potential. Local government can prove just as inefficient as central government and lack the technical competence to administer the programmes for which it is responsible. In this situation, the quality of services can differ greatly from municipality to municipality, with those servicing wealthy areas having the resources and capacity to provide high-quality services, while those in poorer areas lack such capacity or resources. One of the elements of the Argentine crisis which began in 1998 was the high level of indebtedness of provincial governments and the inability of central government to reach agreement with governors about how to manage these debts. This draws attention to the fact that a greater sharing of power can lead to political deadlock between central government and local politicians. As Willis et al. (1999) draw out in their examination of the politics of decentralization in Latin America, the design of decentralized bodies and the balance of powers that emerge is a function of national political bargaining and thus an expression of the strengths and weaknesses of national party systems and political culture.

Furthermore, in considering the Chilean experience, Salazar and Pinto draw attention to the ambiguity of a process of decentralization that has emerged, by and large, from the actions of central government rather than from the pressures and demands of an organized citizenry.[3] They see it as being functional to the needs of a neoliberal economic order that requires weakening the state, privatizing political action (since 'participation' is often reduced to consultative mechanisms involving neighbourhood groups and service providers) and frag-

Box 5.3 Popular participation in Bolivia

In April 1994, Bolivia's Congress enacted the Law of Popular Participation. This established the municipality as the basic unit for local government, authorized the direct election of mayors and municipal councils and recognized for the first time in the country's history the legal standing of indigenous and community organizations and incorporated them into the new local institutions. Furthermore, it mandated that 20 per cent of national tax revenues be transferred to local governments according to a formula based on each municipality's population. Responsibility for investment, administration, maintenance of the infrastructure for health, education and local water supply and sanitation, and for sports, rural roads, culture and irrigation works were all transferred to the local level which was directed to spend no more than 10 per cent of its budget on operating expenses and 90 per cent on developing the local area.

This reform was introduced in a country that had traditionally been highly centralized, with power vested in the hands of bureaucrats and politicians in La Paz. Local government had been limited to departmental and provincial capitals so that 42 per cent of the population, mostly poor rural indigenous *campesinos*, were reliant on national government. Assessing its impact, Grindle writes: 'Overall, the introduction of a new institution created a variety of ripple effects for parties, politicians, and citizens. Most of these changes indicate the creation of new sources of conflict and the emergence of new political actors, new claims for resources, and new sites for contestation. Elections and the interaction of the councils, mayors, and vigilance committees proved to be new spaces for contestation. The efforts of central administrators to control the local use of resources, the parties to reassert control over candidates and campaigns, and the grass-roots organizations to influence investment all suggest the extent to which new institutions can generate new forms of conflict or serve as arenas for old conflicts' (2000a: 144–5).

menting social policies (since these are reduced to local programmes addressing some of the great problems generated by the socio-economic system such as poverty but which do not involve any questioning of that system). In these ways, decentralized government becomes a technical executor of programmes rather than a space through which to mobilize a politically active and aware citizenry (1999: 300–11).

Social reforms: Combating poverty

As the 1990s advanced, it became ever clearer that neoliberal economic policies were failing to reduce poverty and inequality and, in some ways, may even have been exacerbating these problems (see Chapter 7). This recognition led to a growing consensus that state social policy needed to do more to address these acute challenges. Yet, it was also being acknowledged that the traditional ways through which Latin American states had delivered social benefits were over-centralized and bureaucratic, inefficient, often wasteful of resources, poorly accountable and in many cases failed the poor. As Franco put it, 'in many cases, the state has become more of a hindrance than a help to development and to improving the population's living conditions' (1996: 21). Therefore, even though social spending increased throughout Latin America in the 1990s, in most cases more than making up for the decline of the 1980s (Stallings and Peres, 2000: 64–70), attention began to be focused on the need for significant institutional reform in the design and delivery of social programmes, what Franco calls a new social policy paradigm (p. 12). Following Franco, the principal differences between the existing paradigm, inherited from the extensive interventionist state of the days of ISI, and the new emerging paradigm can be outlined as follows:

1   *Institutional form:* from the state having a monopoly on social provision to sharing it with private groups, whether commercial, non-profit or family; this would include a greater decentralization of delivery;
2   *Decision-making process:* from bureaucratic procedures to the involvement of users in the design of social projects;
3   *Financing:* from the state being the source of all financing to contributions coming from other sources such as from private-sector bodies or through users paying fees for services;
4   *Objectives:* from the universal supply by the state of a particular social good (such as education or health care) to an emphasis on ensuring the needs of the population for this good are satisfied, including where necessary a positive discrimination in favour of the poor or minority groups;
5   *Priorities:* from the gradual expansion of a universal service to those most in need, to giving priority to the neediest from the beginning;
6   *Beneficiary population:* from the organized middle classes to the poor;
7   *Means or ends:* from an emphasis on delivering a certain type of service to an emphasis on achieving certain goals;
8   *Indicator:* from emphasizing the amount of social spending to assessing the impact on the target population.

This emerging social paradigm found expression in what Grindle called 'extra-ordinary innovation' in the social policies of many Latin American countries throughout the 1990s (Grindle, 2000b: 44) guided by the principles of decentralization, focalization, privatization, involvement of beneficiaries, flexibility, cost effectiveness and accountability. The widespread use of social funds is probably the best example (Box 5.4).

Box 5.4 Social funds: Models of the new social paradigm?

As part of the reforms of the 1980s, social funds (SFs) began to be used in many Latin American countries to finance programmes for the poorest sectors of the population. Though seen initially as temporary measures to support the poor during the period of structural adjustment, donor enthusiasm (mainly on the part of the World Bank and the Inter-American Development Bank) meant they have become a permanent feature of the neoliberal reformation, operating in 16 Latin American countries. A principal reason for this enthusiasm is that they are seen to embody the principles of the new social policy paradigm, being decentralized, targeted on the poor, cost-effective, partially privatized (in that they contract out to the private sector and to non-governmental organizations (NGOs)) and involve local communities in design and delivery. Roughly a third of funds go to economic infrastructure, another third to education and health, and the remainder to microfinance (usually offering small loans to poor people to establish income-generating enterprises), training and environmental protection. Grants are made available to local communities or municipalities which have a say in designing their project, execution (like construction) is contracted out to private groups, and the local community monitors the project, takes responsibility for its long-term maintenance and contributes a small percentage of project costs, sometimes through free labour.

While donors remain enthusiastic about the superiority of this form of public service provision, Tendler (2000) finds that their own evaluations fail to provide grounds for such a positive evaluation. Though designed as job-creation and poverty-reduction schemes, they have created relatively few jobs and reached less than 1 per cent of the Latin American labour force. The jobs they have created are temporary, of low quality and offer no training, while the wages paid are typically below subsistence level. Neither do the evaluations bear out the claim that they help reduce poverty. Instead, higher expenditures go to better-off communities and regions than to poorer ones since 'better-off communities are better organized, better educated, and have greater access to local decision-makers' (p. 94). Compared to more traditional forms of social service delivery by central government bodies, Tendler finds the social funds may be less cost-effective, have a poor record of longer-term sustainability and maintenance, and can be slower in disbursing funds. NGOs have proved unreliable partners, either because they are not present among poorer communities, have dubious grassroots credentials or are less cost-effective. SFs can also have the perverse effect of undermining central government programmes (in some cases governments have used donor funding of social funds as an excuse to cut social budgets), or they can distract attention from the need for public sector reforms and institution building.

Tendler concludes: 'The most one can say is that SFs and SF-like programmes have not proven to be consistently and sustainedly better than the more traditional supply-driven programmes or the reformed versions of them' (p. 101). Paradoxically, she recommends that to improve them, they should be made more like traditional, government-centred social programmes (Tendler, 2000).

There are many examples of the successful design and implementation of social programmes based on targeting, on decentralization, and on user involvement. Social policy in Chile since the return of democracy has effectively incorporated these principles, though they tend to be integrated into central government programmes rather than being set up parallel to them as in other countries and their success has had a lot to do with the country's high levels of economic growth up to the late 1990s (see Raczynski, 2000). However, as Box 5.4 indicates, a number of fundamental problems can be identified in the attempts to implement social policy reform. Five are outlined here:

1 *Targeting.* As Sheahan points out, part of the problem with evaluating the success of targeted programmes is that it is almost impossible to find out what proportion of the genuinely needy were excluded (1998: 188). In its 1999–2000 *Social Panorama of Latin America*, ECLAC pointed out that, in a context of growing social vulnerability, many middle class and lower middle class Latin Americans are worse off due to the fact that social benefits are being targeted more on the poor (2000b: 49–52). Therefore, while targeting may benefit some, others may suffer as a result.

2 *Contradictory logics.* The widespread support for social policy reforms in Latin America hides the fact that different groups may support them for reasons that are mutually incompatible. For example, neoliberal economists and Finance Ministry bureaucrats may see them as a means of restraining state spending, balancing budgets and privatizing what previously were state activities. Social professionals, activists and some politicians will tend to support them in the hope that they will result in more effective social programmes. Thus, there is a constant tension between the need for efficiency and the need for equity. The evidence of growing poverty and inequality may indicate that the former tends to win out over the latter.

3 *Institutional fragmentation.* Unless reforms are well coordinated, they often result in simply adding on new entities while neglecting to undertake a thorough reform of the main state providers of social services, the education, health, and social welfare ministries. To address this problem, Bolivia has established a Ministry for Human Development and others have established groups coordinating the activities of different social ministries, such as Peru's Interministerial Committee of Social Affairs (CIAS). Hardy (2002) points out, however, that even these have not been able to overcome the

marginalization of social policy in the priorities of Latin American governments.

4   *Priority to the poor.* While the discourse on social reform emphasizes the
    need to target the poor, it is not at all clear that this objective is being met
    through the reforms. In his study of why public social spending in Latin
    America fails the neediest, Lloyd-Sherlock found that the reforms of the
    1990s have done little to reduce what he calls 'inverted targeting' (a bias
    towards the middle classes) 'and often have aggravated it' (1998: 22). In
    general, he concludes: 'Most Latin American social spending is channeled
    into programmes of little relevance to the poor and needy and would appear
    to do more to consolidate inequalities than to ameliorate them' (p. 10).

5   *Social control.* Behind the rhetoric of participation, some see an attempt to
    co-opt marginalized social sectors into the neoliberal development model,
    thereby increasing its legitimacy. For example, Leiva found that interna-
    tionally funded micro-enterprise training programmes in Chile 'sought to
    eradicate from the consciousness of the membership traditional values of
    solidarity, democracy and collective identity, replacing them with individu-
    alism, competition, hierarchy and profit-driven rationality' (2001: 25). This
    is further examined in Box 10.2.

Overall, then, the second generation reforms of the state in Latin America are
proving, at best, to have mixed results. While some successes can be pointed to,
it is still far from clear that they are creating the sort of lean, agile and efficient
state that the reformers hope for. Indeed, as the examples examined in this
section illustrate, the reforms themselves are full of ambiguities and, even if
implemented as planned, may end up weakening and fragmenting the state,
undermining its coherence and its ability to ensure the market serves the needs
of society. Furthermore, there is a tendency to conceive of the process as a
technocratic exercise and a concomitant failure to address the political conditions for success – winning broad political support for the reforms, attending to
the needs of sectors that may lose out, and incorporating elements that might
have broader social appeal. Finally, what is perhaps the greatest weakness of
the reform process is the unresolved tension as to whether it is reforming the
state to make it more amenable to the free operation of the market or to give it
the capacity to direct and control the market for the good of society. This
unresolved tension lies at the heart of the ideological underpinnings of the
reform process.

Beyond the Washington Consensus

If, as outlined in Chapter 4, the Washington Consensus formulated the agenda
guiding the first generation of reforms in Latin America, a new agenda is being
defined to guide the second generation, usually known by the rather clumsy
title, Beyond the Washington Consensus. Indeed, this was the main title of the
World Bank report on institutions mentioned at the beginning of the previous
section. This new agenda lacks the neat formulation of its predecessor, being

largely concerned with the role played by institutions in ensuring economic success and echoing the concerns of institutional economics (see North, 1990). When he was chief economist at the World Bank, Joseph Stiglitz formulated the need for a broader agenda:

> The messages of the Washington consensus in the two core areas [macro-stability and liberalization] are at best incomplete and at worse misguided. While macro-stability is important, for example inflation is not always its most essential component. Trade liberalization and privatization are key parts of sound macro-economic policies, but they are not ends in themselves. They are means to the end of a less distorted, more competitive, more efficient marketplace and must be complemented by effective regulation and competition policies. (1998: 7)

This identifies the objectives of the reforms as being a more competitive and efficient marketplace and the role of institutions as being means to this end. In relation to Latin America, both the Inter-American Development Bank (IADB) and the UN Economic Commission for Latin America and the Caribbean (ECLAC) have been promoting this agenda, though with distinct emphases (see Box 5.5).[4] However, in the World Bank's World Development Reports 2000/01 and 2002 can be found a clear expression of the rationale underlying the new agenda, especially its understanding of the nature and role of institutions and their relationship to markets (World Bank, 2000, 2001).

The title of the 2002 report describes the World Bank's agenda as being that of 'Building Institutions for Markets'. Since it argues that 'income from participating in the market is the key to boosting economic growth for nations and to reducing poverty for individuals', the World Bank sees the objective of institutions as being to make markets work through providing rules, enforcement mechanisms and organizations promoting market transactions: 'Extremely diverse, these institutions transmit information, enforce property rights and contracts, and manage the degree of competition. And in so doing, they give people opportunity and incentives to engage in fruitful market activity' (p. 1). The previous year's report had detailed the key role of markets in alleviating poverty. While acknowledging that 'policies and institutions at the country and local level are the keys to enhancing the opportunity, empowerment, and security of poor people' (p. 179), they fulfil this role through facilitating and, where necessary, complementing the market, not through regulating or restraining it. As the report says, 'while markets are a powerful force for poverty reduction, institutions that ensure that they operate smoothly and that their benefits reach poor people are important as well' (p. 192). In the 2002 report, the Bank states that institutions can promote market development 'that provides benefits for all – inclusive and integrated markets – markets that provide equal opportunity, that reduce risk, and that enable investment in higher-return activities' (p. 4). This clearly identifies the market as the principal means to achieve economic growth and poverty reduction, while the role of institutions is to ensure that it operates efficiently and competitively.

However, empirical evidence from Latin America over the 1990s does not bear out the World Bank's expectation that liberalized markets will result in

Box 5.5 Neoliberalism or neostructuralism?

In response to the implementation of neoliberal structural adjustment policies in the 1980s, the UN Economic Commission for Latin America and the Caribbean (ECLAC) formulated an alternative reform agenda which, drawing on its tradition of advocating a state-led industrialization strategy for the region (briefly outlined in Chapter 3 and often called structuralism), it labelled neostructuralism. While accepting neoliberalism's emphasis on the urgent need for economic reforms, on integration into the global economy, on macroeconomic stability and on a changed role for the state, neostructuralism offered an alternative agenda based on the needs of Latin America.

Formulated in an influential publication entitled *Changing Production Patterns with Social Equity* (1990), ECLAC's proposals centred on the need for the state and the private sector actively to cooperate in improving the region's ability to produce products with a high technological content, to be competitive in cutting-edge international markets, and to distribute the benefits of development widely, thereby reducing poverty and inequality. As Fernando Fajnzylber, one of the principal architects of neostructuralism, put it, it would be a state 'that is going to delegate responsibilities in the area of production to the existing stock of entrepreneurs; a state that is going to concentrate on the task of boosting productivity, the pace of technical progress and the level of training; a state that is going to promote social equity, or social cohesiveness' (Fajnzylber, 1994: 207). Where neoliberalism neglected the importance of technology, neostructuralism saw its acquisition and dissemination as being crucial to boosting productivity and competitiveness; where neoliberalism depended on the market to reduce poverty and inequality, neostructuralism stressed the importance for economic success of reducing poverty and inequality through active social policies; and where neoliberalism accepted low-wage labour as a competitive advantage for the region, neostructuralism emphasized technical innovation as the basis for competitiveness.

By the late 1990s, the term neostructuralism was being less used, though ECLAC continued to promote similar reforms, indicating that many of its proposals still remained to be implemented (see Ocampo, 1998).

higher levels of economic growth and reduced poverty. Instead, the Bank's rationale rests on an assumption that properly functioning competitive markets are beneficial for society as a whole. This assumption derives from the classical economic tradition dating back to Adam Smith and has been challenged by the work of Karl Polanyi who examined how markets functioned in a range of precapitalist societies (for the relevance of Polanyi to Latin America, see Topik, 2001). He concluded that poverty and social dislocation arose from the imposition of the self-regulating market on society as happened for the first time with the advent of the Industrial Revolution in Britain in the nineteenth century. The self-regulating market treated labour, land and money as commodities and therefore led to 'the running of society as an adjunct to the market' (1957: 57) which 'required that the individual respect economic law even if it happened to destroy him' (p. 85). From this arose the baffling paradox for Polanyi that poverty and plenty went hand in hand as constitutive features of this market society, as he called it. Far from market activity being a natural phenomenon, as Adam Smith held, Polanyi contended that 'the market has been the outcome of conscious and often violent intervention on the part of government which imposed the market organization on society' (p. 250). From this he concluded that, instead of fashioning institutions friendly to the market, society needs to put in place 'a network of measures and policies . . . designed *to check the action of the market* relative to labour, land and money' (emphasis added) (p. 76). These concerns of Polanyi are highly relevant to the reform process in Latin America which, through the liberalization of labour, land and financial markets, has opened a range of new possibilities for treating workers, nature and money as commodities to be bought and sold (see Kirby, 2002). The work of Polanyi therefore challenges the assumptions informing the World Bank's agenda, and raises disturbing questions about the nature of its reform project. From a Polanyian perspective, its objective is to impose market principles and mechanisms on society. The conclusions of Williams and Young in this regard remain relevant, namely that the Bank's 'more recent analysis implies the need for a capacity to reach much deeper into Third World societies and mould them more than has ever been contemplated at least in modern times' (1994: 99). Finally, Polanyi's analysis alerts us to the destructive social consequences of such a project.

Conclusions

As quoted in the introduction to this chapter, Falk sees the state in the present era of globalization being pushed in a direction that makes it more responsive to the economic needs of global capital and less responsive to the social needs of its own citizens. The ways in which this has been happening in Latin America have been described, especially the weakening of the state in the first generation of reforms and the attempts now being made to fashion a more efficient state. Attention has also been drawn to the ambiguous rationale informing the reform process. Yet, as Stark reminds us, while the task facing Latin American governments is daunting, the outcomes are not predetermined (1998: 88). The next chapter looks at another area of reforms in which Latin American governments have been very active in response to the pressures of globalization, the process of regional integration.

Notes
[1] US political leaders and Cuban exiles often make the point that Cuba is now the only non-democratic state in the Americas. Indeed, the USA uses this as a justification for excluding Cuba from fora like the Summits of the Americas. This both overlooks the extent to which many Latin American countries are far from being good examples of well-functioning democracies (one thinks of Haiti, Paraguay, Venezuela, Colombia and Chile) and also the fact that Cuba is by no means a military dictatorship of the kind that

has been far too common in other countries of the region. The Cuban political system is a complex mix of democratic and authoritarian elements that require critical assessment rather than ideological dismissal (see Chapter 8).

[2] The Corruption Perceptions Index is a poll of polls and reflects the perceptions of business people and country analysts, both resident and non-resident. It draws on fifteen surveys from nine independent institutions. Results are available at www.transparency.org.

[3] In her study of institutional reforms in Argentina, Bolivia and Venezuela, Merilee S. Grindle emphasizes that 'they were "chosen" by political actors rather than "pushed" on decision makers by societal interests or international pressures' (Grindle, 2000a: 12).

[4] For example, Bull identifies differences in the World Bank's and the IADB's understanding of governance, with the former emphasizing more technical aspects (the provision of clear rules and institutions to enforce them) while the latter has a more political understanding (honesty and accountability of government, and citizen participation in decision-making). (See Bull, 1999: 3.)

6

Regionalization

Regional integration is increasingly being seen by countries large and small as a way of trying to maximize the benefits and avoid the pitfalls of globalization. It can take many forms, from the ambitious institution-building of the European Union (EU) to the looser and more narrowly economic North American Free Trade Agreement (NAFTA) between Canada, the United States and Mexico. But, whatever their forms, regional integration schemes proliferate throughout the world, in Europe and the Americas, in west and southern Africa, in south Asia and in southeastern Asia (for details, see Schulz et al., 2001). Through APEC (Asia-Pacific Economic Cooperation), the United States is attempting to create a large grouping of Asian and Pacific states, including Japan, Australia and, in Latin America, Mexico, Peru and Chile. The motivation for these various efforts is, as Schulz et al. put it, that 'states today experience a lack of capacity to handle global challenges to national interests, and increasingly respond by "pooling sovereignty"' (2001: 4). In Nederveen Pieterse's terms, regionalization is 'a way to negotiate globalization' (2001: 58).

Latin America is no exception to this wave of what is often called the 'new regionalism'. The term has been coined to highlight the differences between the new forms of regional integration now being attempted and other forms of regionalism that characterized the world of the Cold War, often motivated by security concerns (as in the case of the North Atlantic Treaty Organization, NATO) or inter-bloc economic development (the European Economic Community, EEC, and its communist-bloc equivalent, the Council for Mutual Economic Assistance, CMEA). In Latin America, forms of regionalism developed in the 1960s as a way of consolidating the inward-oriented, state-led and protectionist development model of the period (see below). By contrast, the new regionalism is much more open and multifaceted, concerned not just with integrating markets (such as free trade agreements), but creating possibilities for social and cultural integration and experimenting with new forms of shared decision-making. In many cases, it is open-ended, not remaining satisfied with levels of integration already achieved but seeking to extend (through bringing in new members) and deepen integration (through even closer economic, political, social and cultural links). Furthermore, it is taking place in more areas of the world than ever before and shares the characteristic of responding to a common challenge, namely globalization. In the Latin American and

Caribbean region, the new regionalism finds expression in an array of different layers of integration, what Phillips calls a 'patchwork quilt' (1999: 79), at the level of the region as a whole and among different groupings of countries within it. As such, it indicates a third form of neoliberal reformation, alongside economic liberalization and state reform. Indeed, just as economic liberalization and state reform are intimately interlinked as two sides of the one coin, so too is regionalization inseparable from them as it provides the wider international conditions for these other reforms to bear fruit.

This chapter describes the layers of regional integration schemes that are taking place throughout Latin America and the Caribbean. It begins by referring to the aspiration to regional unity that has been present since independence and by describing earlier attempts at integration, particularly in the 1960s. Since US policy and actions towards Latin America have greatly conditioned the region's room for independent manoeuvre, particularly throughout the twentieth century, the following section looks at the region's relationship with its Big Brother. Section three turns to the many new forms of regionalization since the late 1980s, particularly NAFTA and Mercosur, and highlights the regional integration models that now compete for dominance. The final section assesses how the region is responding to the challenges and opportunities of regionalization.

Aspiration to Unity

The idea of Spanish American unity was, says the historian Edwin Williamson, the 'recurrent obsession' (1992: 565) of Simon Bolívar (1783–1830), the liberator from Spanish rule of the northern part of South America (see Box 6.1). Though he was unsuccessful in forging a unity of the newly independent republics, the aspiration has lived on and found expression in various efforts to forge closer ties between the countries of Latin America. Some of these, such as the Congress of Panama in 1826 and the Congress of Lima in 1864, brought together representatives of various Latin American countries who pledged reciprocal respect for the independence and territorial integrity of one another's countries and the use of peaceful means to settle any differences (de Ramón et al., 2001b: 169). Others, however, such as the ambitious attempt to establish the International Union of American Republics, resulted from a US invitation to all the independent states of Latin America to the first Panamerican Conference in Washington DC in 1889. A proposal for a pan-American customs union foundered on Argentine opposition, since it had close economic links with Britain at the time, while Chile rejected a commitment to the obligatory arbitration of political disputes, fearing it would allow Peru and Bolivia to claim back the territory they had lost to Chile in the recently concluded War of the Pacific (1879–83). What did result was the Panamerican Union, which organized meetings of all the American states every five years or so in different capital cities to discuss themes of common interest. This laid the foundations for the emergence of a pan-American system, under US dominance, following the Second World War.

Box 6.1 Bolívar's dream

Following the independence of Peru (1821) and Bolivia (1825), Bolívar dedicated his efforts to establishing the unity of the newly independent Spanish American republics. He had already ensured that Colombia, Venezuela and Ecuador established the unified republic of Gran Colombia on their independence in 1819 and he dreamed of a confederation of Andean peoples which the new states of Chile and the United Provinces (today's Argentina) might later join. At the end of 1824, Bolívar had written to the governments of Mexico, Central America (a unified republic between 1823 and 1839), the United Provinces and Chile inviting them to send representatives to a congress in Panama, since 'it is time that the unity of the American republics which were previously Spanish colonies, based on common interests, be given a solid foundation so that it might endure'. The Congress of Panama met in the Franciscan friary in Panama City in June 1826 but only Mexico, Central America, Peru and Colombia sent delegates. These approved resolutions establishing a federation with a common army and navy to which states not represented could later accede, and with a representative Assembly of the confederated states which would meet at least every two years.

Even though these resolutions remained a dead letter, Bolívar continued to work for an Andean federation that he hoped would be strong enough to challenge the growing power of the United States and to liberate Cuba and Puerto Rico. However, events were moving against him as a civil war in Gran Colombia fragmented the unified state into three independent republics in 1830; months later Bolívar died a broken and disillusioned man. Williamson wrote that 'what a man like Bolívar understood was that a stable national identity could not be achieved other than on the basis of a unifying political ideal. In his efforts to preserve Gran Colombia and in his dream of a pan-American federation, he was striving to rediscover in modern political conditions the fundamental quality that had made the Catholic monarchy of Spain (and indeed Portugal) so stable and resilient – namely, its capacity to reconcile political unity with cultural diversity' (1992: 565).

Meanwhile the aspiration towards Latin American unity (excluding the United States) found expression in the region's political culture. For example, when the Peruvian political activist Victor Raúl Haya de la Torre (1895–1979) founded APRA (Alianza Popular Revolucionaria Americana) while exiled in Mexico in 1924, among its principles was the unity of the peoples of Indoamerica, as he called it. Indeed, he founded APRA as a Latin American political party, though in practice it became a Peruvian party and dominated politics there for most of the twentieth century. Foremost among the sources of the 'doctrine' of the Movement for a Fifth Republic (MVR), the political organization led by President Hugo Chavez of Venezuela, is 'the sovereign unity of Latin American and Caribbean countries, with the aim of making our territories a power centre which could act on the basis of equality with the rest of the world's nations' (Morales, 2001: 53). Meanwhile, a significant step towards establishing a forum through which the states of Latin America could develop a common agenda came with the founding of the UN Economic Commission for Latin America (CEPAL) in 1948 with its headquarters in Santiago, Chile. Washington opposed this, fearing it would develop an agenda for the region independent of US interests. As outlined in Chapter 3, CEPAL promoted a project of state-led, import-substitution industrialization. In order to expand the market for the goods produced by these new industries (previously limited to the domestic market), to stimulate industrial exports, and to open economies to competition, CEPAL also promoted regional integration. As a result the 1960s saw the development of a number of such schemes in the region. Among the most important were the following:

1   *Latin American Free Trade Association (LAFTA)*: founded in 1960, it was renamed the Latin American Integration Association (ALADI) in 1980. This set itself the ambitious target of developing a free trade area by 1973 through periodically negotiated tariff reductions between its members (the countries of South America and Mexico), harmonization and coordination of industrial and agricultural policies, and agreements on complementarity in some industrial sectors (allowing countries to specialize in products for the regional market).

2   *The Central American Common Market (CACM)*: founded in 1960 and including the five countries of Central America (excluding Panama). This was more ambitious than LAFTA in that it sought closer economic integration, a common external tariff, the harmonization of economic policies, and common regional industrialization policies.

3   *The Andean Pact*: founded in 1969 by Colombia, Ecuador, Peru, Bolivia and Chile, and later joined by Venezuela. Chile, once it began to implement economic liberalization under the Pinochet dictatorship, left the pact in 1976. A subgroup within LAFTA, this sought faster progress to establish a free trade zone and closer coordination of industrial policies between countries at similar levels of development (since Latin America's three most industrialized countries, Brazil, Mexico and Argentina, were not members).

4   *The Caribbean Community (Caricom)*: founded in 1973 and comprising 14 small Caribbean states, most of them former British colonies. This has sought to develop trade and economic integration between the members.

This form of regionalism, sometimes called the 'old regionalism', was essentially defensive. As a complement to inward-looking and protectionist development policies, it sought to expand trade and industrial coordination among countries of relatively similar levels of development, while maintaining the regional market protected from outside competition. While it succeeded in boosting intra-regional trade in manufactured goods, its more ambitious plans foundered on a lack of political will among member states and on the enormous difficulties encountered in coordinating policies among countries with highly regulated economies geared to supplying the domestic market. Furthermore, many were producing relatively similar goods so that the scope for complementarity was limited. However, it gave expression to the interests of Latin America and was largely looked upon with suspicion by Washington.

Big Brother

Despite its long-standing aspirations, Latin America has therefore fluctuated between two different conceptions of what regional unity might involve. Clearly, Bolívar intended it to be a unity that excluded the United States and that would limit Washington's power in the region. The second conception, however, not only included the United States but often found expression in forms that subordinated Latin America to US interests. This tension persists into the twenty-first century where it finds expression in competing forms of regional integration (see next section).

Even as Latin America was emerging into independence, the USA asserted in the Monroe Doctrine of 1823 a claim to regional leadership. Referring to European powers, US President James Monroe stated: 'We should consider any attempt on their part to extend their system to any portion of this hemisphere as dangerous to our peace and security.' However, despite the Mexican–American War of 1846–8 in which the USA took from Mexico the territories of California, Arizona and New Mexico, Washington was not strong enough to enforce the Monroe Doctrine until the end of the nineteenth century. By then it had extensive investments and trading interests, particularly in Mexico, Central America and the Caribbean, and, with its military intervention in a civil war in Haiti in 1888, it gave notice of its intention to become the region's policeman. Britain formally recognized US supremacy in the Americas in 1901 following Washington's intervention in a boundary dispute between the British colony of Guiana and Venezuela in 1895–6. Between 1898 and 1932, the US militarily intervened 34 times in nine Central American and Caribbean countries, occupying and administering the Dominican Republic (1916–24), Haiti (1915–34) and Nicaragua (1912–25 and 1926–33), and landing troops for shorter periods in Mexico, Honduras, Guatemala and Costa Rica. During Cuba's independence struggle, Washington sent a military force in 1899 to protect US investments there, occupying the island until 1902. Under intense US pressure, the Platt Amendment was included in the Cuban constitution giving Washington the right to intervene in the country's internal affairs, a right it exercised with military forces from 1906 to 1909, in 1912 and from 1917 to 1922. During the Spanish–American war, it also seized Puerto Rico, which remains under US control. To secure its interests in the building of the Panama Canal, it helped foment Panama's independence from Colombia in 1903 and secured sovereignty over a 10-mile-wide canal zone, cutting the country in two, which it only handed back to Panamanian rule in 2000. In the Roosevelt Corollary to the Monroe Doctrine, President Theodore Roosevelt in 1904 formally declared the right of the United States, as a 'civilized' nation, to end 'chronic wrongdoing' in the region.

By the 1920s, Washington was recognizing the need to use more sophisticated methods to protect its growing economic interests throughout Latin

America. In the Clark Memorandum of 1930, Washington declared that the Roosevelt Corollary had no support in the Monroe Doctrine and that the United States would no longer intervene in the internal affairs of Latin American countries. This found expression in the 'good neighbour' policy, proclaimed by President Franklin D. Roosevelt when he assumed the presidency in 1933 and attested to by the abrogation of the Platt Amendment and the withdrawal of US troops from Nicaragua and Haiti. Instead, Washington sought closer economic ties with Latin America, signing trade agreements with 15 countries between 1934 and 1941. The Second World War strengthened links as both Latin America and the United States relied on one another for trade; furthermore, the foreign ministers of the Americas met in 1939 (in Panama), 1940 (Havana), 1942 (Rio de Janeiro) and 1945 (Mexico City) for consultation on matters relating to the war. Subsequent meetings (in Rio de Janeiro in 1947 and in Bogota in 1948) laid the foundations for what de Ramón et al. calls the constitutional framework of the pan-American system (2001b: 240). This consists of four agreements:

1   The Chapultepec Act of 1945 under which the American states agreed that an attack by an extracontinental power on any one of them would be considered an attack on them all. This de Ramón et al. call the multi-lateralization of the Monroe Doctrine (p. 256);
2   The Interamerican Treaty of Mutual Assistance of 1947 (known as the Rio Treaty), a mutual defence pact between the American states;
3   The Organization of American States (OAS), established in Bogota in 1948; and
4   The American Treaty of Peaceful Resolution (known as the Bogota Pact), also signed in 1948.

These put in place a regional security architecture that was to be put to the test on many occasions over the 40 years of the Cold War during which Washington feared communist subversion in the region, fears greatly heightened after the Cuban Revolution in 1959. As Grugel put it, referring to this period: 'Inter-American relations ... rested on a security agenda, established from Washington, with trade issues and the question of economic development, which mattered far more to [Latin America and the Caribbean], playing a very secondary role' (1996: 134).

Military aid helped modernize the region's armed forces and many of their officers were trained in counterinsurgency techniques in the US School of the Americas in the Panama Canal Zone. The OAS became more an instrument of US policies than a genuinely regional forum, supporting the military overthrow with CIA involvement of the democratically elected Arbenz government in Guatemala in 1954, expelling Cuba in 1962 (a vote on which Argentina, Bolivia, Brazil, Chile, Ecuador and Mexico abstained), supporting the US invasion of the Dominican Republic in 1965 (against Venezuelan protests) and supporting the US invasion of Panama in 1989. These military moves, including the US Bay of Pigs invasion of Cuba in 1961 and US support for Britain in the Falklands/Malvinas war of 1982, all violated the inter-American agreements of the late 1940s, lending support to the claim that this was a form of 'hegemonic regionalism' (Banega et al., 2001: 236). Covert US actions in support of the 1964 Brazilian military coup and in undermining the government of Salvador Allende in Chile (1970–3) offer further evidence. While President John F. Kennedy (1960–3) responded to the challenge of the Cuban Revolution with a broad-ranging development agenda for Latin America, called the Alliance for Progress, the security elements soon took precedence over the developmental ones. US policy took a more benign turn under the presidency of Jimmy Carter (1976–80) who supported human rights in the region and imposed economic and military sanctions on Argentina, Brazil and Chile for grossly violating them. However, this proved short-lived. The Reagan administration (1980–8) took extensive unilateral military action, invading Grenada in 1983 and waging what has been called 'a holy crusade against communist forces' in Central America (Keen and Haynes, 2000: 570). In Nicaragua, the USA created the Contra counter-revolutionary group out of elements of the former Nicaraguan army to wage a terror war against the people of Nicaragua, mined the country's ports (an action found illegal by the World Court in The Hague) and conducted a disinformation campaign against the Sandinista government. Meanwhile, in El Salvador, it spent some US$4.5 billion in trying to defeat the FMLN guerrillas through arming a corrupt military establishment that inflicted terror on its own people and was implicated in the murder of Archbishop Oscar Romero of San Salvador in March 1980. These policies prompted the European Union to give financial aid and to support diplomatic peace moves in the region (see Box 6.2).

Following the end of the Cold War, economic interests have again come to the fore in inter-American relations. President George Bush's Enterprise of the Americas speech in 1990, in which he announced the goal of a free trade zone 'stretching from the port of Anchorage to the Tierra del Fuego', signalled this new agenda. However, continuing US security interests, and Washington's willingness to pursue them through military means, were also signalled in the US invasion of Panama in 1989 to arrest the country's leader, General Manuel Noriega, on drugs trafficking charges, and in President Bill Clinton's increasing support for military moves against drug growers and traffickers, culminating in the five-year $7.5 billion Plan Colombia in 2000 (see Box 9.5) and the Regional Andean Initiative (see Chapter 9). Drugs have thus replaced communism as the justification for US military might in Latin America.

Emerging Regional Architecture

Economic integration dominates the regional agenda of the Americas at the turn of the twenty-first century. Carranza sees the process begun by President Bush's 1990 speech as 'the first US attempt to elaborate a comprehensive policy agenda for the entire Latin American region since President Kennedy's ambitious Alliance for Progress' (2000: 107). For the first time ever, all Latin American states agree on the need to deepen and extend their involvement in regional economic groupings as they face the challenges of globalization, and

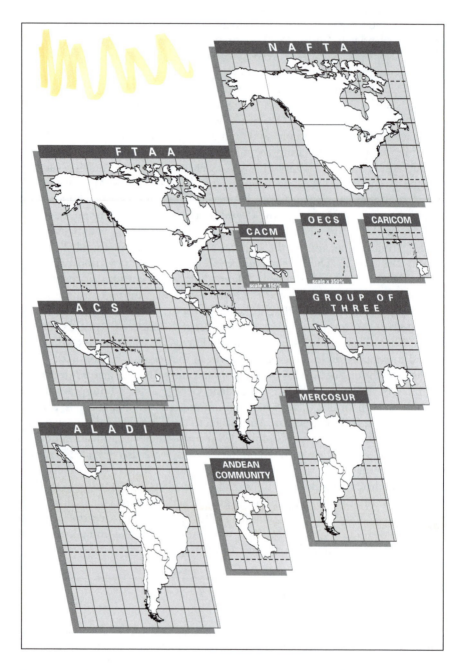

Based on an original map in the Special Report on Regionalisation published by Latin American Newsletters, April, 1988.

Layers of regionalization in Latin America

Box 6.2 The European Union: A counterweight to the USA?

In June 1999, one of the largest ever interregional meetings of heads of state and government at which 48 countries were represented took place in Rio de Janeiro. Significantly, Cuba was present, the United States was not. This was the first summit at this level of the European Union and the Latin American and Caribbean region and marked the coming of age of a growing 'strategic partnership' between both sides. This began in the early 1980s as the EU, with the impending accession of Spain and Portugal, began to turn its attention to Latin America for the first time. Worried at Washington's belligerent role in the civil conflicts in Central America, it developed a relationship with the five Central American countries known as the San José process. The first annual meeting between the foreign ministers of both groups took place in San José, Costa Rica, in September 1984 and has continued since. With the development of the Rio Group in the late 1980s (see Box 6.4), a similar institutionalized relationship developed, this time involving all the countries of Latin America and the Caribbean. By the mid 1990s, EU negotiations were underway with Mercosur, the Andean Community, Chile and Mexico involving ministerial meetings and trade agreements. Programmes to foster investment, academic exchanges, energy cooperation and municipal links between both groups were also developed.

From the beginning, the EU has emphasized the values it shares with Latin America and distinguished its approach from that of the United States. Thus, in dealing with the conflicts in Central America, it shared the Latin American view that these were rooted in poverty, inequality and social injustice rather than in external subversion as Washington believed. On drugs also, the EU stresses coresponsibility including greater efforts to reduce European consumption in contrast to Washington's 'war on drugs'. The EU has become the largest aid donor to the region, as US aid declined over the 1990s. As Crawley puts it, this has fostered an image of the EU as 'cooperative, generous, non-coercive, and development-oriented, rather than security-fixated' (2000: 17). However, behind such generosity lies a concern at weakening trade links between both sides as the EU loses ground to the USA and Asia in the Latin American market and as Latin American exports to the rest of the world grew five times more than those to the EU over the 1990s. One of the difficulties relates to EU protection of its agricultural market, as agricultural and fishery products make up a large share of Latin America's exports to the Union. The future of a promising relationship may depend on how Brussels deals with Europe's farmers.

they have embraced the new US agenda enthusiastically. However, behind this general agreement lurk many differences about what kind of regional integration would best suit countries' interests; some such as Brazil promote an active agenda, while some of the smaller countries are being more passively integrated into the fast changing regional architecture (see Box 6.3). Two models dominate at regional level, Mercosur and NAFTA, though a myriad of different ways of relating to these exist both at subregional levels and at national level.

Mercosur

The origins of Mercosur go back to a mutual pact to support democracy signed by Presidents José Sarney of Brazil and Raúl Alfonsín of Argentina in 1985. Both countries had recently returned to democracy, and the need to prevent a return of the military to power initially overcame the deep historical enmities between both. But the agenda quickly changed to one of economic integration, and by 1991, with the addition of Uruguay and Paraguay, the countries signed a treaty to establish a common market, to be known as the Common Market of the South (Mercosur in Spanish, Mercosul in Portuguese). Though this ambitious goal has yet to be achieved, by the turn of the century Mercosur was a free trade area and imperfect customs union with a common external tariff for trade with countries outside it.[1] Chile and Bolivia joined as associate members in the mid 1990s. With a combined population of 200 million and an aggregate GDP of over US$800 billion, Mercosur constitutes the third largest trading bloc in the world (after the EU and NAFTA). The value of exports within Mercosur increased from US$4.1 billion in 1990 to $17.6 billion in 2000 while those from the bloc to the rest of the world increased from $42.3 billion to $66.7 billion over the same period, indicating that this form of regionalization was not simply a defence against globalization but rather a stepping stone to more successful involvement in the world economy. Meanwhile, foreign direct investment to Mercosur increased from an annual average of $3.8 billion in 1990–3 (2.1 per cent of the world total) to $40 billion in 1997–9 (5.9 per cent) (Rozenwurcel, 2001). However, somewhat like the European Union, Mercosur's agenda goes beyond the economic and includes such issues as integration in the educational and cultural fields, and a charter of social rights. Furthermore, it is an internationally recognized juridical body and negotiates on issues of trade on behalf of its member countries. It has established a number of decision-making bodies such as a Common Market Council made up of member countries' foreign and economy ministers, an executive agency called the Common Market Group, a Trade Commission, a Joint Parliamentary Group and an Economic and Social Consultative Forum. Unlike the EU, however, it remains strongly intergovernmental as effective decision-making rests with the presidents of the member states, and has been criticized for having no body like the European Court of Justice to adjudicate disputes. These weaknesses, together with the fact that consensus is needed for all decisions (unlike the EU which has a complex system of qualified majority voting to arrive at decisions), are seen as blunting its development.

NAFTA

The initiative for NAFTA came from President Carlos Salinas of Mexico who in 1990 requested a free trade agreement with the United States. For Salinas, such an agreement would copper-fasten the neoliberal restructuring of the Mexican economy carried out by his predecessor President Miguel de la Madrid and enthusiastically deepened by himself so that future governments could not reverse liberalization. Sold as Mexico's passport to the First World, the North American Free Trade Agreement was negotiated with the USA and

Canada and came into force at the beginning of 1994. Its goal was a simple one: to eliminate or lower barriers to trade in goods and many services, creating a free trade area 'from the Yukon to the Yucatan'. As well as reducing or abolishing tariffs on many goods produced within the area and facilitating investment between the three members, NAFTA contains agreements on communications, competition and financial services. Mexico failed to have an agreement on labour mobility and a social fund (like the EU's structural and cohesion funds) included. Due to widespread popular opposition in the United States (including labour, environmental, consumer, religious and farm groups), President Clinton on his accession to office in 1992 negotiated labour and environmental 'side agreements' to NAFTA that set up mechanisms to encourage the three countries to enforce existing labour and environmental laws. However, these side agreements 'did not satisfy the more outspoken opponents of NAFTA' (Marchand, 2001: 206). NAFTA is therefore an ambitious free

---

Box 6.3 Different models of regional integration

At the first Summit of the Americas in Miami in 1994, to which all American and Caribbean countries were invited with the exception of Cuba, President Bill Clinton called for the establishment of a Free Trade Area of the Americas (FTAA) and boldly set 2005 as the date for negotiations to finish. The model that the USA had in mind was NAFTA and they envisaged a 'hub-and-spoke' process whereby Washington would negotiate bilaterally with Latin American countries to join the free trade agreement. Chile was then seen as next in line. However, as Carranza put it, it was widely recognized 'that a "hub-and-spoke" model, centred on NAFTA (and its core country, the US), was unfair for the Latin American countries, because the US would be placed in a superior bargaining position. By negotiating separate agreements with each of its smaller partners, the latter would have no chance to make common cause against the US in matters of common interest' (2000: 112).

However, by the time the second Summit of the Americas convened in Santiago, Chile, in 1998, a very different scenario was emerging. In the intervening period, President Clinton had failed to get US Congressional agreement for 'fast track' approval of free trade pacts. Since this meant that the Congress could change agreements that had been carefully negotiated, Latin American countries lost enthusiasm for the process, allowing Brazil to win backing for its counter-proposal of a South American Free Trade Agreement (SAFTA). '[T]he US found itself sitting down to negotiate an FTA with a united South American bloc, with Mercosur as its "hard core"' (Carranza, 2000: 92). This counterposed a 'building blocks' approach to integration, involving collective negotiations with countries on an equal footing and allowing for existing groups, such as Mercosur (or a possible SAFTA if that were to emerge from negotiations between Mercosur and the Andean Community), to continue in existence within an FTAA. At the third Summit of the Americas in Quebec City in 2001 only slow progress was reported from the nine groups negotiating the FTAA.

trade pact but, unlike Mercosur, it contains no aspiration towards deepening integration between the member states; its development is likely to be confined to taking in new members. When signed, it constituted the world's largest trading bloc and the first to join developed countries with a developing country. Not surprisingly, since joining, Mexico has deepened its trade dependence on the United States: the value of its exports to NAFTA grew from $96 billion in 1996 to $150 billion in 2000 and by the latter date almost 91 per cent of these were going to the USA (CEPAL, 2001b: Cuadro 14). Mexico has been trying to lessen this dependence on the US market by negotiating bilateral free trade agreements with Latin American countries and the EU. However, its privileged access to the US market makes it less than enthusiastic at the prospect of more Latin American countries joining the group.

Complementing the emergence of NAFTA and Mercosur as the two poles of attraction for regional integration in the Americas, existing subregional groupings such as the Community of Andean Nations (CAN, as the Andean Pact was renamed), the Central American Common Market (CACM) and Caricom continue in existence. Increasingly, the CAN is drawn to an agreement with Mercosur, while the CACM and Caricom look towards access to the US market. For example, a Central American Free Trade Agreement (CAFTA) is one likelihood. Countries like Colombia and Venezuela are pulled in both directions; they have a tripartite agreement with Mexico, known as the G-3, but Venezuela has also expressed interest in joining Mercosur. Chile has fluctuated between the two: attracted to NAFTA in the mid 1990s, it then considered joining Mercosur but was put off by having to adopt a common external tariff higher than its own and in 2001–2 was negotiating free trade agreements with the United States and with the European Union. Brazil's devaluation in 1999 while Argentina maintained its overvalued currency (due to keeping one-to-one parity with the US dollar) plunged Mercosur into deep crisis as Argentina took unilateral measures to cope with its severe economic crisis. Meanwhile President Fox's ambitious Plan Puebla-Panama (PPP), a 25-year, $20 billion plan to develop transportation and energy infrastructure (including roads, ports, airports, gas and electricity systems, telecommunications, rail lines and tourism infrastructure) integrating a region including the nine southern states of Mexico and the countries of Central America, was attracting major public and private investment. This included an initial pledge of $4 billion from the Inter-American Development Bank. As the new century began, the final shape of the regional architecture that would emerge throughout the Americas was far from clear.

Towards Latin American Unity?

Between the end of the 1940s and the mid 1980s, the presidents of Latin America met twice, both times at the invitation of Washington (Panama in 1956 and Punta del Este, Uruguay, in 1967). Since the 1990s, by contrast, many more fora have been developed, at which they meet, consult, and promote a common Latin American view. Foremost among these is the Rio Group, which fosters active dialogue on a range of economic, political and social concerns (see Box 6.4). Founded in 1987, it grew out of the Contadora Group which brought eight Latin American countries together to assist peace moves in Central America. The presidents of Latin America meet annually in the Rio Group Summit. Since 1991, the annual Iberoamerican Summit takes place between the leaders of the Spanish and Portuguese-speaking countries and those of Spain and Portugal. Presidents also meet at regional level; for example two presidential summits of the Mercosur countries (including Chile

---

Box 6.4 Rio Group: '19 countries with one voice'

As she handed over the year-long presidency of the Rio Group to Costa Rica in January 2002, the Chilean foreign minister Maria Soledad Alvear summed up its role and the year's achievements:

> The nineteen-country Rio Group is today the most representative and flexible mechanism for dialogue and political coordination in the region and the principal interlocutor with countries and groups of countries in other regions.
>
> In its fifteen years of existence, the Rio Group has contributed to the consolidation of peace in our region, to advancing democracy, to the protection of human rights and to the progressive integration of our economies.

Among the year's achievements, she mentioned:

1   At their annual summit, the region's presidents called for Latin America to 'strengthen its voice and its presence at international level so that development and globalization might be more equitable'.
2   The presidents also agreed to coordinate their positions and actions as far as possible so as to be a more effective presence at the International Monetary Fund, the World Bank, and the World Trade Organization.
3   The Rio Group expressed the position of Latin America on multilateral issues at various UN conferences.
4   It continued its institutionalized dialogue with the European Union and looked forward to the second summit of European and Latin American heads of state and government in Madrid, in May 2002.
5   It called on the G-8 countries to intensify their efforts to overcome poverty in the most needy countries.
6   It expressed Latin American solidarity to the US people following the terrorist attacks of 11 September and took part in various consultative meetings to coordinate action against terrorism.
7   It expressed solidarity with the peace process in Colombia, preoccupation at the situation in the Middle East and support for an independent Palestinian state, and 'constant backing for Argentina amid the gravity of its crisis' (Alvear, 2002).

and Bolivia) take place every year. More irregularly, the Summits of the Americas bring all the leaders of Latin America and the Caribbean (except for Cuba) together with those of the USA and Canada. Political groupings also exist at subregional level and new ones are emerging. Within the Caribbean, the Organization of Eastern Caribbean States (OECS) groups the small microstates of the region, all of them former British colonies, while the Association of Caribbean States (ACS) was founded in 1994 to join the Caribbean states with those of Central America, Mexico, Venezuela and Colombia. Significantly, Cuba was a founder member of ACS, signifying its attempt to find a new role for itself as part of the Caribbean region (see Chapter 8).

Latin America appears therefore more united than ever, and less dominated by the United States than it has been for over a century. Even the Organization of American States (OAS) has taken on a new role, promoting democracy and human rights. However, despite the grand sentiments of the Rio Group, the countries of Latin America are not acting in concert on the major issues that will determine their future – the nature of the emerging global economic order and their place within it. As Peter H. Smith recognizes, 'there are too many incentives for too many countries to pursue their own alternatives' (2001: 64–5). And, while Muñoz argues that 'the region no longer sees its present and future as inevitably dependent on the United States' (2001: 82), Smith counters that for Asia and Europe (where countries of the region are seeking to build closer links) Latin America holds little importance – its future will depend on the United States (pp. 52–62).

Recognizing this, different countries pursue different strategies according to opportunities presented, largely dictated by their economic relationship to the USA. Mexico finds itself more and more dependent on the USA, even aligning its foreign policy stances with those of Washington (Gonzalez, 2001: 161–6), while different South American states pursue different strategies, though most continue to pay close attention to opportunities that might be offered by Washington. The exceptions are Venezuela and Brazil. The former, under President Hugo Chavez, seemed deliberately to antagonize the USA through its leading role in the Organization of Petroleum Exporting Countries (OPEC) and through Chavez taking on the presidency of the Group of 77 in 2002 (comprising Third World countries), which he used as a platform to mount swinging attacks on neoliberalism. Brazil, on the other hand, seeks a leadership role as the dominant state in South America, aspiring to counteract the dominant role of the USA. Many smaller countries, especially in Central America and the Caribbean, see few options other than closer economic links with the United States. This lends credibility to Guedes da Costa's doubts about the validity of conceiving of Latin America as a coherent entity 'since the region has not developed a uniform identity in world politics' (2001: 92).

What is largely missing in this complex manoeuvring is the voice of civil society. Paradoxically, this found more expression in relation to NAFTA because of the major protest movement that emerged against it particularly in the United States, but creating links with civil society groups in Mexico. This highlighted the fact that NAFTA was largely the creation of big business and responded to its needs, rather than to wider social needs, particularly those of the poor and marginalized (Marchand, 2001). In South America, on the other hand, regional integration has been promoted by governments, though big business actively supports them (Banega et al., 2001). Here, however, the voice of civil society has been mostly silent and the debate about regionalization is confined to political, business and academic elites. But this is not to say that the neoliberal reformation has had a beneficial impact on civil society. Assessing its human impact is the subject of Chapter 7.

Note

[1] There are many stages to regional economic integration, though few of the integration processes underway anywhere in the world move to the higher stages. As described by Schulz et al., these are as follows: 'At the lowest stage there is a preferential trade area whereby member countries charge each other lower tariffs than those applicable to non-members, while preventing the free movement of goods within the area. The second stage is a free trade area in which tariffs and quotas are eliminated among members, but each country retains its own tariffs against imports from non-members [NAFTA]. A customs union goes further; in addition to sharing a free trade area, members erect a common external tariff [Mercosur]. The common market is a more developed stage of integration. It combines the features of the customs union with the elimination of obstacles for the free movement of labour, capital, services and persons (and entre-preneurship) [the European Community before it then became the European Union]. The next step on the ladder is an economic union, which involves a common currency and/or the harmonization and unification of monetary, fiscal and social policies [the European Union]. Political integration constitutes the ultimate stage of economic inte-gration, and it presupposes the unification of economic and political policies, and that the central supranational authority not only controls economic policy but is also respon-sible to a common parliament' (2001: 10).

7

The Human Impact

I n discussing economic growth, and the conditions that help generate and
maintain it, economists have a tendency to see it as an end in itself rather
than as a means to individual and social well-being. Yet, if the functioning of
the economy does not improve the livelihood of large sections of society, not
only is it questionable in itself but it generates the conditions that will in time
undermine it. These issues are particularly pertinent in a region like Latin
America that, as we saw in Chapter 2, displays high levels of poverty and
inequality. The real test of the neoliberal reformation, therefore, and its ability
to endure, rests on its success in improving the livelihood of the majority of
Latin Americans. The purpose of this chapter is to assess its performance in this
regard.

The chapter opens by looking in more detail at trends in poverty and
inequality throughout the region in the 1990s and at the different ways in
which poverty is understood and measured. The following section examines
the changing levels and nature of employment, and it closes with an outline of
the ways in which a liberalized economy is reshaping the social structure of
Latin America. Section three turns to the topic of environmental destruction
and how this affects the lives of Latin Americans, especially the poor. The
quality of people's participation in their societies is the subject of section
four which describes the impact of reform on the region's social and cultural
fabric. The chapter ends with a discussion of the causes of social deterioration
in Latin America and asks the fundamental question: is neoliberal reform serving to improve or to worsen the quality of life of most Latin Americans?

Human Development

As has already been shown in Chapter 2, both poverty and inequality tended to
worsen throughout Latin America over the 1990s. Examining the data in more
detail, a more variegated picture emerges as it shows that the percentage of
households in poverty actually declined significantly over the decade, from 41
per cent in 1990 to 35.3 per cent in 1999, while the percentage of persons in
poverty declined from 48.3 per cent to 43.8 per cent over the same period.
However, due to population increase, the actual numbers in poverty increased

with 41.3 million households in poverty in 1999 as against 39.1 million a decade earlier, while 211.4 million people were living in poverty in 1999 as against 200.2 million in 1990. Furthermore, the percentage of the population living in poverty, after falling between 1990 and 1997, showed a slight increase between 1997 and 1999 (from 43.5 per cent to 43.8 per cent). Even with the rather ambiguous improvement over the course of the 1990s, poverty was worse at the turn of the new century than it had been in 1980, generally considered as marking the end of the protectionist model of import-substitution industrialization (ISI), when 40.5 per cent of the population or 135.9 million people were living in poverty. Some countries, however, showed a notable improvement, with Brazil, Chile and Panama reducing the proportion of poor households by more than 10 per cent, while Costa Rica, Guatemala and Uruguay reduced it by between 5 and 10 per cent. On the other hand, the proportion of poor households in Venezuela rose from 22 per cent in 1981, to 34 per cent in 1990 and to 44 per cent by the end of the century. Colombia, Honduras and Mexico showed only slight improvements, while in Paraguay and Ecuador, where figures for urban poverty only are available, the percentage of urban households in poverty increased substantially. The majority of poor households in Latin America lack drinking water and, on average, contain more than three persons per room. They are characterized by low levels of education, with the head of household having on average less then three years of schooling, and by high levels of unemployment or underemployment.

Inequality has also worsened over the 1990s so that by the turn of the century Latin America maintained its distinction of being the region with the highest levels of inequality in the world. The concentration of wealth and income among the richest 10 per cent of the population, and the gap between this group and the poorest groups, is what characterizes the region's distributional situation. Except for Costa Rica and Uruguay, the richest 10 per cent receives over 30 per cent of income in all countries, and in some cases this reaches 40 per cent and over (Chile, Colombia, Nicaragua, Guatemala, and Brazil where it reaches 47 per cent). At the other end of the distribution, the bottom 40 per cent receive between 9 and 15 per cent of income, except for Uruguay where they receive 22 per cent. Over the decade of the 1990s, inequality (as measured by the Gini coefficient)[1] improved in only three countries (Colombia, Honduras and Uruguay), remained more or less the same in five countries (Nicaragua, Guatemala, Chile, Panama and Mexico) and worsened in Brazil, Bolivia, Paraguay, Argentina, Ecuador, El Salvador, Venezuela and Costa Rica. Furthermore, the percentage of the population with incomes lower than half the national average increased in nine countries, remained the same in four, and decreased in only three. In most countries, more than 40 per cent of the population receives incomes less than half the average income, while in Brazil almost 55 per cent are in this situation. CEPAL concludes that, of the 17 countries it analysed, only two succeeded in reducing inequality over the 1990s and holds out little hope for a substantial improvement in this situation over the short or medium term (CEPAL, 2001a: 20).

Data on poverty and inequality, however, offer only rough guidance as to the quality of life of the majority, what can be called social well-being. For example, to what extent does a reduction in poverty improve people's sense of well-being? Is a reduction in poverty or a reduction in inequality more important in improving the well-being of society? These questions touch on understandings of poverty and how it relates to people's quality of life, understandings that have changed considerably over the past two decades. From this evolution in thinking has emerged a fuller appreciation of the elements that constitute social well-being. Three different stages can be identified in the evolution of thinking about poverty. The first stage involved an exclusive focus on people's income and on measuring how this has increased or decreased. Yet, as Nobel economics laureate Amartya Sen reminds us in his work, this avoids how people translate income into well-being. For example, he highlights the fact that African American men, though far better off in income terms, have a far lower chance of reaching an advanced age than do men in China, Sri Lanka, Costa Rica, Jamaica or the Indian state of Kerala, thus drawing attention to 'social arrangements and community relations such as medical coverage, public health care, school education, law and order, prevalence of violence and so on' (Sen, 1999: 22–3). For Sen, therefore, what has to be evaluated is the actual quality of life that people manage to achieve, what he calls 'our capability to lead the kind of lives we have reason to value' (p. 285). People's income is only one crude indicator of this quality of life; others are elementary things like nourishment, health, avoiding early death (see Box 7.1) or more complex achievements like being happy, having self-respect and taking part in the life of the community. Obviously some of these are far easier to measure than are others, though central to them all is the importance of equality, both of opportunities but also of the material conditions needed to achieve these. This broader understanding of what constitutes social well-being led to the development of the UNDP's Human Development Index based on indicators of health and education as well as income (see Box 2.1). This has proved very influential in broadening our understanding of well-being beyond a simple measure of income levels. However, it is not sufficient, as emerged from participatory surveys of some 60,000 poor people in 60 countries carried out for the World Bank's World Development Report on poverty in 2000 (see Narayan et al., 2000). These surveys highlighted two key aspects of poverty not captured by previous understandings. The first was a concern with risk and volatility of incomes, often expressed as a feeling of vulnerability. As Kanbur and Squire put it: 'From these descriptions, we come to understand the particular importance of poverty not just as a state of having little, but also of being vulnerable to losing the little one has' (1999: 21). The second was the lack of power they experienced in their interaction with government employees and institutions. At times, these elements were more important for the poor than increased incomes. Assessment of the human impact of the neoliberal reformation, therefore, needs to devote attention to its impact on the vulnerability and powerlessness experienced by Latin Americans.

Despite this broader understanding of the elements that constitute well-being, measures of poverty based on income alone exercise major influence on policy-makers. For example, much of the policy discussion on reducing poverty in Latin America concentrates on the levels of growth that would be

Box 7.1 Income and nutrition in Mexico

While official biannual surveys show an increase in the nominal incomes of all strata of Mexican society since the mid 1980s, this hides the growing inequality in income distribution and its effects on the nutritional spending of households. For example, between 1989 and 1998 the income of the richest 10 per cent of Mexican households increased from being 17 times greater than that of the poorest 40 per cent to being 18.5 times greater (CEPAL, 2001a: Table 2.1, p. 69). In 2000, the minimum salary was worth just 30 per cent of what it was in 1980, while the average manufacturing wage was 76 per cent of the value it had in 1980 (CEPAL, 2001b: Table 22, p. 40).

In their study of the effects of this on Mexicans' spending on nutrition, Torres Torres and Gasca Zamora found that the poorest 20 per cent spent a significantly increased percentage of their income on foodstuffs between 1984 and 1996, while the spending of higher income groups on foodstuffs remained the same or declined. Despite this, through estimating the cost of a basket of foods that would satisfy basic energy and protein needs, what they call 'nutritional security', they find that in 1996 the incomes of 50 per cent of Mexican households were not sufficient to purchase such a basket of foods. This included 40 per cent of the urban population and 80 per cent of the rural population. They therefore conclude that 46 million Mexicans were suffering from malnutrition of some form (Torres Torres and Gasca Zamora, 2001).

required to achieve this.[2] Furthermore, the ways in which poverty is measured result in very different estimates of its levels. The World Bank bases its estimates on the percentages of the population falling below two poverty lines; the first measures those on less than one US dollar a day (extreme poverty) and the second those on less than two dollars a day (poverty). CEPAL, on the other hand, measures the percentage of the population whose income is insufficient to buy a basket of essential foods (indigence) and those whose income is up to double the value of this basket (poverty), thus allowing for expenditure on non-food items. The values are derived from household surveys and in 1997 the indigence line varied from US$74 a month for Argentina to $25.8 a month for Nicaragua, while the poverty line varied from $148 for Argentina to $51.5 for Nicaragua (ECLAC, 1999: Box 1.2, p. 53). Not surprisingly, the World Bank estimates for both extreme poverty and poverty are in most cases far lower than are CEPAL's estimates of indigence and poverty, in some cases the former are less than half the latter (see CEPAL, 2001a: Box 1.5, p. 51).

For these reasons it is important to find ways of capturing the impact of economic processes on people's quality of life instead of concentrating on headcounts of the poor and how growth may improve their incomes. For, as ECLAC acknowledges, raw data on poverty fail to capture the changing nature of social vulnerability that affects large sectors of the population throughout Latin America. 'In the 1990s ... social vulnerability took its place alongside poverty as a dominant feature in the lives of vast segments of the population including the middle income strata who, in the previous development stage, had come to symbolize upward social mobility' (ECLAC, 2000b: 49–50). It identifies four elements that have created a greater risk of insecurity and sense of vulnerability for the majority:

1 *The changing nature of employment.* Most of the jobs being created are in low-wage, low-productivity sectors characterized by insecure conditions of employment.
2 *Reduced social services.* Many middle class and lower middle class sectors have lost social benefits as these are being targeted more on the poor.
3 *Erosion of traditional forms of collective organization.* Declining networks of social solidarity such as trade unions, political parties and community groups throw people back on their own resources to survive.
4 *The growth of microenterprises.* As public employment declines, more and more rely on small private-sector enterprises for employment which are weak and vulnerable to competitive pressures.

As a result, it estimates that more households were at risk of falling into poverty in the 1990s than previously and that these risks are likely to continue increasing if present policies continue. Paradoxically, in this situation, growth may increase people's vulnerability if it exacerbates the conditions causing it. This captures in a fuller way how the neoliberal reformation is undermining the quality of life of the majority of Latin Americans and highlights the central role being played by the labour market in this.

Precarious Existences

Employment is the principal way in which the economy can improve people's livelihoods, both through the income it provides and through its contribution to quality of life and social participation. Proponents of the neoliberal reformation held out high hopes that it would increase employment and incomes, especially for unskilled workers, and reduce the gap between the highest and the lowest wages, what are called wage differentials. The results, however, have been quite different to what was expected. This section firstly examines trends in levels of employment and in wages before turning to look at the nature of employment under the neoliberal development model. It ends by outlining their implications for Latin America's social structure.

The region's economically active population has grown steadily throughout the 1990s, from 167.4 million in 1990 to 211.8 million in 1999, that is from 39 per cent of the population to 42 per cent. A large part of the growth was accounted for by growing female participation, from 37.9 per cent of women (who are at an economically active age) at the beginning of the period to 42 per cent at its end. This means that the number of Latin American women in the labour force rose from 53 million to 73 million over the period. However, demand for labour did not increase to the same extent and the region entered the twenty-first century with an urban unemployment rate of 8.3 per cent in 2000 which had increased virtually steadily (with some fluctuations) since 1990 when it had stood at 5.7 per cent (ILO, 2001: Table 1-A, p. 55).[3] Table 7.1 shows how growing unemployment has especially affected women, young people and the poor, indicating the failure of the neoliberal reformation to create jobs for more vulnerable groups.

Broken down by countries, those of South America have fared worst with Argentina, Brazil and Colombia, its three largest countries, showing a persistent increase in unemployment at the turn of the century. Increases were also evident in Bolivia, Chile, Ecuador, Paraguay, Uruguay and Venezuela. In Mexico and Central America, on the other hand, unemployment was decreasing; urban unemployment in Mexico was a mere 2.2 per cent in 2000, the lowest in the region. In the Caribbean also, unemployment was decreasing though, with the exception of Cuba, levels here remained high (between 9 and 15 per cent).

Neither have wages behaved as expected. Overall, the real industrial wage in Latin America was only slightly higher in 2000 than it had been in 1980 and in some countries it was substantially lower. In Mexico, real industrial wages in 2000 were less than 60 per cent of what they had been in 1980 and had declined from their levels in the early 1990s. Of 15 countries in the region for which the ILO gives data, in seven of them the real industrial wage in 2000 was still below what it had been in 1980. The real urban minimum wage was also far lower: the average for the region stood in 2000 at 73 per cent of what it had been in 1980, while in only six countries on an ILO list of 18 Latin American countries was it higher (ILO, 2001: Tables 9-A and 10-A, pp. 69–70). ECLAC estimates that whereas at the beginning of the 1990s some 66 per cent of households received incomes less than the average income, by the end of the decade some 75 per cent of households found themselves in this situation (2000b: 68). Its *Social Panorama 2000–01* contained evidence from Uruguay that, following a

TABLE 7.1 IMPACT OF UNEMPLOYMENT ON DIFFERENT GROUPS IN LATIN AMERICA, 1994 AND 1999 (% OF EACH GROUP UNEMPLOYED)

Groups	1994	1999
Both sexes	7.1	10.6
Men	6.7	9.4
Women	7.7	12.3
Youth (15–24 years)	14	20
Poorest 20%	14.8	22.3
Second poorest 20%	8.1	12.7
Middle 20%	5.6	9.4
Second richest 20%	3.9	6.5
Richest 20%	2.3	4.3

Source: CEPAL, 2001a: Table III.8, p. 106

period of unemployment, workers' incomes fell by between 23 per cent and 34 per cent and that this tendency had increased over the course of the 1990s (2001a: 111). Furthermore, wage differentials have widened with the neoliberal reformation. Firstly, the gap between minimum and industrial wages has grown as the former increased by only 0.3 per cent a year between 1990 and 1997 while the latter increased by 1.4 per cent a year. Secondly, Klein and Tokman chart how the wages of high and low-skilled workers have fared:

> Across Latin America, income differentials between professional and technical workers and those employed in low-productivity sectors increased from 40 per cent to 60 per cent on average between 1990 and 1994. This was the result of substantial growth in the real incomes of high-skilled workers in modern activities and slow increases or even declines in the wages of unskilled labour in low-productivity sectors. In eight out of ten countries for which data were available, the wage gap by skill level widened. The same can also be seen when the wages of skilled workers are compared with those of blue-collar workers since 1988. (2000: 18)

It can therefore be concluded that employment trends under the neoliberal reformation are exacerbating poverty and inequality. A similar polarization is evident when the nature of the employment being created under the new model is examined. Following Klein and Tokman, four interrelated processes can be identified:

1 *Privatization.* With the privatization of state companies and the downsizing of the state, the public sector ceased being a contributor to employment growth in the 1990s. During the decade, its share of urban employment fell from 15.5 per cent to 13 per cent.
2 *Services.* The shift to the private sector, however, did not result in major job creation by large private companies. Altogether, companies with over 100 employees only created 17 out of every 100 new jobs created during the 1990s while 90 out of every 100 new jobs were created in the services sector. Of these, 70 per cent were in low-productivity services, mostly personal, retail trade and transportation services in the informal sector.
3 *Informality.* The limited job-creation capacity of the formal economy, both public and private, left more and more workers reliant on the informal economy for a livelihood (see Box 7.2).
4 *Insecurity.* More and more workers were employed on short-term contracts or with no contracts at all. This left many with no social security cover. ECLAC found that in all countries the incomes from employment of non-permanent and non-contract workers are significantly lower than those of permanent and contract workers (ECLAC, 2000b: 100). Klein and Tokman conclude that 'in most countries insecure employment accounts for all job growth in the 1990s' (2000: 17).

In 2001, the Latin American section of the International Labour Office published for the first time its Decent Work Development Index, comprising seven

Box 7.2 The informal economy: Engine of job creation

The informal economy emerged in the 1990s as the main engine of job creation in Latin America, accounting for 61 of every 100 jobs created. The proportion of the region's non-agricultural workforce in informal employment increased from 43 per cent in 1990 to 47 per cent in 2000, an increase equivalent to some 20 million people. Furthermore, its importance seemed to be growing as the informal economy's share of all new jobs created rose from 67.3 per cent in 1990–4 to 70.7 per cent in 1997–9.

The term 'informal economy' covers a range of activities, including self-employed workers, unpaid workers in family enterprises, domestic servants, and microenterprises with no more than five employees. Examples of such enterprises include workshops making clothes, shoes, and metal or wood products, sometimes under contract from larger firms, or restaurants and repair shops. While sometimes regarded as illegal, studies have shown that the informal economy operates in a realm between the underground economy and legality, frequently evading labour regulations.

Of every 10 new informal jobs in the 1990s, three were in microenterprises where workers' incomes can reach about 90 per cent of average incomes in the formal economy and therefore tend to be higher than in other informal activities. However, 'between 65 per cent and 95 per cent of those working in microenterprises do not have a written contract, and between 65 per cent and 80 per cent are not covered for health risks or old age. They tend to work longer hours and are more likely to have accidents at work' (Klein and Tokman, 2000: 16).

indicators. These relate to employment (unemployment rate and informality), income (industrial wage, minimum wage and women/men income gap) and the social protection of workers (social security coverage and the number of working hours). This found that, between 1990 and 2000, seven countries recorded progress in decent work conditions (Chile, Colombia, Costa Rica, El Salvador, Honduras, Panama and Paraguay), two countries remained constant (Bolivia and Peru) and in six countries work conditions worsened (Argentina, Brazil, Ecuador, Mexico, Uruguay and Venezuela). However, these six countries represent about 75 per cent of the economically active population of Latin America and the Caribbean (ILO, 2001: 45–7).

The changing nature of employment is reshaping the social structure of Latin America and reversing previous trends towards upwards social mobility, a process which was described as the emergence of 'middle class societies' as manual and rural occupations gave way to non-manual and urban ones (ECLAC, 2000b: 67). According to ECLAC, in the 1990s the non-manual and urban occupations that are expanding offer, for the most part, low-productivity, insecure and low-wage employment. As a result, it concludes that 'there is every indication that the occupational structure has become the foundation for an unyielding and stable polarization of income' (p. 68). It identifies the emerging occupational stratification of the Latin American workforce at the turn of the century as follows:

1   an upper group, comprising 9.4 per cent of the workforce, made up of employers, high-level management in the public and private sectors, and high-level professionals, with incomes almost 14 times higher than the poverty line and an average of over 11 years of schooling;
2   an intermediate group, comprising 13.9 per cent of the workforce, made up of lower-level professionals and technical and administrative employees, with incomes five times higher than the poverty line and an average of 11 years of schooling;
3   a lower group, comprising 73.2 per cent of the workforce, made up of traders, manual workers, service workers and agricultural workers. Their average incomes are 2.8 times the poverty line and they have an average 5.3 years of schooling. 'The great majority of workers at this level do not earn enough to raise an average-sized Latin American household out of poverty,' concludes ECLAC (p. 66).

This echoes Cox's description, outlined in Chapter 1, of how globalization is dividing the world's workforce into three categories:

1   the *integrated*, comprising highly skilled people who maintain the productive apparatus;
2   the *precarious*, comprising those workers whose lower levels of skills make them more easily disposable and replaceable and who are employed under flexible conditions;
3   the *excluded*, comprising the unemployed and those who work in small, low-productivity enterprises (Cox, 1999: 9).

The long-term implications of this polarization for the quality of life of Latin Americans are well captured by O'Donnell:

> The sharp, and deepening, dualism of our countries severely hinders the emergence of broad and effective solidarity. Social distances have increased, and the rich tend to isolate themselves from the strange and disquieting world of the dispossessed. The fortified ghettos of the rich and the secluded schools of their children bear witness to their incorporation into the transnationalized networks of modernity, as well as to the gulf that separates them from large segments of the national population. (Quoted in Klein and Tokman, 2000: 28)

It has been shown in this section that, over the course of the 1990s, unemployment has tended to increase especially in South America, wage levels have fallen for most people and the quality of employment has worsened. These tendencies have contributed to a growing polarization of Latin American societies between a relatively small elite which is benefiting from the neoliberal reformation and the majority who are relatively worse off. This has increased the vulnerability of most Latin Americans and, in particular, the risks they face of falling into poverty.

Environmental Destruction

The concept of vulnerability has also come to be used by CEPAL to express the magnitude of human and material damages caused to communities by natural disasters. Latin America is a region particularly prone to natural disasters such as earthquakes, hurricanes and volcanic explosions and the incidence of such disasters showed a significant increase at the end of the twentieth century. Over the final three decades of that century, almost all the countries of the region suffered a significant natural disaster and, with the exception of Asia, it had the highest number of victims of such disasters. In Latin America between 1972 and 1999, they caused 108,000 deaths and directly affected over 12 million people, while damages were conservatively estimated at US$50 billion. Between 1900 and 1989, the average was 8.3 disasters per year whereas between 1990 and 1998 this rose to 40.7 per year, while the damage caused rose from $8.5bn in 1972–80 to $23.7bn in 1990–2000 (estimated in dollar values of 1998) (CEPAL, 2000: 10–11).

The causes are complex but they include environmental change and the socio-economic vulnerability of many communities. Among the environmental causes that most affect countries of Latin America are changes in maritime currents and in the pattern of winds. The changes in currents off the west coast of South America known as El Niño, which has made ever more frequent appearances over the final decades of the twentieth century, cause severe rainfall in some regions, drought in others, and the disappearance of some species of fish for a long period. The countries of the Caribbean and Central America are in the path of hurricanes that can have an intense impact in a short period of time over an extended region. For example, between 23 October and 4 November 1998, Hurricane Mitch, with winds of up to 285 km per hour and intense rainfall, hit Guatemala, El Salvador, Honduras, Nicaragua and Costa Rica, leaving 9,214 people dead and 1.2 million people directly affected. Honduras, one of the poorest countries in Latin America, was worst hit, as Mitch left in its wake 5,657 deaths, 620,000 people directly affected and damage estimated at $3.8 billion. As a result, the GDP of Honduras fell by 7.5 per cent. Most of the region's countries lie on a tectonic faultline that runs down through Mexico, Central America and the west coast of South America, resulting in regular earthquakes throughout this area. While the causes of all these disasters are natural, the level of impact that they have on people, their communities and their livelihoods results from the social conditions in which people live (see Box 7.3). For this reason, experts are beginning to use the term 'socio-natural disaster' to indicate the reasons why natural disasters have far more severe impacts on poor countries than on rich countries and, within them, on the poorer sections of the population (Gómez, 2001: 14).

Box 7.3 Venezuela: Turning a natural disaster into a human one

Between 14 and 16 December 1999 the small Venezuelan state of Vargas covering the narrow hilly strip between Caracas and the Caribbean coast experienced the worst natural disaster in the country's history. In the course of 72 hours, 911 millimetres of water per square metre fell, more than the average annual rainfall over the previous 87 years. This led to avalanches of mud, carrying rocks and even tree trunks, rolling down the hillsides on which tens of thousands of poor people lived in informal settlements. As a result, 11 million cubic metres of mud, in places up to 4 metres deep, covered 807 hectares of the state or 16 per cent of its urbanized area. It is estimated that some 250,000 people, around 80 per cent of the state's resident population, were affected directly or indirectly, while the death toll may be as high as 30,000. Damage was estimated at almost $2bn.

While the cause of the disaster was the exceptional and intense rainfall, its impact resulted from the unplanned expansion of Caracas over the previous 40 years when the population of Vargas grew from 100,000 to 300,000 between 1961 and 1990. Poor people arriving in the capital received no support from the state to find housing and so settled on the steep hillsides around Caracas which, being unsuitable for building, had no value in the housing market. Basic services only arrived to these densely populated, unplanned and precarious settlements when it was too late to provide adequate drainage, sewerage systems or access routes. It is estimated that almost 50 per cent of Caracas's population live in these settlements. For architect Marco Negrón, it was this lack of a policy of urban development on the part of the Venezuelan state that turned a natural disaster into an economic, social and human one (Negrón, 2000).

The growing vulnerability of poorer Latin Americans, therefore, results from the interaction of natural and human causes. However, while some disasters such as earthquakes or volcanoes result from the geophysical make-up of the region and will continue to occur at a rhythm dictated by nature, there is growing evidence that others are occurring more frequently due to the impact on the environment of human activities, resulting in global warming and the depletion of the ozone layer. The industrialized world is the greatest culprit in these matters (see Held et al., 1999: 396–9). But within Latin America, such activities as intensive agriculture, industrialization and unplanned urban settlements are severely affecting the capacity of the natural environment to absorb the impact of some disasters. For example, Gómez points out that one cannot understand the severe impact of Mitch in Central America without taking into account prior environmental degradation due to deforestation, the obstruction of river beds by construction and inadequate waste disposal (p. 33). Furthermore, poverty makes people more vulnerable to the impact of natural disasters. As CEPAL says, 'the poor live in zones of high risk, use cultivation techniques which damage the environment or work on marginal lands, and have less access to information, to basic services and to pre- and post-disaster protection' (2000: 2). Finally, the disasters themselves further weaken the environment, thus resulting in a vicious circle, since they contribute to exacerbating social and environmental vulnerability. Thus, drought and forest fires in Central America in 1997 caused by El Niño are seen as contributing to the severe impact of Mitch the following year, while the migration of people due to disasters exacerbates overcrowding in vulnerable urban settlements and puts even more pressure on land use. In the twenty-first century, a more frequent occurrence of extreme natural events is predicted for Latin America, among them more intense rainfall, stronger winds and more intense drought. These are likely to lead to reduced crop yields, a greater incidence of infectious diseases such as malaria, dengue and cholera, a rise in sea levels affecting coastal settlements, and a decrease in biodiversity (Gómez, 2001: 35). The combination of increased threats due to climate change and increased susceptibility to such threats due to poverty and intense land cultivation will result in greater vulnerability among many poor Latin American communities over the coming decades.

Quality of Citizenship

If the life experience of most Latin Americans is marked by ever greater vulnerability and if their societies display evidence of growing poverty and inequality, it is often asked why there is not more interest and involvement in organized politics as a way of changing this situation. Increased violence in many Latin American countries suggests that the response is coming in the form of more delinquency rather than through organized opposition (see Box 7.4). Indeed, the widespread conformism that seems to mark many Latin American societies at the beginning of the twenty-first century points to the changing nature of citizenship under the impact of the neoliberal reformation. This has been well analysed by sociologist Tomás Moulian, whose book on contemporary Chile subtitled 'Anatomy of a Myth' (1997) became a best-seller in that country. But such changes are also evident to a greater or lesser extent in all Latin American societies as neoliberal reforms introduce a pervasive culture of consumerism that is replacing a collective practice of citizenship with an individualistic one. Under the previous statist model of import-substitution industrialization (ISI), citizenship was practised through collective associations, such as trade unions, political parties or social movements, which promoted alternative projects of social change. Such a practice of citizenship found expression in different forms of social solidarity, among them protests, strikes, high levels of participation in politics, neighbourhood activities, even public festivals. Participants shared the common conviction that, through their collective actions, they could achieve significant and beneficial social change.

While evidence of such a practice of citizenship has not entirely disappeared in Latin America, it has been greatly weakened. In its place is emerging a practice of citizenship based on individual consumption as more and more Latin Americans find their identity and define their progress through the acquisition of goods, from microwave ovens and satellite TV to cars and package holidays paid for in quotas over periods of up to four years. This Moulian calls

Box 7.4 'Breakdown in community life'

'One manifestation of the breakdown in community life in urban centres is the
rise in violence seen in most Latin American cities. Crimes are being committed
with impunity at an alarming rate, and the population therefore has a growing
sense of insecurity which is further amplified by the media' (ECLAC, 2001b: 95).
The Panamerican Health Organization regards Latin America as having the
highest homicide rate in the world at over 20 per 100,000 inhabitants. While
countries such as Argentina, Chile, Costa Rica, Paraguay and Uruguay maintain
relatively low rates of around four homicides per 100,000 people (though in
these countries crime rates are also rising), between 1980 and 1995 the rate in
Brazil increased from 11.5 to over 30, in Colombia from 20.5 to 65, and in
Venezuela from 11.7 to 22. In the Caribbean, rising crime is associated with
drug trafficking: in Trinidad and Tobago the homicide rate per 100,000
inhabitants increased from 2.1 in 1980 to 12.6 in 1990.

Some 60 per cent of Latin America's urban population are estimated to have
been victims of crime between 1990 and 1995, while UN data suggest that
more than half of all Latin American women have been assaulted in their homes
at some time during their lives. Six million children and adolescents are
estimated to be attacked by family members each year, 80,000 of whom die as
a result of mistreatment. Young men living in poor areas are particular targets; in
Rio de Janeiro 65 per cent of all deaths among adolescents aged between 10
and 19 are homicides (ECLAC, 2001b; del Olmo, 2000).

'credit-card citizenship', since the widespread availability of credit cards provides the medium through which many can access levels of consumption
beyond what their incomes would permit (Moulian, 1997: 102–10). While
there are credit limits on each individual card, in Chile the pervasive use of
such cards (which are actively marketed by retail outlets) allows individual
consumers to hold as many as they wish. The cost of this form of instant
gratification is that it severely constrains an individual's future options, since
it results in high levels of indebtedness. As analysed by Moulian, this practice
leads to an individualistic and conformist culture restricting horizons of progress to what an individual can buy and severely constraining the ability or
desire to be critical or to engage in collective political actions, since these might
put at risk the employment on which the possibility of future consumption
rests. As he writes: 'Alienated by the individualistic illusion of consumerism
it is difficult to rediscover the lost practices of collective action' (p. 103).
Moulian further argues that the practice of consumerism has now become
the means through which many forge their identity, providing them not just
with material goods but also with a sense of self-esteem and credibility –
excluded from it, a person would feel a nobody with her or his path to progress
closed (p. 106). The culture of consumerism opens a world of seemingly endless
and seductive possibilities to reinforce constantly the values and practices on
which credit-card citizenship rests. Elaborate shopping malls, now a feature of
all large Latin American cities, provide 'grand temples of consumption'

(Moulian: 113) amid the chaos and social breakdown of the societies around them. Here the illusion is created of a safe and classless world in which all have equal access to the right to consume. Goods are displayed, not in their naked form as in traditional markets, but attractively packaged and presented, thus emphasizing their desirability. In these ways, the mall provides a world equivalent to the fantasy world of the 'tele-novelas', the TV soap operas that are a central feature of contemporary Latin American culture. 'Here are presented all the conditions for consumption to become a passion' (Moulian: 114).

However, consumerism rests on illusions that hide the harsh world of flexible employment and growing vulnerability experienced by most Latin Americans. Access to consumption does not offer opportunities for upward social mobility, and the sense of classless equality that characterizes the temples of consumption hides the constant vigilance and discrimination which ensures the poor or troublesome are instantly ejected. The desire to possess more goods distracts attention from deeper forms of self-realization whether through fulfilling work, through collective activities or through cultivating an interior life, while the need to pay their credit card bills forces many to become workaholics, working extended hours or seeking second jobs in their off-hours. Moulian therefore identifies consumerism as a mechanism of domination through which people internalize a submissiveness to the neoliberal model and exercise a 'self-exploitation' (p. 120) as they impose on themselves the disciplines needed for the success of the model. Finally, the mortgaging of the future on which credit-card citizenship depends closes off critical options, inducing high levels of stress, an anxiety and insecurity about what the future holds, and a sense of being powerless to do anything about it. In this way it contributes to the second dimension of poverty identified earlier in this chapter, namely powerlessness.

A year after Moulian's book was published, the Chilean section of the United Nations Development Programme (UNDP, or PNUD in Spanish) published a report on human development which contained survey evidence showing high levels of human insecurity among Chileans despite the country's economic success (PNUD, 1998). The UNDP defines human security as incorporating both objective and subjective elements and therefore reflects not just objective conditions but also how people experience these. The six dimensions of human security measured in the Chilean survey covered delinquency, employment, social provision, health, information and sociability. In follow-up discussion groups, three basic fears were expressed: fear of the other, fear of social exclusion and fear of meaninglessness. The UNDP found widespread concern at the weakening of social bonds and the narrowing of relationships of confidence more and more to intimate circles of family and friends. It found feelings of insecurity widely shared among Chileans in each of the areas covered: 'Despite modern advances, or perhaps because of them, the empirical results show that the majority of people feel insecure about getting employment, they are not convinced the education given their children will secure their future, they have little confidence in being able to afford timely and good quality medical attention and they fear they will not have sufficient income to live adequately in old age' (p. 24). Furthermore, a recognition of inequality was found to be widely shared: 'The majority of those interviewed, with the exception of those in the high socio-economic group, feared not being in a condition to make the most of development opportunities and of securing themselves against risks' (p. 24). While this survey does not touch on the culture of consumerism, it does serve to confirm many of the elements identified by Moulian, most especially the erosion of social bonds and a sense of anxiety and insecurity about the future.[4] It is striking that these were found in the country that was regarded as the most successful economy in Latin America for most of the 1990s and where the neoliberal reformation had advanced furthest. They point therefore to a grave weakening of the quality of citizenship, leaving many with a sense of powerlessness to do anything to change the conditions in which they live. This was confirmed in the UNDP's subsequent report on Chile, in 2000, which showed marked changes in the types of groups to which Chileans belonged, with far fewer involved in groups concerned with social change and more involved in associations for self-betterment or in consumer groups (PNUD, 2000: 170).

Neoliberalism: Cause or Cure?

The quantitative evidence reviewed in this chapter shows growing poverty and inequality in most Latin American countries in the 1990s, while the qualitative evidence points to an increase in the vulnerability and powerlessness of most Latin Americans over the same period. Inevitably the causes of such phenomena are highly complex and not amenable to brief summation. However, in drawing to a close this four-chapter section on the neoliberal reformation, it is important to address the fundamental question: is neoliberal reform serving to improve or to worsen the quality of life of most Latin Americans? If the answer is positive, then it points to the need to deepen and extend the neoliberal reformation, even if this may cause pain for a period to some sectors. If it is negative, however, then it presents the challenge of modifying and revising it in fundamental ways.

The theoretical case for the positive social impact of neoliberal reforms is cogently made by the World Bank. For example, in its 2000–1 World Development Report on poverty, the Bank asserts that 'market-friendly policies' such as openness to international trade, low inflation, a moderate-sized government and strong rule of law 'on average benefit poor people as much as anyone else'. The means through which these policies deliver benefits is economic growth from which 'all income groups on average benefit equally' (World Bank, 2000: 66). The case therefore rests on two claims: (1) that neoliberal reforms result in higher economic growth rates, and (2) that growth benefits the poor as much as anyone else. The evidence presented by the Bank to support its case is given in the form of macroeconomic regressions (essentially mathematical exercises correlating generalized world data on economic growth and poverty) (see Dollar and Kraay, 2000). For Latin America, such a case finds expression in the claim that the reforms had a positive impact on growth (World Bank, 2000: 64) and that they had a positive effect on reducing poverty and inequality (see Londoño and Székely, 1997: 9, 20–5).

However, at the beginning of the twenty-first century a consensus seemed to be emerging among authoritative sources in the region that disputed both claims. Some of the evidence on which this was based has already been presented in the section of Chapter 4 entitled 'Towards Dynamic Growth?' Reviewing economic growth rates over the 1990s led ECLAC to comment: 'the fact that growth slowed down in comparison to pre-debt patterns raises questions as to whether reforms have had the strong positive effect on economic growth that some analysts believe they have' (2000a: 54). Examining the impact of reforms on employment and equity, Stallings and Peres identify four groups among the nine countries they examine which show different outcomes. Chile and Costa Rica show a positive performance on both; Argentina, Brazil and Colombia show a negative performance on both; Bolivia and Mexico show strong employment growth but increased inequality; while Jamaica and Peru show poor labour market performance but a decline in inequality. Yet none of these outcomes can be easily correlated with these countries' status as reformers: according to the same author's classification, Chile, Argentina, Bolivia and Peru were all 'aggressive reformers' while the others were 'cautious reformers' (2000: 48, 110–52).

A similar conclusion can be drawn from the evidence presented earlier in this chapter. Among the six countries that were most successful in the 1990s in reducing poverty, only Chile had an exceptionally high average growth rate of 6.1 per cent over the decade and was an aggressive reformer. Costa Rica (4.9 per cent growth), Panama (4.5 per cent) and Guatemala (4.1 per cent) were all reluctant and incomplete reformers, while Uruguay (2.9 per cent) and Brazil (2.6 per cent) fell into the same category but achieved significantly lower growth rates. Mexico (3.6 per cent growth) and Colombia (2.5 per cent) were more thorough reformers than many of those who achieved more success in reducing poverty. However, the three countries which had least success in reducing poverty were all ones in which attempts at neoliberal reforms were blocked or reversed – Venezuela (2.4 per cent growth), Paraguay (1.8 per cent) and Ecuador (1.7 per cent). Furthermore, there was virtually no correlation between success in reducing poverty and success in reducing inequality. Only Uruguay (a reluctant reformer with a relatively sluggish growth rate) managed success in both, while the more aggressive reformers, Chile, Argentina and Bolivia, were unsuccessful. Again, however, Venezuela, Paraguay and Ecuador were among the failures in this regard. The only additional conclusion that can be drawn from this examination is that while being an aggressive reformer with a relatively high growth rate by no means led to reduced poverty and inequality, being a blocked reformer with a poor growth rate seemed a recipe for increased poverty and inequality.

This points therefore to factors other than neoliberal reforms in helping decrease poverty and inequality, factors such as a country's political culture and system, effective social policies, and the political complexion of ruling parties. But it tempts the conclusion that, while neoliberal reforms may not be a sufficient condition for decreasing poverty, they are a necessary one, as the countries in which neoliberal reforms were blocked performed worst. Such a conclusion could only be maintained, however, if consideration of the impact of reforms were limited to the quantitative data presented so far in this section. When the qualitative evidence presented earlier in this chapter on growing vulnerability and powerlessness is taken into account, then a rather more negative conclusion about the impact of the neoliberal reformation is warranted. This shows that, even where reforms have helped create a situation in which the income of the poor is increasing, such reforms are directly contributing to worsening the vulnerability of large sections of the population through their impact on the quality and permanence of employment, on the growth in social polarization, and on environmental vulnerability. Indirectly, through promoting a culture of consumerism, they are increasing the sense of powerlessness that, evidence suggests, is a characteristic of this culture. In the face of such evidence, it seems safer to conclude that economic reforms of some kind are a necessary condition for reducing poverty but that the particular kind of reforms undertaken in Latin America, namely neoliberal reforms, are on balance exacerbating rather than resolving poverty. It is noteworthy, for example, that the evidence of growing vulnerability and powerlessness comes not just from countries where the neoliberal reformation may have failed but from those where it has been most successfully and thoroughly implemented.

Notes

[1] The Gini coefficient is an international measure of inequality that charts the degree to which different groups fall below a line of perfect equality.

[2] For example, in its *Social Panorama of Latin America 2000–2001*, CEPAL estimates that an average annual growth rate of 2.9 per cent per capita, or 4.5 per cent GDP growth, would be required for the following 15 years to halve the rate of poverty (CEPAL, 2001a: 17).

[3] Rates of unemployment in Latin America tend to be lower than they are in North America and Western Europe, since the lack of state welfare benefits means that many workers have no option but to eke out a living in the informal sector. Those who are formally unemployed tend to be people who had formal sector jobs and were made redundant.

[4] Evidence quoted by the Inter-American Development Bank (IADB) indicates that this anxiety and insecurity are widely shared. It reports survey evidence about how Latin Americans view trends in poverty over the 1990s taken from Latinobarometro 2001, an opinion survey carried out yearly in the urban areas of 17 countries in the region: 'Imagine a country or region where 60 per cent of the population think the economy is in trouble and 70 per cent see no possibility of improvement in the near future. Three out of four people think there are more poor people today than five years ago and 86 per cent believe the distribution of income is unjust. About 67 per cent view their chances of finding work today worse than five years ago and 62 per cent fear they will lose their job in the next 12 months. A full 58 per cent of the population thinks their parents were better off then they are and, for nearly half, their economic situation has deteriorated in the past 10 years' (IADB, 2001: 1).

Interlude

8   Cuba: Uncertain Transition

Cuba: Uncertain Transition

S ince its revolution in 1959, Cuba has taken a road to development very different from that of the rest of Latin America. With its state-controlled socialist economy and society, and its authoritarian political system, it was in many ways more similar to other socialist developing countries such as Vietnam or North Korea than to the rest of Latin America, though its socialism maintained a very distinctive Caribbean flavour. Furthermore, Washington's implacable hostility to the revolution, and its economic embargo on trade with or investment in the island's economy, served to isolate Cuba from the rest of the Americas. Finally, the collapse of the Eastern bloc and the Soviet Union in the late 1980s and early 1990s cut Cuba off virtually overnight from its main trading and investment partners, plunging its economy into deep crisis and forcing a painful and profound adjustment that was still underway at the beginning of the twenty-first century. For these reasons Cuba warrants a chapter to itself. This chapter firstly outlines the distinctive nature of Cuba's economic and political system, and its social conditions, as these developed under the revolution. In its second section, it describes the impact on this model of the collapse of Eastern European communism and the authorities' responses to this situation. The following section looks at the emergence of new social actors with new values, indicating that beyond its economic challenges, the revolution faces a crisis of legitimacy. Finally, the chapter discusses the prospects for a post-communist Cuba as Fidel Castro ages and the issue of transition looms large.

A Place Apart

The overthrow of Cuban dictator Fulgencio Batista by Fidel Castro's 26th of July guerrilla movement on 1 January 1959 seemed a typically Latin American form of regime change. Initially, the measures implemented by the new government, such as agrarian reform and supports for national industry, reflected the agenda of moderate progressive sectors throughout Latin America. However, as radicals replaced moderates in key state posts during the first year (such as Che Guevara becoming director of the National Bank), the stage was set for a wave of more radical reforms over the course of 1960, including a trade agreement with the Soviet Union, the expropriation of Texaco, Standard Oil and Shell when they refused to refine Soviet oil, and the nationalization of US properties after Washington eliminated Cuba's sugar quota. By October 1960, President Eisenhower had implemented an embargo on all US exports to Cuba, still in place over 40 years later, and the following January he broke off diplomatic relations. After the Bay of Pigs invasion by a CIA-trained force in April 1961, which was easily defeated by Cuba's armed forces, Fidel Castro proclaimed his revolution socialist. This opened the way for the widespread expropriation not only of US-owned factories, utilities and other properties but also of domestically owned ones and the establishment of a central planning agency in an attempt to diversify the economy away from its overwhelming dependence on the export of sugar (it constituted about 80 per cent of the value of exports at the time of the revolution) towards other food crops and the industrial development of sugar cane by-products. Declining sugar harvests in 1962–3 and growing trade deficits as a result soon reversed the attempt at diversification and there was a renewed emphasis on sugar production, stimulated by the objective of reaching a 10-million-ton harvest in 1970. The attempt failed (8.5 million tons were harvested), damaging Castro's prestige and the country's economy, but it marked a turning point for the revolution and led to a greater institutionalization of the economy and the political system. A system of material rewards was introduced for workers in a bid to raise productivity and in 1972 Cuba joined the socialist trading bloc, the Council for Mutual Economic Assistance (CMEA), formalizing its economic dependence on guaranteed Soviet preferential prices for its sugar exports and on low-price Soviet oil imports, as well as on low-interest loans and the ability to import consumer and military goods from Eastern European markets. Though this institutionalized dependence reinforced the centrality of sugar in the Cuban economy, it also permitted a moderate diversification of the domestic economy with industrial inputs replacing consumer goods as the main imports and led to a period of sustained economic growth in the early to mid 1970s (Pérez-Stable, 1999: 86–8).

If Cuba's state-run and Soviet-dependent economy marked it out as being entirely different from the rest of Latin America, so too did its political system, what are called the Organs of Political Power (OPP). On the basis that social transformation was more important than holding elections, Fidel Castro announced their indefinite postponement a few months after taking power. Following an emphasis on the charismatic leadership of the revolutionary leaders in the 1960s, an institutionalized electoral system was established in the mid 1970s that allows citizens to elect local delegates to municipal assemblies. These assemblies then elect members of provincial assemblies who in turn elect delegates to the national parliament, the National Assembly. Direct elections to provincial assemblies and the National Assembly were introduced in the 1990s, though demands for greater electoral plurality (including proposals that dissidents be allowed to stand for election) were rejected.[1] Electors also have the power to recall their delegates at each level, while those elected are required to submit to public scrutiny in six-monthly accountability meetings. Some 50 to 60 per cent of constituents usually turn out for these meetings. Municipal assemblies have extensive powers over schools, clinics, grocery stores, and small local industries. By Western standards, it falls far short of a fully democratic system as candidates for election are not allowed to campaign and parties other than the Communist Party are not permitted. Despite this, a study of how the electoral system worked in four different municipalities concluded that elections take place in a climate of sufficient freedom to have legitimacy in the eyes of citizens for whom the moral quality of candidates is the major criterion in casting their vote. The study concluded that, despite excessive formality and bureaucracy, 'Cuban municipalities have become effective mechanisms for local development and for meeting the everyday needs of the population' (Dilla Alfonso and González Núñez, 1997: 77). Though delegates do not have to be party members, in practice about 75 per cent are (Pérez-Stable, 1999: 123).

However, the characteristic that most clearly distinguishes Cuba in the eyes of many Latin Americans is the social transformation brought about by the revolution. As detailed in Table 8.1, in many spheres social conditions are comparable to those in some of the world's most developed countries. A situation of effective full employment prevailed until the economic crisis of the 1990s, with unemployment rates of between 2.4 and 3.8 per cent in the 1970s and 3.4 per cent in the 1981 census. However, this hid significant underemployment which Pérez-Stable reports as being as high as one-third of the labour force and which is linked to low levels of productivity (p. 91). Educational levels improved markedly and more than 95 per cent of 6- to 14-year-olds were enrolled in school. Furthermore, as Pérez-Stable writes, 'at the beginning of the 1990s, Cuba had one of the most skilled labour forces in Latin America. At least 35 per cent had graduated from high school, vocational training, teacher training, or higher education' (p. 94). Health care was a particular priority for the government and was available free to all citizens. Primary care was widely available in all provinces and regions. Major efforts were made to construct housing, in both rural and urban areas. Two-thirds of all rural housing was built since 1959 and two-fifths of urban housing, though only about 55 per cent of this was regarded as solidly constructed (Pérez-Stable: 93). Greater equality for women was also a goal of the Cuban revolution and, after 1970, female participation in the labour force expanded significantly. However, the Cuban Women's Federation (FMC), a mass organization with a membership of some 3 million, had regular disagreements with the government which tended to give priority to male employment. It helped secure passage of the 1975 Family Code requiring men to share equally in household duties and childcare, though FMC leader Vilma Espín was complaining a decade later that this goal was far from being reached (Pérez-Stable: 139–42).

In its annual Human Development Report, the UNDP compares the ranking of countries on its human development index with their ranking according to per capita GDP. This allows an estimate of how well countries are using their resources to promote social development. Countries that gain a minus score on this ranking have a lower level of human development than might be expected from their level of wealth. On the other hand, countries that gain a positive score are using their wealth, even if it is relatively little, to promote higher levels of human development than would be expected. Some developed countries rate poorly in this regard. For example, in the midst of booming economic growth

TABLE 8.1 CUBA'S SOCIAL ACHIEVEMENTS

	Life expectancy	Infant mortality per 1,000 live births	Adult literacy (%)	Enrolment in education[a] (%)	Doctors per 1,000 people	Women parliamentarians (% of total)
Cuba	75.8	7	96.4	73	518	27.6
Latin America	69.7	32	87.7	74	132	12.9
United States	76.8	7	99	94	245	12.5
OECD	76.4	12	97.4	86	222	15.1

[a]Combined primary, secondary and tertiary enrolment.

Source: UNDP: Human Development Report 2000

at the end of the 1990s, Ireland gained a score of −11, equal to Luxembourg, and the worst among developed countries. On the other hand, Latin American countries like Chile and Uruguay achieved a score of 9, indicating substantial achievement in the field of human development. Of the 174 countries listed in the UNDP's 2000 Human Development Index, Cuba with 40 achieved the second highest score, while the United States achieved −1.

Economic Reorientation, Social Strains

By the late 1980s, nearly 70 per cent of Cuba's trade was with the Soviet Union and the country received 85 per cent of its imports from the Eastern bloc. Guaranteed prices and easy Soviet finance provided the Cuban economy with an effective subsidy that has been estimated as being worth 20 per cent of GDP (M. Pastor, 2000: 32). Furthermore, Cuba received 12 to 13 million tons of oil annually from the Soviet Union at prices below those on the world market. With the collapse of much of the Eastern bloc in 1989 and of the Soviet Union itself in 1991, this relationship quickly ended and Cuba was plunged into its worst economic crisis since the revolution. It is estimated that between 1989 and 1993 GDP fell by 35 per cent in real terms, real salaries by around 18 per cent and consumption by 13 per cent (Ibarra and Mattar, 1998: 30). Furthermore, this happened at a time when the US embargo on trade and investment with Cuba was being tightened: the 1992 Cuban Democracy Act (called the Torricelli bill after its congressional sponsor) prohibited subsidiaries of US corporations from trading with Cuba and tightened restrictions on sending dollars to the island, while the 1996 Cuban Liberty and Democratic Solidarity Act (the Helms-Burton bill) allows lawsuits be brought against foreign governments, companies and individuals who deal in Cuban property that was expropriated after the revolution, and also transformed into law (and therefore beyond presidential discretion) all existing economic sanctions against Cuba. Furthermore the bill contained the explicit objective of instituting a formal democratic system and removing both Fidel Castro and his brother and heir-apparent, Raul, from power (Purcell, 2000).

Cuba's response to this situation was designed to reactivate the economy through reinserting the country into the international trade and financial systems from which it had been isolated since the 1960s. A series of economic reforms in the early 1990s sought to attract foreign investment, particularly into tourism and export sectors, expanded opportunities for self-employment, legalized the use of the US dollar and opened currency exchanges, created free trade zones on terms very favourable to foreign companies and reformed the country's banking sector. A determined attempt was made to forge stronger economic and political links with Latin American countries, the European Union and, in particular, Cuba's Caribbean neighbours through membership of the Association of Caribbean States (ACS) and an agreement for increased trade and joint efforts in the sugar industry, livestock and fisheries with Caricom, the economic grouping of mostly English-speaking Caribbean states (see Chapter 6) (Domínguez, 2001). In an attempt to reduce a huge budget deficit, subsidies to state industries were cut, new taxes introduced, prices increased for consumer goods and services, and charges introduced for some services that had been free. In 1993, the state created Basic Units of Cooperative Production (UBPCs) which allowed workers on state farms to lease their lands permanently, effectively handing over to private production over 40 per cent of the country's cultivable land. Agricultural markets were created throughout the country, allowing these farmers to sell their produce at prices not controlled by the state.[2] By 1997, private initiative supplied almost 75 per cent of the produce sold in these markets (Ibarra and Mattar: 35). As Zimbalist put it: 'Each of these reforms represented a small step toward promoting decentralization, individual initiative, market incentives, and greater efficiency' (2000: 18).

In a bid to limit the extent of these reforms, however, the state has prohibited the hiring of wage labour in many of the small enterprises in the new informal sector (for example, small family-run restaurants) and has imposed draconian taxes on their earnings.[3] For this reason, the growth of tourism has not led to a flowering of small businesses serving the tourism sector and the number of registered self-employed fell at the end of the 1990s. Companies setting up in the new free trade zones are not allowed to hire their own labour and must use workers selected by a government agency. Due to these limitations (and to the US embargo), such zones 'seem to have attracted little more than warehousing' (M. Pastor: 49). Severe legislation against dissidents and journalists in 1999 marked an attempt to impose greater orthodoxy on the population. Yet, while amounts of foreign investment have been much lower than was hoped for, the economic reforms have greatly reduced the budget deficit and led to a significant recovery of economic growth with rates of 6.8 per cent in 1999 and 5.7 per cent in 2000, well above the average for Latin America.

But analysts point to the fact that economic reform has been somewhat contradictory, combining limited liberalization with the maintenance of state control. As a result, Zimbalist identifies three distinct economies in Cuba:

1   The traditional state sector which accounts for more than three-quarters of the official labour force. Despite around 200,000 layoffs in the late 1990s, this sector is seen as still being heavily overstaffed and has received little investment to modernize it.
2   The export enclave sector with both state companies and joint companies (involving the state and foreign capital), relying on foreign technology, capital, management and marketing skills. These cater to the international market and are limited to a small number of sectors: tourism, nickel, tobacco, citrus fruits, fishing and biotechnology.
3   The informal and market sector that has grown up as a result of the liberalization of farmers' markets, the opening of hard-currency shops and self-employment (pp. 18–19).

The emerging Cuban economy therefore bears more and more resemblance to the rest of Latin America, as outlined in Chapter 4. This pointed to certain structural features of the new economic model in the region such as its dependence on dynamic subsectors, usually those receiving foreign investment, and the fact that these subsectors link more with sectors external to the region rather than with other sectors of the national economy (for example, through using imported inputs rather than ones produced domestically). As was pointed out in Chapter 4, this results in a growing trade deficit as the region imports more than it exports; in Cuba also the trade deficit has been growing steadily throughout the 1990s, from $215 million in 1992 to $780 million in 2000 (CEPAL, 2001d: 165). However, the pace of change remains slower in Cuba. As Manuel Pastor states: 'The sorry truth is that reform is grudging. Privatization has been mostly ruled out and, while subsidies to state firms have been cut by 80 per cent since 1993, modernization of this sector has been modest at best' (2000: 42). Despite considerable liberalization, therefore, the state still maintains a dominant economic role, though more and more it exercises this not through central planning as in the past but through coordinating the activities of state companies and entities which have had considerable decision-making power devolved to them. 'As a result, central planning and the market coexist in a tense relationship in more and more areas of the economy' (Ibarra and Mattar: 34).

Another way in which the Cuban reforms differ from those in most Latin American countries is the government's attempt to spread the burden of adjustment more equitably throughout the population and to cushion the population from the full extent of the economic shock. Spending on health and education as a percentage of GDP has been more or less maintained, while defence spending was severely cut, though the quality of social services has deteriorated. But the severity of the crisis has caused new problems: for example in 1992–3, more than 50,000 people suffered from optic neuropathy, largely caused by poor nutrition (Pérez-Stable: 93). Unemployment grew to almost 8 per cent in 1995 but had declined to 5.5 per cent by 2000, one of the lowest rates in Latin America. However, Ibarra and Mattar report that some state companies keep workers on their payrolls in case they might be needed (p. 33), while CEPAL estimates that some 400,000 further redundancies are required in state companies if they are to be competitive. In 1997, CEPAL put total Cuban unemployment and underemployment at 34.1 per cent of the labour force. In terms of living standards, it estimates that real wages fell by over 80 per cent between 1989 and 1995 (Zimbalist: 18, 26). Taking the recovery since 1995 into account, GDP per capita still fell by 2 per cent over the 1991–2000 period, well below the average increase of 1.6 per cent for Latin America as a whole over the same period and, after Haiti, the worst performance in the region. The percentage of the population in poverty has increased from less than 2 per cent in 1988 to nearly 10 per cent in 1996, still low by Latin American standards (see Chapter 7). Significantly, however, the emergence of a dollar economy has resulted in the growth of inequality, since Cubans with access to dollars can enjoy a higher standard of living and purchase goods in dollar shops not available to other Cubans. This means that people working in tourism (such as hotel staff, guides, taxi drivers, prostitutes) or families who receive remittances from relatives in the United States (and such remittances are now valued at up to $800 million a year, equivalent to one-sixth of Cuba's export earnings) earn far more than highly qualified doctors, engineers or scientists. Some of this latter group are opting to move into relatively unskilled work in the dollar economy. Zimbalist writes that the egalitarianism that characterized Cuban society and was one of the revolution's great achievements has been thoroughly undermined with the share of income going to the top 5 per cent of income earners rising from 10.1 per cent in 1986 to 31 per cent in 1995. 'Cuba has become a class society, defined by access to hard currency through work, politics, or family abroad,' he concludes (p. 13).

Emerging Actors, New Values

With the economic reorientation required by the fall of Eastern European communism, there emerged from the heart of Cuban society itself in the 1990s a challenge to the totalizing dominance of the state over social life. For the revolutionary state established since 1959 had imposed a single integrating logic on society that found expression in forcefully articulated and constantly reiterated values such as equality over liberty, and sovereignty and national independence over legal procedures and representative mechanisms, and which equated Cuban identity with support for the socialist order. This revolutionary nationalist value system monopolized public life to such an extent that any autonomous public sphere effectively disappeared. In this situation, the expression of alternative values such as liberty, individualism and autonomous expression was limited to hidden, submerged and intimate spaces. Thus there existed what Bobes calls 'a submerged society' (2000: 265) in which particularistic solidarities (such as, for example, the gay subculture depicted in the film *Before Night Falls*) and individual and autonomous strategies of survival prevailed.[4] In this society also were emerging new generational attitudes towards the revolution (see Box 8.1 on blacks). As long as the state maintained its monopoly, this submerged society had virtually no public spaces in which it could express itself, a situation that served to fuel 'pessimism, apathy and cynicism' (Suchlicki, 2000: 57). However, the fall of the Berlin Wall and the delegitimation of Marxism associated with it, as well as the liberalizing reforms introduced in Cuba as a result, undermined the dominant monopoly the state had enjoyed and opened new spaces for social actors to emerge. This happened in two main ways:

1 The economic reforms emphatically eroded the fundamental values on which the state's legitimacy had rested, such as equality, national sovereignty and the ability of the revolution to provide first-class social services.
2 The reforms helped constitute new actors no longer totally controlled by the state, such as economic actors (foreign investors, small businesses and the self-employed; the cooperative farming sector), social actors (non-governmental organizations established to receive outside funding; communal social movements established to address local social problems), political actors (dissident political and human rights groups), cultural actors (sports and cultural groups; the churches) and academic actors (centres of research and publication) (Dilla and Oxhorn, 2001: 162–71).

Box 8.1 Are Cuba's blacks deserting the revolution?

Cuba's black population, which had gained considerable material benefits from the revolution, was long considered by the government as a loyal base of support. However, riots in Havana's black neighbourhood of Malecon in August 1994, in which several state-owned dollar shops were destroyed and greater freedom and political changes demanded, worried authorities, since many of the rioters were blacks or *mulattos*. It raised the fear that racial tensions might become a destabilizing factor in Cuba's changing society.

To assess blacks' attitudes towards the Cuban revolution and what lies ahead for their country, two Harvard researchers undertook an independent survey of black people on the island. This revealed a widespread negative perception of the situation of blacks before the revolution and a similarly widespread positive perception of the benefits of the revolution for blacks, as it resulted in significant educational advances and upward social mobility for them.

Looking to the future, however, a clear generational difference emerged. Older blacks have a far greater fear that the collapse of the socialist order in Cuba would mean a return to racism, while younger respondents do not equate the end of socialism with the end of racial equality. A similar divide is evident in perceptions of the Cuban-American exile community, a predominantly white group, since blacks have been heavily underrepresented in those fleeing Cuba. Older blacks are more fearful that the return of these exiles following a regime change would result in greater racism, whereas younger blacks are unconcerned, an attitude indistinguishable from that of white Cubans. As the researchers conclude: 'The current crisis has eroded some of the emblematic achievements of the Cuban revolution to such a degree that young blacks no longer perceive the restoration of capitalism as a major reverse. The future might be dark, as one of our respondents stated, but the present is dark enough already' (de la Fuente and Glasco, 1997: 69).

While many of these new actors created by the reforms are, to a greater or lesser degree, dependent on the Cuban state, Bobes sees in them the means whereby a civil society independent of the state can be constituted and strengthened, giving expression to new forms of solidarity and institutionalizing new mechanisms through which state and society can relate. They constitute an arena for new forms of collective identity, new principles of organization and new ways of reproducing society (pp. 267–8). This found expression and was strengthened by the visit of Pope John Paul II in 1998 during which, for the first time in almost four decades, an autonomous discourse different to that of the state was communicated through the mass media. There is therefore a cultural struggle taking place in Cuba between the state and an emerging civil society. Some of the emerging actors are clearly having a positive impact. For example, LeoGrande underlines the significance of the role being played by the Cuban Catholic Church in which it is careful not to challenge the regime too directly, but neither is it uncritical of the state's actions. He writes that 'it thereby constitutes living proof that one can be a loyal Cuban, not a pawn of the United States, and still disagree with Fidel Castro', something that marks 'a significant change in Cuban political culture' (2000a: 6). On the other hand, Dilla and Oxhorn warn that state bureaucrats seem to favour emerging economic actors (such as foreign investors and their local agents, technocrats, the incipient domestic private sector) over social actors that promote more collective projects of social change. 'In doing this, they paradoxically encourage the emergence of those civil society actors whose options lead inexorably to the restoration of capitalism' (2001: 173).

Una Salida Cubana?

As Cuba enters the twenty-first century, one of the few certainties is that it is undergoing a fundamental economic, political and social transition. As Zimbalist puts it, the economic model is no longer viable and the longer it is rigidly pursued, the more likely it is that the present system will come to a violent and destructive end (2000: 14). Furthermore, as LeoGrande writes, 'the reinsertion of Cuba into the global economy has set in motion internal economic processes that are corroding the regime's monopoly on power. For the first time in forty years, politics outside the regime are at least as interesting and portentous as politics inside it' (2000b: 129). But what is less certain is how this transition will take place or what new development model will emerge from it. It looks increasingly unlikely that the sudden collapse of communism that took place in many Eastern European countries will happen in Cuba. Such a scenario would have been most likely during the most difficult years of the transition in the early 1990s, but these passed with remarkably few expressions of major public discontent. With the economy growing, there are fewer grounds now for an explosion of mass protest. China provides a different model of transition but so far Cuba has proved unwilling to allow the same level of economic freedoms on which China's success in attracting significant foreign investment rests. Instead, some Cuban intellectuals are studying Spain's political transition from the Franco dictatorship to democracy in the 1970s, finding lessons there for their present situation. The likelihood therefore is that the transition will be distinctively Cuban, as captured by the term *salida cubana*. Perhaps the most important question about a distinctively Cuban transition, however, is the extent to which it can maintain the major social achievements of the revolution or whether it will lead to the imposition of a socially corrosive form of free-market capitalism.

While economic collapse is highly unlikely, questions remain about the depth and permanence of liberalizing economic reforms, not helped by the stop–go nature of their implementation. As LeoGrande writes, commentators are agreed that 'they do not amount to a Cuban transition to capitalism' (2000a: 3). At least three major challenges face Cuban decision-makers. The first is that 'it is difficult to determine where the island's competitive advantage may eventually emerge' (M. Pastor, 2000: 44). Sugar is still its most important product (constituting just under 50 per cent of exports), but this faces declining prices and saturated world markets. It maintains a high-quality niche market for its tobacco products (Cuban cigars) but there are limited opportunities for major expansion. Nickel has emerged as an important export item but here too international prices are falling. Other non-traditional exports such as seafoods and citrus fruits face intense competition from many Latin American countries. Finally, Cuba has had a major success in developing biotechnology and pharmaceutical products, but international markets for these are controlled by a few multinational companies which would be likely to buy out Cuban capacity in these areas, thus greatly reducing their contribution to the island's economy. The second major challenge is access to the US market. Any success in capturing other markets is minor compared to the potential of the huge and lucrative US market on its doorstep. While it is excluded from this, Cuba's options for major economic success are severely constrained. Thirdly, there is the challenge of making the large state industrial sector competitive, so that it can generate high-quality jobs and make a positive contribution to Cuba's economy and society. One of the many contradictions of the present situation is that foreigners are allowed to own productive assets and employ workers in Cuba, whereas Cubans are not. Thus there is no attempt to develop industries owned by Cubans, whether privately or jointly with the state, which might help modernize Cuban industry and offer a base of support for some continuity between the present model and whatever model will emerge in future. The longer constructive, imaginative and determined reforms are postponed, the more likely will be the prospect that more and more of Cuba's productive assets will be bought by foreigners, including members of the Cuban American exile community, who have no interest in, or are actively hostile to, maintaining as far as possible the social achievements of the Cuban revolution. Since a significant part of Cuba's industry can only become competitive by cutting costs and shedding many workers, the issue of how the social costs are going to be contained and ameliorated lies at the heart of a successful transition.

The key to how the transition will take place, however, rests not in economics but in politics, in LeoGrande's words 'how the economic imperative for reform ... will be translated through the Cuban political system' (2000a: 4). As civil society remains too weak and fragmented to drive a transition and as there is no charismatic figure emerging who might unite opposition to the present system, significant change is most likely to emerge from within the higher echelons of the Cuban state. The stop–go nature of economic reform points to a struggle for dominance between reformers and more hard-line elements, and Fidel Castro's obvious dislike of economic liberalization strengthens the position of the latter group. Yet, despite this, even he has to recognize that the state cannot do without the productivity, employment and tax revenues provided by the private sector. 'Thus the government must put up with people whose self-interest places them in conflict with it – over tax rates, regulations, supply distribution, and, ultimately, fundamental ideology,' writes LeoGrande (2000a: 5). The continuing strength of the Cuban state, and the relative weakness of the private sector, means these tensions do not translate into instability, at least for the present. Indeed, for all the uncertainties of its present transition, Cuba is characterized by a remarkable political stability that rests on two principal foundations, one institutional and the other popular. There are three pillars to the regime's institutional strength – the military, the security apparatus and the Communist Party. The armed forces, which have not been used for internal security and are therefore not tainted by associations with state repression, are respected by much of the population. Some commentators point to their growing involvement in political and administrative affairs, including military officers in high-level party posts and military technocrats taking key positions in tourism, telecommunications, and various industries. For Suchlicki, this marks a 'growing trend toward the militarization of Cuban society' (2000: 69), whereas Erisman believes that such a view seriously underestimates the party's position and ignores civilian control of the armed forces (Erisman, 2002: 148–9). Both positions point to the continuing institutional strengths of the regime. These are complemented by the second source of stability, the popular identification with the nationalist values with which the regime constantly identifies itself. As Bobes writes about resistance to fundamental change:

> Especially, the identification of the state socialist order with a complex of values associated with nationalism and social justice plays a critical role. This is strengthened by the hostility of the US, reinforcing the sense of a nation under siege and having to defend itself, as well as giving an enemy that can be blamed for economic failures. Fidel's charisma, the widespread attachment to social justice and the perception that the rights obtained could be lost in a radical change, linked to the existence of a revengeful and politically intolerant exile group which Cubans identify with corruption and immorality, also constitute important reserves for continuity. (2000: 268–9)

Given these conditions, it seems unlikely that any major change will come before Fidel Castro steps down or dies. In this event, it is planned that power will pass to Raul Castro who is head of the armed forces and deputy to Fidel in top state and party posts. It is possible that civilian party leaders like Ricardo Alarcón or Carlos Lage might occupy some senior positions, like state president. This transition is likely to happen quite smoothly, not least because loyalty to Raul Castro has been one of the conditions for promotion within the armed forces. Though attention is focused on the transfer of power once Fidel leaves, more uncertain will be a transfer following a period in office by Raul Castro. Since he is reported to be in failing health, he may have little time to consolidate his rule, therefore opening the prospect of greater instability in such a situation. Apart from any disruptive effects of instability on the economy and on society, these political transitions are going to be crucial in determining the outcome of the balance of forces between reformers and hard-liners in the bureaucracy and the political system. For Cuba's potential derives from the fact that it has maintained a state with real capacity in both economic and social terms. This distinguishes it from most Latin American countries where the first generation neoliberal reforms of the 1980s and 1990s greatly weakened the state and constituted the market as the principal agent of economic and social organization (see Chapter 5). In the Cuban case, it is still unclear how state capacity will be used in future. Three possible scenarios seem likely:

1   The state is used to block the sort of audacious economic and social reforms that are required if Cuba is to achieve a new, sustainable and socially egalitarian development model. This scenario would entail a continuation of the present stop–go nature of reform.
2   The state squanders its capacity through favouring private interests (both foreign and domestic) over public ones, thereby marginalizing the state as the key agent of a new development model. From what Dilla and Oxhorn write about the bureaucracy favouring private business interests, this may be the most likely long-term outcome.
3   The state is used to develop a coherent model of economic and social development harnessing market forces in a way that helps consolidate and perpetuate the social benefits of the revolution. In the present neoliberal ideological climate this is far from easy, but such an option has the potential not only to benefit most Cubans but to offer an alternative path for the rest of Latin America.

The other major element influencing a transition will be the posture of the United States. Though publicly this is as hostile as ever, contacts and cooperation behind the scenes are growing, as for example between the coastguards of both countries in targeting drugs traffickers (Domínguez, 2001: 194). Increasingly also, senior political and business leaders are voicing the need for a more constructive engagement by Washington, symbolized by the visit of former President Jimmy Carter to Cuba in May 2002. Whether these are strong enough to counter the strong political influence of the Cuban American lobby remains to be seen, but at least for the first time there is emerging a counterweight to its intransigent and hostile position.

There is, therefore, much that is uncertain about Cuba's future. It depends on a highly complex set of factors, both domestic and international, both economic and political. Reducing it to the overthrow of Fidel Castro and the communist system is a myopic view that fails to appreciate the real strengths of what the Cuban revolution achieved, and arrogantly dismisses the wishes of the Cuban people themselves. For, as Centeno puts it, 'Whatever body establishes authority – a reconstituted army, some civic alliance of technocrats and popular groups, or a Miami-led exile vanguard backed by US marines – will have to deal with the dilemma of how, after many years of sacrifice and hope, to satisfy the population's political and economic aspirations' (Centeno, 1997: 24). Failure to satisfy these aspirations could be the source of long-term instability, long after the transition has taken place.

Notes

[1] In the first elections under the new system, in December 1992, it is estimated that up to one-third of voters cast blank or defaced ballots, effectively an anti-government vote. This led the regime to mount a major mobilization effort for the second-round elections the following February which resulted in a return to more normal patterns of mass support, though 7.2 per cent cast invalid ballots, a figure which rose to 14.3 per cent in Havana (Pérez-Stable, 1999: 186–8).

[2] Such markets had been permitted between 1980 and 1986 but were closed by Fidel Castro who was concerned that they were leading to increased social inequality and reducing state control.

[3] These measures derive from Marxist fears of workers' exploitation and dislike of the profit motive.

[4] For example, Bobes reports the positive value given in submerged social networks to such activities as prostitution linked to tourism, the stealing of state resources, or black market involvement as these are seen as expressing individualism, self-interest and rational calculation (2000: 241–3).

Section III

Popular Responses

9

Political Strains

In covering the neoliberal reformation, the four chapters of Section II have outlined the principal features of the structural context in which Latin Americans find themselves at the beginning of the twenty-first century. As mentioned in Chapter 1, sociologists use the term 'structure' to refer to what can be called the given 'objective' realities facing actors, be they individuals (such as political leaders) or, more often, collective actors such as political parties, trade unions or social movements.[1] Section III, on political responses to the neoliberal reformation, concentrates on what sociologists call 'agency', namely the potential for actors to change the given structural situation. It describes various ways in which Latin Americans are responding to the new globalized world in which they find themselves. The focus is on *political* responses, since politics is the activity through which people aspire to influence and change in a desired direction the decisions that affect their lives and the lives of their societies. Obviously there are spheres other than politics, such as business or entertainment, that affect profoundly the life of society, but these effects happen as an indirect result of their primary activities (producing and exchanging goods and services in the case of business and, in the latter case, providing entertainment). Politics is the activity that seeks as its principal objective to change society and it does this through taking political power (winning elections, forming governments) or through seeking to influence the decisions of those who have power (lobbying, influencing public opinion, protesting). Throughout the twentieth century, the principal form of political action was through political parties which developed strong collective identities among significant sectors of national populations (such as the links between organized labour and left-wing parties or populist parties in many countries). This form of political activity, oriented to winning power within formal political systems, is the subject of this chapter. Chapter 10 looks at another form of politics, namely groups that operate outside the formal political system and do not seek to win political power but rather to influence how power is used. This form of politics, expressed through social movements of various kinds, has exercised a major influence in many Latin American societies (for example, through strong trade union movements, or through popular mobilizations against military dictatorships). In this way, the principal forms of 'agency', being utilized by Latin Americans to influence the structural situation created by the neoliberal reformation, will be examined.

This chapter begins by outlining the political turbulence that marks Latin America at the beginning of the twenty-first century as the formal democratic systems consolidated in the 1990s lose legitimacy and people resort more and more to street protest as a way of making and unmaking governments. This is one way in which the political strains alluded to in the chapter's title are manifested, namely the stresses and strains of Latin American politics. The second meaning of political strains, namely the different currents of political orientation that manifest themselves, is the subject of the subsequent sections of the chapter. Section two looks at how the Latin American left is responding to the neoliberal reformation, both through adapting to it (as has the Chilean Socialist Party) and through fashioning critical responses (as the Brazilian Workers Party is doing). The ways in which the distinctive current of politics known as Latin American populism has responded, through the emergence of what is often called neopopulism, is the subject of section three. Section four looks at political groups who seek to safeguard the economic status quo, namely right-wing parties; since in many countries the armed forces have played this role, the section examines how committed to democracy are the region's military. The fifth section concentrates on Colombia where powerful guerrilla groups, right-wing paramilitary squads and the Colombian state battle for the country's future with the growing military involvement of the United States. A final brief section draws conclusions about politics in the era of neoliberalism.

Political Turbulence

The section of Chapter 5 entitled 'Democratization' has outlined the contrast that exists between the widespread consolidation of formal democratic regimes throughout Latin America and the growing disenchantment with this system of electoral politics as it fails to improve the well-being of most social sectors. This is consistent with the view that globalization is resituating states so that they respond more to the requirements of international competitiveness and less to the welfare of their own citizens, as outlined in Chapter 1. As mentioned there, and described in Box 5.2, this tends to reduce politics to the marketing of political personalities rather than it being the arena where different programmes and projects for organizing society are argued over and win public support. Popular perception that political elites are corrupt is also undermining politics.[2] This section describes how citizens are responding to this situation throughout Latin America. It begins by offering evidence that the democratic political system is losing legitimacy among Latin Americans and goes on to outline two resulting characteristics that can be observed in the politics of the region at the turn of the twenty-first century: firstly, the weakening of the ability of political parties to represent social demands, and, secondly, the resort to direct action outside the political system.

Political legitimacy is difficult to measure. Sometimes resort is had to levels of political abstention as these are taken as indicating levels of alienation from the political system. Box 5.2 has offered some data for Chile and a general trend towards ever higher levels of political abstention has been noted throughout Latin America in the 1990s (see Hellinger, 1999: 54). Survey evidence is another way to measure levels of dissatisfaction with the political system and offers the benefit of measuring this directly rather than inferring it from levels of abstention. Tables 9.1 and 9.2 offer evidence from the annual Latinobarometro survey of over 18,000 people in 17 Latin American countries, chosen as a representative sample of the general population. Table 9.1 measures support for democracy (the percentage who support it as a system) and satisfaction with it (the percentage who are satisfied with how it operates). Latin American respondents report lower levels of support for and satisfaction with democracy than do those in other regions similarly surveyed. Table 9.2 shows a low and declining level of confidence in political leaders and parties among Latin Americans.

These worrying attitudes have found expression in a weakening of the central role political parties have played in mediating between citizens and the state. This characteristic can be seen in a number of tendencies evident in Latin American politics during the 1990s. Firstly, in a number of countries, long-established and major parties have seen their support base suddenly migrating to new leaders and political groups. This happened most notably in Peru and Venezuela where outsiders to the political system, Alberto Fujimori in Peru in the 1990 presidential elections and Hugo Chavez in Venezuela in the 1998 presidential elections, won mass popular support at the expense of such parties as APRA and Izquierda Unida (IU) in Peru[3] and Acción Democratica (AD) and COPEI in Venezuela. Alongside this, a second tendency is evident, in the fragmentation of political representation among a large number of small parties, some of them restricted to particular regions. This was evident in the congressional elections in Argentina in 2001 and in Colombia in 2002 where the combined vote of a large number of small parties was greater than the vote for the large established parties, such as the Peronists in Argentina and the Liberal Party in Colombia.[4] Thirdly, most of the new parties emerging, whether Cambio 90 of Fujimori or the Movement for the Fifth Republic (MVR) of Chavez which became majority parties virtually overnight, or smal-

TABLE 9.1 SUPPORT FOR AND SATISFACTION WITH DEMOCRACY, 2000–1

Regions	Support (%)	Satisfaction (%)
European Union	78	53
Africa	69	58
India	60	40
Eastern Europe	53	29
Latin America	48	25

Source: Latinobarometro, 2001

TABLE 9.2   LEVELS OF CONFIDENCE IN
                 INSTITUTIONS, PERSONS, 1996
                 AND 2001

Confidence in	1996 (%)	2001 (%)
Church	76	72
Television	60	49
Armed forces	42	38
President	39	30
Police	30	30
Judicial system	33	27
National Congress	27	24
Political parties	20	19
Fellow citizens	20	17

Source: Latinobarometro, 2001

ler parties, many of them newly founded, offer ill-defined policies, often differ on only relatively minor points among one another, are weakly institutionalized, and depend on the appeal of their leader and founder. Thus, if the leader exits the political stage (as did Fujimori in 2000 when he resigned the presidency by e-mail during a visit to Japan) the party virtually disappears as an electoral force.

These trends may in some situations indicate a greater democratization of political systems, as is evident in Mexico (see Box 9.1). However, in other situations, as Hartlyn points out in the case of Venezuela, 'the possibility for a more institutionalized and accountable democracy is reduced' (2002: 125). This is because of the weakening of the central role parties play in a successful democratic system, socializing supporters into the system, canalizing their interests and demands, and holding leaders accountable. Roberts sums up these characteristics of contemporary Latin American politics:

> In a context of social fragmentation engendered by the collapse of state-led development models and the subsequent spread of free market reforms, heterogeneous and decentralized forms of collective action have not been able to generate a stable electoral majority or a compelling programmatic alternative to undergird a radical democratic project. These forms of collective action remain too segmented and localized to develop a critical mass for a national political alternative, much less to challenge increasingly transnationalized concentrations of political and economic power. In such a context, electoral support is likely to flow toward populist figures or amorphous catch-all parties that appeal to the mass of unattached individual voters but provide little impetus for a deepening of popular sovereignty. (1998: 5)

In this situation, a second characteristic is evident, namely the tendency to bypass the political system altogether and to resort to direct street protest as a way of changing unpopular governments. By mid 2002, in five South American countries, street protests had succeeded in replacing presidents, though Pedro Carmona who replaced Hugo Chavez in Venezuela in April 2002 lasted less than 48 hours before Chavez himself returned. However, in

Box 9.1 Offering Mexicans 'democracy *lite*'

In July 2000, the candidate of the right-wing PAN party, Vicente Fox, won Mexico's presidential election, thus ending the 71-year-rule of the Institutional Revolutionary Party (PRI). Though the PRI had submitted its candidates to popular elections every six years and presidential re-election was not possible, the party's longevity relied on what Schedler calls 'a combination of fine-tuned antidemocratic restrictions [such as restrictions on party and candidate registration, electoral fraud and corruption, and a near monopoly by the ruling party on access to the media and electoral resources] and genuine popular support' (2000: 6). However, a series of electoral reforms between 1987 and 1996 which created an independent and transparent system, coupled with the impact of the neoliberal reformation, resulted in the PRI slowly losing power at municipal, state and congressional levels. Only in 1989 did a state governorship fall to a candidate of an opposition party for the first time but, by the time of the 2000 elections, one-third of governorships and most municipalities were in the hands of opposition parties.

The PAN (National Action Party) was founded in 1939 and represented the only genuine political opposition to the PRI until the founding of the left-wing PRD (Party of the Democratic Revolution) by dissidents of the PRI in 1989. PRD founder Cuauhtemoc Cardenas, son of legendary Mexican president Lazaro Cardenas (1934–40), was widely believed to have been robbed of the presidency by fraud in 1988 when PRI candidate Carlos Salinas was declared the winner after electoral computers failed on election night. The PAN was traditionally seen as a mouthpiece for northern Mexican business and conservative Catholicism. However, Vicente Fox, the former head of Coca Cola in Latin America, succeeded in broadening the party's appeal, emphasizing its social and political as well as its economic liberalism and pledging poverty reduction through economic growth and targeted social programmes. As Mexican political scientist Denise Dresser put it: 'Fox consciously eluded easy classifications. He staked out a position one day and embraced its alter ego the next; he catered to the right, then flirted with the left' (2002: 85). Beginning his campaign early, he gained a lead in the polls which made him the most credible possibility for ousting the PRI in the minds of uncommitted voters, and he charmed US business leaders, politicians and the media by his 'charisma and denim-and-boots cowboy demeanor' (Shirk, 2000: 29). In the event, he won 42 per cent of the vote, to 36 per cent for the PRI and 16 per cent for the PRD. So amazing were the results for Mexicans that even as they came through on election night Fox himself was not convinced that the PRI would concede defeat (R. Pastor, 2000).

In Dresser's view, Fox won the presidency through skilful marketing and sought to use the same formula to govern Mexico. What he lacks, however, 'is a clear grasp of the political bartering necessary to transform positions into policies', which has led to him alienating not only opposition legislators but even those of his own party. A year after he took power, she wrote: 'Peace in Chiapas remains elusive, fiscal reform is bogged down in Congress, social programmes are at a standstill, the economy is grinding to a halt, and the president still spends more

> time promoting himself than getting the job done. ... Fox's governance style,
> wherein image trumps substantive policy, suggests that Mexicans may be offered
> little more than democracy *lite*' (pp. 84, 86).

Argentina, Ecuador and Paraguay, presidents unelected by popular vote were
finishing out the mandates of their predecessors who had resigned due to
massive street protests, while in Peru, Fujimori had fled to Japan and resigned
in November 2000 only months after his re-election in a vote that was widely
seen as fraudulent. In that situation, Congress president Valentin Paniagua
took power, organized new elections in April 2001 and handed power over
to the victor, Alejandro Toledo, whom Fujimori had 'defeated' a year earlier. In
Colombia and Bolivia also, social unrest had reached dramatic proportions
though without overthrowing presidents. The collapse of the Colombian
peace process in early 2002 had intensified the political killings, bombing
and kidnappings that characterize the country's political life (see below),
while waves of urban and rural protests in Bolivia in 2000 had greatly weakened the government of Hugo Banzer who resigned a year early due to cancer,
handing power over to his vice-president, Jorge Quiroga, to serve the remainder of his term. Benavente and Jaraquemada see this widespread 'social rebel-
liousness' in South America as occurring in situations of acute social problems
which governments prove unable to resolve. However, such mass street protests express not a coherent ideological view nor a set of proposals for change
but 'a mood of anger and frustration, a growing loss of the legitimacy of
government and of democratic institutions that are seen as inefficient, and
the inability of political parties to represent' popular demands. As such, they
reflect 'a profound crisis of governability in Latin America for which no viable
institutional solutions are apparent' (2002: 7).

The Left: Diverging Responses

If the political scene in Latin America at the turn of the twenty-first century is
characterized by a failure of political parties to channel citizens' demands for
economic and social change, by elitist control of democratic systems, and by
the seeming lack of alternatives to neoliberal reformation, this suggests that
left-wing parties are failing to respond to the challenges posed by this new
situation. For the left has traditionally seen itself as the political force best
positioned to channel demands for radical social and economic change, to
deepen democracy and to propose alternatives. If these are requirements of
the present moment, why is the left not more successful in winning adherents
through responding to popular discontent against the neoliberal reformation?
The question is best answered by looking at the ways the left has tried to
respond. Following Vilas (1998) and Lievesley (1999), three main left-wing
responses to the neoliberal reformation can be identified. The first Lievesley
calls 'the intransigents' (p. 73) who denounce the existing neoliberal model and
proclaim the need for the overthrow of capitalism. Yet, as Vilas puts it, they

reduce politics to a 'self-marginalizing dogmatism' (p. 68) that has proved incapable of winning any significant base of adherents. In different ways the Chilean Communist Party and Peru's United Left (IU) illustrate the fate of this option. The former has lost its traditionally significant place in the Chilean political system and, though still in existence and contesting elections, it no longer has any members in the Chilean Congress. The latter, by making the option in the late 1980s to deepen the revolutionary struggle and overthrow capitalism, found itself losing its base of support as a profound economic crisis in the late 1980s and neoliberal restructuring in the early 1990s under Fujimori made individual survival rather than social revolution the main preoccupation of the poor. The IU's vote declined from a high of 30 per cent in the 1986 municipal elections to 0.6 per cent in the 1995 presidential elections. The other two ways in which the left is responding deserve rather more attention, however. These are what can be called 'Third Way' politics and a popular radicalism.

By 'Third Way' politics is meant the option to accept the neoliberal order, believing that it is possible to make it serve the interests of the poor and marginalized by better managing it through more efficient regulation of capitalist enterprises, an equitable taxation system and targeted social programmes. This approach therefore is not interested in alternatives to neoliberalism, believing them illusory, but rather in its more efficient and compassionate management. Taking its inspiration from Britain's New Labour government of Tony Blair, 'Third Way' politics have been explicitly endorsed by centre-left presidents such as Ricardo Lagos of Chile (2000–6), Fernando Henrique Cardoso of Brazil (1994–2002) and Fernando de la Rua of Argentina (1999–2001). Indeed Hugo Chavez of Venezuela (1998–) has also adopted the mantle of the Third Way, though the style and substance of his policies are better seen as a radical neopopulism (see Box 9.3). Despite the Third Way's promise as a modernizing social democracy in response to the challenges of globalization (see Giddens, 1998 and 2000), Power's examination of the record of Cardoso's Party of Brazilian Social Democracy (PSDB) following its foundation in 1988 shows a steady move to the right of centre and a pronounced shift towards a liberal, pro-market orientation in economic policy (2001–2: 625–6). The party's record leads Power to identify a number of obstacles that face left-wing attempts in Latin America to manage neoliberalism in a progressive way. The first of these is the need for left-wing parties to find allies with whom they can get into power. Without these they are shut out of power forever, but building alliances can mean the dilution of ideology. This was true of Cardoso (who allied with the right-wing Liberal Front Party (PFL)) and of the alliance between the centre-left Frepaso and the centre-right Radical Party which brought Fernando de la Rua to the presidency of Argentina. In the Chilean case, the Concertacion alliance grouping the President's Socialist Party, the centre-left Pro-Democracy Party (PPD) and the centrist Christian Democrats is less of a restraint. However, a senior Socialist Party deputy, Sergio Aguilo, issued a public document in March 2002 accusing the government of following right-wing policies so that the only electoral choice facing Chileans is 'to choose between two rights' (Aguilo, 2002). The second obstacle identified by Power is the weakness of political parties and the more fluid, unpredictable nature of electoral politics in Latin America which condition the manner parties can maintain the coherence necessary for a Third Way approach. Finally, Power points to the extent of policy challenges in Latin America where poverty and inequality are endemic and economic crises are life-and-death dramas with total macroeconomic and social collapse a real possibility. This clearly describes the ignominious collapse of the de la Rua presidency at the end of 2001 under mounting economic crisis and determined street protests. In an interview towards the end of his presidency, Cardoso recognized that the Third Way is in retreat but that the challenges for progressive governance remain as people's social situation has failed to improve in pace with market reforms (Aravena Bolivar, 2002).

The third left-wing response to the challenges of the neoliberal reformation is by way of popular radicalism. This label covers a group of left-wing parties that in different countries are attempting creatively to develop alternatives to neoliberalism through a politics of popular participation and through novel responses to the huge social challenges they face. The principal parties or alliances included under this label are the Frente Amplio (FA) in Uruguay, the PRD in Mexico, the Workers Party (PT) in Brazil (see Box 9.2), and the FMLN in El Salvador. All of these parties have reached power at municipal level where they have had a chance to practise a new form of politics, availing of the increased powers given to local government under second generation reforms (see Chapter 5). As Vilas puts it, this new form of politics attempts to link representative with participative democracy and to open up practical proposals for transforming society (1998: 72). With strong roots in social movements, these parties use their control of municipal governments to foster new forms of participation, particularly by marginalized sectors. However, they also devote considerable attention to developing innovative and efficient services, particularly for the poor. In some cases, such as has happened in Mexico City since the PRD took control of the city government, the left's efforts have been hampered by central state control over funds. In other cases, centre-left parties or alliances that were emerging as important political actors proved unable to carve out an enduring role amid political and economic volatility. This is true of Venezuela's Movimiento al Socialismo (MAS) and Causa R, which were weakened by their support for the presidency of Rafael Caldera (1993–9) and which then split in response to the emergence of Hugo Chavez, with one faction supporting him and another opposing. In Argentina, the Frepaso alliance was greatly weakened by its involvement in the disastrous de la Rua administration. Yet, even where the left has proved capable of effective and imaginative governance at municipal level, such as in the case of the FA in Montevideo and the PT in various Brazilian cities, it has found it much more difficult to win power at national level. Though the FA won the highest vote in Uruguay's presidential elections in 1999, supporters of the two traditional parties joined ranks to ensure the election of a conservative president, Jorge Battle, in the second round runoff. Finally, and perhaps most significantly, the left even at its most successful has proved better at channelling discontent than at proposing alternatives. As Lievesley writes: 'Although reno-

Box 9.2 The PT and popular participation in Porto Alegre

In 1989, the Workers Party won control of the municipal government of Porto Alegre, capital city of the southern Brazilian state of Rio Grande do Sul (with 1.3 million inhabitants). The city was virtually bankrupt, burdened with debts, and with current costs greater than its income. Broad sectors of its population had only limited access to basic services. The new government immediately set about cutting costs and implemented a progressive tax reform (taxing the rich more highly to fund basic services for the poor) that soon gave it access to greatly increased financial resources. But, more importantly, it developed new institutions of genuine popular participation, giving real decision-making power to civil society and involving a large number of civil organizations – from neighbourhood groups to non-governmental organizations (NGOs), and from cultural groups to education, health and housing pressure groups – in running the city. The most important institution established was the participative budget, a process involving city officials, elected representatives and tens of thousands of local people in their neighbourhoods who meet throughout each year in working groups, neighbourhood and zonal meetings, and plenary assemblies to analyse budgetary figures and define spending priorities. It is estimated that over 100,000 people participate in this process in which the city government is but one actor alongside many others, though one that actively seeks to safeguard the overall interests of the city.

Other participative institutions include the 'constituent city', a biannual congress of delegates from the participative budget process, of the city council, and of representatives of NGOs, architects, technicians, engineers and urban planners, to develop guidelines and strategies for the economic, social, environmental and cultural development of the city. A commission that includes representatives of civil society has the power to hire and fire city functionaries and to decide on their salaries. The city has developed a strategy to avail of the opportunities opened by Mercosur (see Chapter 6) to become a regional development pole, and various city programmes seek to develop technological innovation and create high-quality jobs. Investment has been channelled to improve infrastructure and services in poor districts: the percentage of homes with drinking water and sewerage has risen considerably while primary and secondary school enrolment rose by 159 per cent between 1989 and 1997 (Kliksberg, 1999: 94).

The Workers Party has seen its vote in Porto Alegre's municipal elections increase throughout the 1990s. More importantly, it has developed a new relationship between the state and civil society, in which the latter is an active partner in a reinvigorated public sphere. As Utzig put it, the PT in Porto Alegre has learnt that the great challenge for the democratic left is to implement practical policies capable of reforming society while at the same time inventing new institutions that have the potential of overcoming the status quo and transforming society (1998: 109).

vated and new left-wing parties have moved – with greater or lesser degrees of commitment and effectiveness – into the terrain of radical democratic politics, they have not as yet been capable of formulating a coherent political vision which could act as an alternative to neo-liberalism' (1999: 75).

Neopopulism and the Politics of Anti-politics

In many Latin American countries, populist politicians have proved much more successful than the left at mobilizing and maintaining a mass following. On the wane in most countries in the 1970s and early 1980s, populist politics made a surprising comeback in the 1990s, usually in a neoliberal form known as neopopulism. Classical populist politics had emerged in the 1920s and 1930s as incipient industrialization and migration to the cities, coupled with the extension of the franchise, resulted in a large new group of voters, disorganized and potentially destabilizing for society. Through their direct appeal to these masses, populist leaders such as Lazaro Cardenas in Mexico (1934–40), Getulio Vargas in Brazil (1930–45 and 1951–4), Victor Raul Haya de la Torre in Peru (who never reached the presidency), Victor Paz Estenssoro in Bolivia (1952–6, 1960–4 and 1985–9), José Maria Velasco Ibarra in Ecuador (1934–5, 1944–7, 1952–6, 1960–1 and 1968–72), and Juan Domingo Perón in Argentina (1946–55 and 1973–4) succeeded in integrating them into society and creating solid bases of political support through a direct identification between the leader and the people that proved remarkably enduring. This came to be characterized by analysts as Latin American populism (to be distinguished from American or Russian populism). Though each case of populist politics has its own distinctive features dependent on the style of the particular leader and the context in which he operated, common institutional, ideological and political elements can be identified. Since populist politics rested on a sense of direct and emotional identification between the leader and his followers, the political parties created tended to be poorly institutionalized, being entirely controlled by the leader and subject to his wishes. The dominant role of the charismatic leader also meant that the parties' ideology was ill-defined and even incoherent, often being little more than a vague set of slogans appealing to wide, cross-class support. For their followers, what mattered was not party ideology but a deep sense of trust in the populist leader. Finally, the classical populists all followed strong, state-led industrialization policies coupled with the redistribution of benefits to the poor (see Conniff, 1999, for an overview of populism in Latin America).

   Since neoliberal reforms weakened the state, imposed greater austerity on the poor and restricted the potential for redistributive policies, they were seen as marking a move away from populism. Indeed a literature developed in the 1980s castigating populists for overspending and irresponsible macroeconomic management which plunged their countries into economic recession (see Dornbusch and Edwards, 1991). However, in the early 1990s, leaders such as Alberto Fujimori in Peru (1990–2000), Carlos Menem in Argentina (1989–99) and Fernando Collor de Melo in Brazil (1990–2) discovered remarkable affinities between neoliberalism and elements of populism. Four elements of this neopopulism can be identified:

1   *Charismatic leadership and direct appeal to the people.* Fujimori and Collor de Melo were both outsiders to national politics in their countries and took the political establishment by surprise in winning the presidency. Menem, though the candidate of the Peronist Party, had been a relative outsider within the party and relied more on his personal appeal than on the party machine. Menem and Collor de Melo used television skilfully to enhance their appeal. As Weyland writes: 'They depicted themselves as outsiders who would clean up the existing mess. They attacked the incumbent governments, politicians in general, powerful interest groups, and socioeconomic elites. They claimed to be benefactors of the downtrodden' (1999: 180).

2   *Bypassing existing structures and centralizing power.* Once in power, all three centralized power in the presidency, often resorting to rule by decree to implement their neoliberal reforms. When opposed by the Peruvian Congress where he did not have majority support, Fujimori closed it down in 1992, winning wide popular support through his depiction of the politicians as corrupt obstacles to his reforms. Collor de Melo had less success in his attempt to bypass parliament and finally resigned in 1992 as the Brazilian Congress moved to impeach him for corruption.

3   *Appeal to unorganized masses.* Though implementing harsh austerity programmes of neoliberal reform, the neopopulists won mass support among the unorganized poor in the growing informal sector as they directly appealed to them against the organized interests of trade unions, political parties and other vested interest groups. Where the austerity programmes were seen to work, as in Peru and Argentina where they reduced soaring inflation, attracted investment and led to economic growth, they allowed Fujimori and Menem to win re-election (both in 1995) with strong support from the poor. Where the policies showed poor results, as in Brazil, the president's support collapsed.

4   *Use of social policies to shore up support.* Both Menem and Fujimori used part of the proceeds of their wide-ranging privatization of state companies for social spending, ensuring that they were personally visible as the source of the benefits. Fujimori made well-publicized trips to shanty towns and rural areas to open new schools and health centres built by funding from the Ministry of the Presidency (Cotler and Grompone, 2000: 37).

Paradoxically, therefore, elements of populist politics aided the implementation of thorough neoliberal restructuring in these countries, winning the support of economic elites and the multilateral agencies for what were, especially in the case of Peru, authoritarian regimes with weak democratic legitimacy. In the case of Hugo Chavez in Venezuela, however, neopopulist politics has been used to resist neoliberal reforms and to strengthen the state (see Box 9.3).

The politics of bypassing existing parties and, at times, political institutions in a direct appeal to the people against the political establishment has come to be called 'anti-politics'. A group of political leaders emerged in Latin America

Box 9.3 Hugo Chavez: The last revolution of the twentieth century?

The political style and practice of Venezuela's President Hugo Chavez contains much that is quintessentially neopopulist. The popularity that won him election in 1998 as a political outsider was based on the unsuccessful coup he led against the neoliberal government of President Carlos Andrés Pérez in 1992. His first 18 months in office were dominated by a refounding of the country's political system, including a new constitution and renaming the country the Bolivarian Republic of Venezuela. His Movement for a Fifth Republic (MVR) party, whose electoral appeal rests largely on his charisma, espouses an eclectic 'humanistic, revolutionary and Bolivarian doctrine' proposing a 'self-managed and competitive economy', an inclusive social policy, protection by the state of socio-economic rights and 'the obligation that public powers, freely elected, control, correct and direct the play of the economy and the market' (Caponi, 2001: 31–2). His denunciation, in popular and abrasive language, of the political and economic elites which had ruled Venezuela over the previous 50 years helped unite employers, trade union leaders and the Catholic Church in a pact to overthrow him, which briefly succeeded in a 48-hour coup in April 2002 until a military revolt and popular pressure returned him to power. In a weekly radio programme 'Alo, Presidente' he receives phone calls from people about their problems and telephones government ministers on air ordering them to resolve them.

Chavez, however, does not use his appeal to introduce neoliberal policies, but rather to strengthen the state's control over the economy. This is most evident in his petroleum policy. Since this provides some 80 per cent of the country's export earnings, his decision to resurrect the Organization of Petroleum Exporting Countries (OPEC), and to coordinate controls over oil production in order to raise prices, has seen the price of a barrel rise from US$8 in early 1999 to $23 a year later. This policy has transformed the country's prospects and completely reversed his predecessor's attempts to prepare the huge state oil company, PDVSA, for privatization. Instead of a unipolar world dominated by the economic needs of the United States, President Chavez seeks a multipolar world. Towards this end, he has fostered close relations with China, maintains an active diplomacy with oil states Iraq, Iran and Libya, and has taken over the leadership of the Group of 77, a large grouping of developing countries. To ensure the benefits of this policy flow to other countries, Venezuela provides oil on concessional terms to a number of small Central American countries and Cuba. This has led to growing opposition by Washington which was implicated in the April 2002 coup against him.

For Venezuelan political scientists Luis E. Lander and Margarita López Maya, Chavez's petroleum policy is an essential part of his political project which, 'with all its insufficiencies, ambiguities, improvisations and indefinitions, is trying to construct an alternative to neoliberal globalization' (2002: 4). Colombian historian Medófilo Medina sees Venezuela as having 'broken in an original way from the convention that issues of world importance are left to the competence of the leaders and officials of countries belonging to the financial and industrial centres of the world, and to transnational technocrats'. For this reason, he calls it 'the last revolution of the twentieth century' (2001: 127–8).

in the 1990s basing their appeal on a rejection of the existing political party system. Both Fujimori and Chavez referred scathingly to the parties that had dominated their countries' political life over the proceeding decades as *partidocracia* (partidocracy rather than democracy) (see Ellner, 1998: 136) and their success was based on an astonishing popular rejection of these parties. A similar, though not as extreme, emergence of new personalist parties can be identified in Brazil (with Collor de Melo)[5] and in Bolivia. In the latter case, the appeal of broadcaster Carlos Palenque, through his radio and TV shows highlighting discrimination and injustices, led to the founding of his CONDEPA (Conscience of the Patria) party in 1988, while beer baron Max Fernandez the following year founded the UCS (Unidad Civica Solidaridad) based directly on his country-wide beer distribution network. In the 1993 elections, both received a little over 14 per cent of the vote, the third and fourth most voted parties in the country respectively. Despite such rhetoric as Fernandez's statement in 1995 that 'it would be much better if political parties did not exist ... I wish politicians would disappear from our country' (quoted in Mayorga, 1995: 120), both parties worked within the political system, even initially being part of the coalition that voted former military dictator Hugo Banzer into power following the 1997 presidential elections. The deaths of both Palenque and Fernandez in the late 1990s, however, weakened the two parties whose support was based very much on their personal profile, but the politics of anti-politics has endured and found expression in the remarkable success of coca farmers' leader Evo Morales, who, with 21 per cent of the vote, came in just behind the front-runner, former President Gonzolo Sanchez de Lozada, in the 2002 Bolivian presidential elections.

The emergence of such 'anti-politics', writes Mayorga, marks a relatively new political logic that negates the need for intermediate institutions such as political parties between the people and the state, as they are seen as distorting the popular will. 'In consequence, this form of politics is eminently anti-institutional, elitist and personalist in its focus on the figures of the outsiders. To these are attributed messianic qualities and they present themselves as saviours of the nation, incarnating the popular will and united by direct links with the popular masses' (1995: 34–5). Hellinger lists the ranks from which Latin American political leaders have emerged in recent years: 'as the prestige of the parties falls personalist leaders are as likely to come from the ranks of technocrats, beauty queens, failed coup-plotters, media personalities, sharp politicians who have turned against their own parties, former scholars, guerrilla chiefs and businessmen' (1999: 67). The economic problems and political turbulence in many Latin American countries at the turn of the twenty-first century provide perfect conditions for the practice of anti-politics to thrive.

Safeguarding the Status Quo

Political life in most Latin American countries was, in the nineteenth century, divided between liberals and conservatives. The former were anti-clerical, urban-based and reflected the interests of middle class and business sectors while the latter supported the Catholic Church, were more rural in their base of support, and expressed the interests of large land-owners and other rich elites. In some countries, such as Honduras and Colombia, Liberal and Conservative parties still dominate political life, though in most countries this divide has been superseded by the emergence of left-wing parties, populist parties, Christian democratic parties (particularly in Chile, Venezuela and Costa Rica) and, more recently, personalist parties. Most of these were seeking fundamental changes in their countries' economic and social structures (or at least claimed they were) as a way of incorporating the large sectors of the population living in poverty and marginalization. In this situation, elites who felt their interests threatened relied on the armed forces to intervene on their behalf. The democratization of the region in the 1980s and 1990s with the strong backing of the United States ruled this option out. However, the tendency of business elites to opt for authoritarian solutions was seen in Venezuela in April 2002 when the high command of the armed forces responded to the pressure of business, the trade union confederation and the Catholic Church (with, it appears, the urging of the United States) to force President Chavez out and replace him with the head of the main business group, Fedecameras, Pedro Carmona, who instantly closed Congress and revoked the country's Bolivarian constitution. Though revolts within the armed forces as well as popular opposition to the coup forced Carmona to step down within 48 hours and a return to constitutional rule, the public equivocation of Washington and some Latin American countries (such as Chile), and their unwillingness to even call what happened a coup, carried vivid reminders of past practice. However, Chavez is a rare exception in early twenty-first century Latin America in attacking the interests of business elites. Elsewhere, governments of whatever political complexion give priority to safeguarding the interests of big business, closely monitered by the International Monetary Fund, the World Bank and international credit rating agencies. In such a situation, it is perhaps not surprising that few noteworthy new parties of the right have emerged in Latin America, with the exception of Chile's UDI (see Box 9.4). The Action for the Republic party of Argentina's technocratic economy minister under both the Menem and de la Rua administrations, Domingo Cavallo, only gained 10 per cent of the vote in the 1999 presidential elections, while to win the Mexican presidency in 2000, the PAN had to broaden its base of support and blur its identity as a party of business sectors.

While the military have returned to barracks in Latin America, questions remain about their subordination to civilian authority and their commitment to democracy. As political instability grows, might they once again see themselves as having a responsibility to impose order and safeguard elite economic interests? This question is best answered by examining the extent to which the region's military institutions have submitted themselves to civilian control and the rule of law. Following the return to democracy, accountability for crimes committed by military personnel became a tense public issue in many countries with the high command resisting any investigation. In Argentina, the former military rulers were submitted to trial and imprisoned but all those under their command given an amnesty. The government of Raul Alfonsin (1983–9) faced a

Box 9.4 The UDI: The rise and rise of Chile's new right

Chile's 1999 presidential election, the third since the return to democracy in 1990, marked the emergence of the new right as a serious contender for government. The youthful right-wing candidate and member of the Union Democratica Independiente (UDI), Joaquín Lavin, came within 31,142 votes of the candidate of the governing centre-left coalition, Ricardo Lagos, an experienced senior politician, winning 47.5 per cent of the vote to Lagos's 47.9 per cent. In the second round runoff, Lagos received 51.3 per cent to Lavin's 48.6 per cent. During the Lagos presidency, Lavin, a member of the conservative Catholic society Opus Dei, astutely used his position as mayor of Santiago to project an image of national leadership, positioning himself to become President of Chile in 2006.

Founded in the early 1980s by Jaimé Guzman, also an Opus Dei member, and a key civilian ideologue of the Pinochet dictatorship, the UDI captured around 15 per cent of the popular vote in elections between 1989 and 1996. It is led by an homogeneous and disciplined group of young politicians, most of whom were graduates of the Catholic University in the 1960s and had held government positions, at both national and local level, under the dictatorship. In contrast to Chile's traditional right-wing party, the Renovacion Nacional (RN) with its internal divisions between liberals and conservatives and its willingness to reform some of the authoritarian legacies of the dictatorship, the UDI positioned itself as a defender of the 'protected democracy' which General Pinochet bequeathed to his civilian successors, especially in the form of the 1980 Constitution. Three elements constitute the basis of its political outlook – neoliberal economics, conservative Catholic social doctrine, and a nationalist belief in national unity, including support for the armed forces.

Another factor distinguishing the UDI from the traditional right has been its active work among poorer sectors of the population, based in part on its Catholic identity and on a practical desire to solve social problems. This steady work, together with skilful use of the media and a populist style, allowed it to overtake RN (with which it has been in alliance throughout the 1990s) as the largest party of the right. In the 2000 municipal elections, it won 21 per cent of the vote to RN's 18.5 per cent, and in the 2001 congressional elections became the largest party in the Chilean Congress (see Box 5.2). Morales and Bugueño show that, in contrast to its image as a party of the rich, the UDI receives high levels of electoral support in poor areas, both urban and rural (2001: 237–41). Furthermore, as its success in Chile grew, so too did its international profile, and its advice on electoral strategy was being sought by conservative parties in many Latin American countries, including Colombia, Honduras, Argentina, Bolivia and the Dominican Republic (Insunza and Urrutia, 2002).

number of military uprisings as a result. In Chile, the armed forces resisted any acknowledgement that they had done wrong and, up until the arrest of General Pinochet in London in 1998, little progress had been made in holding them accountable. The arrest opened the way for an avalanche of cases against military personnel before the country's courts for human rights abuses, including cases against the former dictator. Only in this situation did the armed forces grudgingly and reluctantly move to acknowledge their past abuses. On other issues also, such as promotions, budgets, training and deployment, military institutions have resisted civilian control, leading to what Hunter describes as 'mutual testing' between politicians and military officers as both sides probed how far they could go in promoting or resisting change (1998: 302). Where the military had left government in disarray, such as in Argentina after defeat in the Malvinas/Falklands war, and with the economy in decline, civilian control was easier to achieve. Where the transition to democracy took place in a way and at a pace controlled by the military and amid economic growth, such as in Chile and Brazil, military resistance to civilian control was greater. In most countries, a stable coexistence has been reached in which the military maintain considerable autonomy but show themselves more willing to cooperate with civilian governments. However, there are also many indications that the armed forces continue to see a role for themselves in maintaining internal order in their countries. It has been alleged in Peru that when President Fujimori came to power in 1990 he adopted a plan that the country's armed forces had prepared amid the economic and social chaos of the final years of the Garcia administration to take over the reins of government and implement neoliberal restructuring. Fujimori relied heavily on the armed forces during his period in office, promoting officers loyal to him and protecting the institution from investigations of human rights abuses in the war against the Sendero Luminoso guerrillas (Cotler and Grompone, 2000: 96–102). Under Hugo Chavez in Venezuela, the military have been heavily involved in development and social projects while many military personnel hold government posts. In Ecuador, middle ranking officers played an active role in the indigenous uprising that led to the overthrow of President Jamil Mahuad in 2000, though the army took a harder line against indigenous protests in 2001 (Lucero, 2001). In Brazil, the military have been used to raid *favelas* (shanty towns) to root out gang violence, racketeering and the trafficking of drugs and arms. A major exception in this regard is Argentina where, despite a history of active military intervention in politics, the armed forces and their budgets have been greatly reduced and their role in internal affairs severely circumscribed. After the trauma of the 1980s, senior Argentine officers appear unwilling to challenge this situation. In summary, it can be concluded that despite progress, the armed forces in many Latin American countries maintain prerogatives and freedoms, a role in the internal life of their countries, and even attitudes and values that indicate less than full commitment to democratic subordination. In a situation where internal economic and social order might break down and where the posture of the United States might be willing to accept it (as appeared to be the case during the brief Venezuelan coup in April 2002), a return of the military to power in some Latin American countries is not inconceivable.

Colombia: Imploding State?

Colombia presents very different political strains, unique in Latin America for their persistence and intensity. Indeed, by the beginning of the twenty-first century, its political and criminal violence had so worsened that fears were being expressed that it had become uncontainable. As the USA became more preoccupied and drawn into the situation (see Box 9.5), media comparisons with Vietnam and Kosovo became common (Pizarro Leongómez, 1999). The Colombian state has been under attack since the 1960s by the Revolutionary Armed Forces of Colombia (FARC) and Army of National Liberation (ELN) guerrilla groups, though historians identify two phases of violence prior to the emergence of the guerrillas. The first is the period known as *la Violencia*, usually dated from the growing clashes between Liberal and Conservative groups during the electoral campaigns of 1945–6, which reached a new intensity following the murder of Liberal presidential candidate Jorge Gaitan in 1948, and lasted until 1953. The second phase is characterized as 'mafia' violence, usually for control of land, and this is dated as 1954–64. The emergence of guerrilla groups in the 1960s is a third phase and the fourth phase is seen to begin in the late 1980s as the growth of the right-wing AUC paramilitary group added a lethal new intensity, neoliberal restructuring further weakened the state, and lucrative drug-trafficking provided resources to many of the warring groups (Safford and Palacios, 2002: 345–67). Over the 1990s about 10 people a day died due to political violence and over 4,000 were made to disappear. Between 1995 and 2000 there were 12,000 kidnappings by armed groups, while some 2 million people have been internally displaced due to violence over the last 15 years of the twentieth century. These chronic levels of violence are but the latest manifestations of deep-rooted problems of instability and recurrent political violence that have plagued Colombia since independence. As Browitt writes: 'The long-term crisis of the nation-state has created a vacuum of legitimacy into which have flowed military and paramilitary forces and the drug industry, especially over the past 15 to 20 years, all of which have virtually destroyed the successful functioning of electoral politics and the rule of law' (2001: 1064).[6] The collapse at the end of the presidency of Andrés Pastrana (1998–2002) of peace processes with both guerrilla groups and the wave of violence unleashed as a result appeared to leave no option other than a military one. The resounding victory of the hard-line opponent of the peace process, Alvaro Uribe, in the 2002 presidential elections showed that most Colombians seemed to support such an option.

While Colombia's violence bears some resemblance to the guerrilla wars of the 1980s in Central America, at least two elements distinguish it and make it particularly difficult to resolve. Firstly, it involves a complex array of actors and interests. On the one hand are the two left-wing guerrilla groups, the FARC with about 15,000 fighters and the ELN with about 3,500. The frustrated efforts of President Pastrana to advance the peace process with the FARC left commentators wondering whether, after 40 years of armed struggle, the guerrillas had a coherent project to advance (Biehl, 2002). On the other hand, the United Autodefence groups of Colombia (AUC), which traces its

Box 9.5 Plan Colombia: Towards another Vietnam?

Plan Colombia, drawn up between Washington and Bogota in the early years of the Pastrana administration, is presented as a multidimensional plan to help resolve the country's difficulties. Its main objectives include the negotiation of peace agreements with the armed insurgents, combating drugs trafficking and revitalizing the economy through increasing foreign investment and creating employment. To this end, Washington has pledged $1.3 billion in aid over two years, more than the total amount it gave over the previous decade, while the plan's overall budget is put at $7.5 billion over five years. However, most of the US contribution is going to be channelled through the Colombian armed forces to strengthen their fight against drugs traffickers. This includes three new and specially trained battalions, a large quantity of helicopters and improved combat and communications equipment. The Plan makes Colombia the second largest recipient of US military assistance in the world and the third largest recipient of US foreign aid.

These aspects have led critics to fear that the Plan is a cloak for deeper US involvement in the war against guerrilla groups, which runs the risk of drawing US troops into the fighting, thus deepening rather than resolving Colombia's problems. Though the direct involvement of US military personnel is limited to 500 advisers, among their roles are those of providing intelligence and selecting targets for anti-drugs operations. Based on these fears the European Union has limited its contribution to Plan Colombia to $750 million to be spent on improving social conditions in isolated zones of the country. It has been pointed out that 56 per cent of the Plan's budget goes on military assistance and a further 26 per cent on the police, while only 9 per cent is earmarked for alternative development, 3 per cent for the displaced, and 1 per cent for human rights (APDH, 2002: 5). The Plan has been criticized for reducing Colombia's problems to those of narco-trafficking and guerrillas, to which military solutions are proposed, while avoiding such problems as inequitable landholding and human rights abuses.

origins back to self-defence groups organized in the 1980s by drugs traffickers and cattle ranchers, unified in the 1990s and grew rapidly from about 1,600 at its unification to between 8,000 and 11,000 at the end of the decade. Their vicious tactics, involving massacres, assassinations, disappearances and mass evictions, led the authorities to declare them illegal in 1989, though close links between them and state forces have been documented by Americas Watch, including the involvement of senior serving army officers in the paramilitary group (Latin American Newsletters, 2001). State forces, including the armed forces and the police, number about 160,000. It has been estimated that almost 70 per cent of the assassinations, massacres and disappearances have been committed by the army and the police, or by paramilitary groups operating with the army (Sánchez and Avilés, 2001: 5). Involvement in the lucrative drugs trade marks the second difference with the guerrilla wars of the 1980s, since it provides both sides with secure sources of sizeable income which, if anything, increase the incentive for war rather than peace. Both the FARC and the AUC 'tax' drugs producers and offer them security for their activities, while the pervasive use of kidnappings for ransom provides another source of income. For these reasons, the Colombian situation more and more resembles the so-called 'new wars' of a globalized world which are not fought for principles but rather reflect the weakening of state power and the growth of alternative sources of violence such as organized crime and mercenary groups (Tokatlian, 2001: 80).

The intensification of Colombia's violence is having a growing impact on its neighbours. Armed incursions by all the armed groups involved, including state forces, have occurred in each of its neighbouring countries, but especially in Venezuela and Ecuador. Growing numbers of displaced Colombians are migrating across borders, 1 million into Ecuador alone, while the destruction of drug cultivation by fumigation from the air is forcing cultivation more and more into border areas. Drug processing laboratories have been discovered in northern Ecuador. Finally, levels of violence such as homicides and kidnappings similar to those in Colombia are now found in border areas of neighbouring countries. Though Colombia's neighbours prefer to deal with these problems on a bilateral basis rather than a regional basis through moving military units to secure their borders with Colombia, the USA is pressing for a regional response, especially through the Regional Andean Initiative, known as IRA in Spanish. This places the military combating of drug trafficking as a high priority on Washington's agenda for the Andean region. Bonilla fears that this constitutes 'a threat to the security of the Andean countries both because of its direct effects on them and because they have had to hand over to Washington a leading role in confronting drug trafficking' (Bonilla, 2001: 23). Among the practical effects of this strategy is that US military forces are ever more active in the region; Ecuador, for example, has given them use of its base at Manta on the Pacific coast. In these ways, growing US involvement in Colombia is drawing in its neighbours also.

Conclusions

Amid the urgent need for coherent responses to the impact of the neoliberal reformation and the challenges of globalization, political systems throughout Latin America are proving unable to represent widely expressed frustration and a desire for change, and to channel these in a positive direction. Instead, representation is fragmenting as new political parties emerge based on colourful personalities rather than on developed political programmes. As traditional parties are weakened, it is possible to identify only a small number of parties that seem capable of mobilizing electorates around political projects offering significant social change, among them Brazil's PT on the left and Chile's UDI on the right. Parties such as Chile's Socialists or Brazil's Social Democrats that have aspired to manage neoliberalism in an efficient but socially progressive way have failed to offer a real alternative. Meanwhile, a growing tendency to resort to street protest to undermine unpopular governments is evident, leading some commentators to speak of a crisis of governability. Amid such a crisis, the focus falls on other social actors, such as social movements, that offer the possibility of responding to the needs of society in novel and creative ways.

Notes

[1] This is not to imply that the structural situation has fallen ready-made from the heavens. Obviously, it was formed through the agency of particular groups but, as was often the case with neoliberal reforms, these were introduced by elites not in response to strong popular support for them but under certain pressure from international agencies (such as the World Bank) and as responses to wider international changes (the liberalization of markets and financial flows, for example). 'Structure' is therefore a complex concept but it captures the constraints and limitations imposed by a particular historical situation.

[2] Corruption among politicians is nothing new in Latin America and there is no way of knowing whether it is more widespread at the beginning of the twenty-first century than it was previously. However, as political parties and people's sense of allegiance to them are weakened, more electors may be more willing to believe allegations of corruption than were previously.

[3] The four parties which between them had got 95 per cent of all votes cast in the 1980 and 1985 elections in Peru (AP and PPC on the right, APRA in the centre-left and IU on the left) received between them just 9.4 per cent of all votes in the 1995 elections, with the result that they were all eliminated from the electoral register of parties, since none had received 5 per cent or more of the vote.

[4] In Colombia, the smaller parties won just under 50 per cent of the vote as against around 30 per cent for the Liberals and around 8 per cent for the Conservatives. In Argentina, the smaller parties won 40 per cent of the vote in the elections for the Chamber of Deputies as against 37 per cent for the Peronists and 23 per cent for the alliance of the Radical party and the Frepaso.

[5] Indeed, the Brazilian party system as a whole is weakly institutionalized. As Mainwaring puts it: 'For a nation that has had considerable experience with democratic government and that has attained a medium per capita income level, Brazil is an exceptional case of party weakness. ... Parties have appeared and disappeared with stunning frequency.' Apart from three electorally insignificant parties, the oldest party in Brazil, the Party of the Brazilian Democratic Movement (PMDB), dates from 1966 and has had its current name only since 1979. 'Parties have weak roots in society and limited legitimacy, and exercise little influence over congressional representatives' (Mainwaring, 1999: 4–5).

[6] Neither should the contribution of high levels of poverty and inequality be neglected. As Guerrero Barón writes: 'No one can really ignore the explosive conditions of poverty, unemployment, and marginalization in which large parts of the population live, granted that many of these conditions are themselves worsened by the war. In addition to these are the social effects of the structural adjustments brought about by the liberalization and globalization of trade, with its sequel of privatizations, the introduction of new technology, the replacement of stable employment by temporary contracts, the forma-tion of large monopolistic consortia dominated by international financial capital, the unprecedented weakening of trade unions and the repositioning of the relation between labour and capital, and so on' (2001: 13).

10

New Social Actors

O ver the final decades of the twentieth century, Latin America saw the emergence of a vibrant civil society as new collective actors such as shanty town organizations, human rights movements, Christian base communities and various forms of self-help groups made their presence felt in the social and political life of their countries. Usually referred to as 'social movements', these groups were seen by analysts as embodying a new form of politics, not concerned with taking political power but rather with democratizing society, claiming rights and pressing demands on the state. Though highly diverse in the forms they took, difficult to quantify and define, and with a presence in public life that could at times be strong and combative and at other times apparently insignificant, these social movements awakened immense hopes that they were the building blocks of a qualitatively different and more participatory society. Furthermore, since the poor formed the core of many social movements, they were thought to mark the 'irruption of the poor' challenging the well-developed forms of elitist control that were a characteristic of most Latin American societies since colonial times.

The 1990s, however, saw a more sober assessment of the potential of these new social actors as their limitations were identified and their contribution to Latin American society more carefully delineated. The purpose of this chapter is to examine Latin America's new social movements, their responses to the neoliberal reformation and their prospects in a more globalized world order. It begins by outlining their emergence under military dictatorships and the promise they were then seen to hold. Section two examines the challenges they have faced as countries returned to democratic rule and how they have adapted to this new situation. In particular, it asks whether these movements have the potential to confront neoliberalism and offer an alternative or whether they more often constitute survival strategies for the poor and vulnerable. The following section examines the emergence of strong indigenous movements in the 1990s as these seem to embody a more combative approach towards neoliberalism, especially in countries with a large indigenous population. The fourth section looks at the emergence of a transnational civil society in Latin America in response to globalization, asking whether this constitutes a form of 'globalization-from-below' as a counterweight to the impact of 'globalization-from-above', namely from the large corporations. The final section draws conclusions about the potential of Latin America's more activist civil society in the twenty-first century.

Grassroots Democratization

The term 'social movements' is used in Latin America to refer to a wide variety of different forms of social organization and community association that emerged from the 1960s onwards, giving voice to the needs of marginalized social sectors. They are distinguished from the large class-based political organizations like trade unions or peasant movements that had become predominant in the period of import-substitution industrialization (ISI) and populist politics from the 1930s to the 1960s (see Chapter 3). Their emergence is linked to the growing crisis of this economic and political model as it proved less and less able to satisfy the material demands of the increasingly urbanized poor majority, and also to the wave of military dictatorships which suppressed trade unions and political parties. As Foweraker put it, 'the combination of urban expansion and repressive government did prove a fecund context for the emergence of new social actors, especially women; for the discovery of new forms of organization and new strategic initiatives; and for the increasing statement of demands in terms of *rights* that became widespread throughout Latin America from the 1970s onwards' (1995: 5; emphasis in original). Escobar and Alvarez doubt a single label can encompass them all, so diverse have been the different forms of social organization and struggle that emerged. They list them as follows:

> From squatters to ecologists, from popular kitchens in poor urban neighbourhoods to Socialist feminist groups, from human rights and defence of life mobilizations to gay and lesbian coalitions, the spectrum of Latin American collective action covers a broad range. It includes, as well, the movements of black and indigenous peoples; new modalities of workers' cooperatives and peasant struggles; middle- and lower-middle-class civic movements; the defence of the rain forest; and even cultural manifestations embodied, for instance, in Afro-Caribbean musical forms (such as salsa and reggae) and incipient antinuclear protest in some countries. (1992: 2)

A number of common features can be identified, however, that allow them be grouped as a collective concept. Firstly, and perhaps most importantly, social movements have 'restored social actors in modern society to a fully conscious life' (Foweraker, 1995: 36), thus counteracting the rather deterministic emphasis on social structure that marked both modernization and dependency theory (see Chapter 1). Secondly, their forms of organization are looser and more informal, as well as less hierarchical and more democratic, than those of most trade unions and political parties. Thirdly, they combine struggles for material resources with a cultural politics that seeks to contest dominant meanings. As Alvarez et al. write, 'the cultural politics enacted by social movements, in challenging and resignifying what counts as political and who – besides the "democratic elite" – gets to define the rules of the political game, can be crucial, we maintain, to fostering alternative political cultures and, potentially, to extending and deepening democracy in Latin America' (1998a: 12). Fourthly, social movements are often rooted in local issues but link these to wider national and even international struggles through networking and establishing two-way channels of communication. Finally, social movements help constitute and reinforce new social identities as people are 'motivated to mobilize as women and teachers, as Indians and peasants, as students and democrats, as workers and socialists, or as any other more or less complex multiple identity' (Foweraker: 60), thereby resisting the reduction of social struggle to one dimension such as class as had tended to predominate in the major social struggles of the pervious period. All of these elements are illustrated in the contribution made by social movements to the return to democracy in many countries of the region (see Box 10.1 on Haiti).

Box 10.1 Democratizing Haiti: Civil society's role

The small Caribbean state of Haiti (population 8 million) was the first Latin American country to gain independence when Toussaint L'Ouverture, inspired by the ideals of the French Revolution, led a slave revolt and established the world's first black-ruled modern state in 1804. However, a functioning democracy was never established; the long occupation by US marines from 1915 to 1934 solidified the state and provided it with a trained army, but left a weakened civil society. The army imposed 'Papa Doc' Duvalier as Haiti's president in 1957 and he organized two parallel organizations, a militia and the dreaded Tontons Macoutes secret police. On his death in 1971, his 18-year-old son, Jean-Claude Duvalier, became president with US support. From the mid 1970s, a more independent and critical civil society began to emerge, firstly through the work of journalists and writers. Following a wave of state repression in 1980, the Catholic Church's Radio Soleil emerged as a focal point of opposition to the regime. 'Dissemination of the social gospel of liberation theology fanned sentiments of justice, dignity, equality and solidarity' which reached to remote corners of the country (Smarth, 1997: 103). Alongside this, priests and sisters were organizing Christian base communities among the poor. A series of popular protests in 1984 and 1985 finally forced Duvalier to flee the country in February 1986. However, this only marked the beginning of the struggle for democracy in Haiti.

While political parties emerged in this new situation, they were weak and poorly organized. Instead democracy was strengthened by a wide network of Popular Organizations (POs) that sprang up throughout the country, especially in poor areas. Though POs appeared spontaneous and amorphous from the outside, they developed internal structures, electing leaders and forming committees charged with communications, education, public relations, finance, and secretarial duties. Some had human rights, cultural, security, international relations and popular economics committees. At regular general meetings, the current national and international situation was discussed, 'with rank and file members being encouraged to participate actively and express their point of view with no restrictions' (Smarth: 119). POs took upon themselves a wide range of tasks such as paving local streets, running literacy courses, putting pressure on the state for better services, denouncing unjustified black marketeering and, in some cases, establishing schools. They played a leading role in identifying Tontons Macoutes and at times meted out rough justice to them. Their vigilance against a return of the old order helped mobilize a widespread public reaction against a coup attempt by former Tontons Macoutes leader Roger Lafontant in January 1991. This social activism formed the base of support for Lavalas (Flood), the political movement that persuaded liberation theology priest Jean-Bertrand Aristide to run for the presidency in 1990, which he won with 67 per cent of the vote against his technocratic rival, Marc Bazin, who had spent $36 million on his campaign.

However, the changes being ushered in by an activist civil society proved too much for the old guard who overthrew Aristide in September 1991, just nine months into his presidency. Vicious repression was directed at the popular movement: estimates of deaths range from 3,000 to 10,000 and 'the appearance of dozens of horribly mutilated bodies in Haiti's streets became an almost daily occurrence' (Kumar, 2000: 129). Some 30,000 Lavalas supporters became internal refugees while tens of thousands took to the sea in rafts to try to reach the USA. Many who survived were sent back, often to a brutal death. The Bush administration showed little interest in restoring Aristide so a network of civil society groups in the USA uniting the Haitian diaspora and local human rights groups sprang into action, publicizing the atrocities being committed by the military regime in Haiti and lobbying members of Congress and the incoming Clinton administration. This helped produce a change of US policy, a UN embargo on Haiti and talks between President Aristide and the military leader, General Raoul Cedras, in July 1993. Though the terror continued for a further year as Cedras refused to honour his agreement to leave power, and further public pressure had to be put on the US administration to act more decisively, President Aristide was finally returned to power in October 1994 with the backing of a large UN force. Parliamentary and municipal elections held in June 1995 and presidential elections in December 1995 indicated that, for the first time, a functioning democracy was being consolidated in Haiti. An activist civil society, both national and transnational, played a key role in achieving this.

The diversity of social movements also makes definition difficult and many analysts resist offering one. Having said at the beginning of their edited collection that they would also resist the temptation, Escobar and Alvarez in the book's conclusion define social movements as 'organized collective actors who engage in sustained political or cultural contestation through recourse to institutional and extrainstitutional forms of action' (Alvarez and Escobar, 1992: 321). Such a definition does not, however, resolve some of the continuing debates about the application of the term. For example, trade unions are regarded by some as old social movements to distinguish them from the new forms that have arisen since the 1960s. As Zapata recognizes, rates of union-ization are at an historic low, many of their hard-won gains such as job security, collective negotiation and workers' protection are being fast eroded and workers in key areas of the new globalized economies (the *maquiladoras* and fruit exports) don't have unions to defend them. These developments constitute 'a very serious threat to their survival' (Zapata, 2001: 16). In other cases, however, trade union movements that played a key role in opposi-tion to military rule and emerged as strong movements alongside other social movements, such as happened in Brazil, are included under the rubric of new social movements. Indeed, the distinction between 'old' and 'new' social move-ments is seen by some leading theorists as too sharp; for Foweraker, in opening up the political sphere, articulating popular demands and politicizing what were previously private issues, new social movements simply continue the job of the old ones (p. 44). Furthermore, the definition fails to acknowledge that outside forces such as political militants, church personnel, or non-govern-mental organizations (NGOs) have usually played a critical role in the emer-gence of social movements (Alvarez and Escobar: 322). Under the conditions of the military dictatorships of the 1970s and 1980s, many of these outside forces were committed to the growth of strong social movements; with the return to democracy, their attention was often directed elsewhere. For all its imprecision, however, the term social movement has come to signify the emergence of an activist civil society in Latin America and the potential for social change this was seen to embody. This is the sense in which it is used here.

The novel promise of these movements is that they embodied a new under-standing of politics with new values, new ways of working for social change and new organizational forms. As Roberts describes it, their struggle for social transformation 'occurs at multiple points in civil society and is driven by the political protagonism of diverse social actors, from labour unions to neigh-bourhood associations, ecclesial base communities, women's groups, human rights organizations, and other forms of grass-roots collective action. For this new conception of political agency, social transformation is not directed from above following the conquest of state power by a party or guerrilla vanguard. Instead, it occurs in a decentralized manner through a multiplicity of grass-roots initiatives and eventually percolates upward through the cumulative modification of power relations' (1998: 68–9). In their forms of action, there-fore, social movements expressed the values of the society they aspired to create: it would be inclusive and not hierarchical, transform society through transforming values and social relations from below rather than imposing changes from above, and create small-scale, decentralized and participatory organizations rather than large ones in which power was centralized and con-trolling. For these reasons, left-wing parties saw them as key protagonists for the society they aspired to build – deepening democracy, fostering equality, and mobilizing the discontented.

This understanding of social movements, however, tended to focus on their potential rather than examine their practice. It was heavily influenced by European theorists of new social movements such as Alain Touraine, Jurgen Habermas, Claus Offe and Chantal Mouffe who identified the women's movement, the peace movement or the ecology movement as reactions against the inroads of state and market into people's lives in post-industrial society. For these theorists, the emphasis was on the assertion of new identities (such as gender, sexual orientation), the rejection of traditional roles (worker, consumer, client) and the redefinition of relationships with nature. For this reason, they labelled them *new* social movements to distinguish them from trade unions and political parties. This literature, therefore, with its emphasis on identity, has been seen as dealing with the 'why' of new social movements, seeking to understand the reasons for their emergence. It is contrasted with a literature that emerged in the United States which focused on issues such as how movements mobilize, organize and make decisions, issues of strategy or the 'how' of social movements. Though neither dealt with the Latin American experience, early understandings of the region's new social movements and their potential were heavily influenced by the new social movement literature from Europe, while the insights into organizational issues offered by the US literature were 'comprehensively ignored' (Foweraker: 16). This helps to explain some of the emphases in the Latin American literature, but this overlooked some of the major differences between the European and the Latin American situations. Among these is the fact that the European movements were a reaction against some of the consequences of successful development and took for granted the rule of law and other democratic freedoms; in Latin America on the other hand social movements were a response to underdevelopment and the failure of the state to integrate the majority into the benefits of modernity, and they were often responding to harsh military regimes that violated the law with impunity and eliminated democratic freedoms. An appreciation of these differences, as well as a more critical engagement with the new social movements literature, has led theorists of Latin American social movements to advocate 'a careful blending of the two prevailing theoretical and methodological approaches' (Alvarez and Escobar: 319). Furthermore, as Radcliffe writes, it came to be recognized that 'the transformatory potential of social movements was often celebrated too soon' (1999: 214) and a new emphasis became evident in the literature whose objective is 'to understand actual mobilizational experiences – warts and all' (Oxhorn, 2001a: 164).

Confronting or Surviving Neoliberalism?

The return to democracy throughout Latin America in the 1980s and 1990s was to show up what Lievesley calls 'the fragmented, defensive and vulnerable character of much popular organization' (1999: 122). While in a number of cases, social movements had played a key role in popular mobilization against military dictatorships (Chile, Uruguay, Peru, Argentina, Brazil, El Salvador), 'the movements begin to lose impetus once negotiations begin with the incumbent regime, and parties or proto-parties begin to move to centre stage' (Foweraker: 104). In this new situation, parties and state elites set institutional agendas that have the effect of marginalizing social movements from policy-making and influence. Indeed, in the eyes of many who previously looked to them for leadership, their *raison d'être* is lost as political activism is channelled through institutionalized political systems. In a context where the state was more responsive to popular demands, where less NGO funding was available, and where the Catholic Church was returning to the sacristy feeling itself under threat from the inroads of evangelical groups, a new and more difficult situation was created for social movements.

If military dictatorships presented social movements with an antagonistic and often repressive state against which to mobilize and unite, the return to democracy presented them with a state offering funding and a response to their demands. This was to prove a far more difficult terrain in which to operate: 'Since social movements are often competing for the same scarce resources, the state responds selectively to their demands, so separating them and even setting them one against the other' (Foweraker: 68). What is presented as an offer of partnership can often have the effect of co-opting and controlling (see Box 10.2). Political parties, which under dictatorships looked to social movements as providing spaces for political mobilization, seek to control and demobilize them once democracy is reinstated. This is because they provide competition for political loyalties and, in the tense political situation following a return to democracy, offer the potential for destabilizing the agreement reached between military and civilian elites. Foweraker writes: 'In general it appears that political party activity is always potentially divisive of social movements at the local and community level in Latin America' (p. 84). The return to democracy, therefore, has served to highlight that social movements have limits to their autonomy and do not constitute a homogeneous collective social actor with shared aims and means. As Lievesley points out, they are heterogeneous, 'with groups mobilizing around diverse agendas which may not always be compatible' (1999: 104). The divisions may stem from identity issues such as gender, class or ethnicity, or from different levels of consciousness. Susan Stokes found out in her examination of attitudes of social activists in a Lima shanty town in the 1980s that some espoused direct action, leading the people on marches to the city centre to occupy offices, while others had a clientelistic outlook and sought favours from political leaders and state officials. The former were democratic in their practice and saw their struggles for social improvements as steps on the way to greater social transformation while the latter were hierarchical and their objectives limited to winning improved social conditions for their neighbours (Stokes, 1991). Yet, for Alvarez and Escobar, the very fluidity of social movements' practices can allow them to engage with the state without necessarily being co-opted nor losing their socially transformative goals. As they write, 'when no single organization can claim to represent a movement, it is more difficult for politicians or policymakers to manipulate or distort the goals of the movement as a whole. Moreover, the existence of numerous groups or organizations, pursuing similar overall goals through different strategies and tactics, may simply mean that a given movement's sociocultural and political agenda is being articulated simultaneously in a wide range of institutional and extrainstitutional arenas – and this can have potentially salutary effects' (pp. 323–4). Radcliffe identifies the common features that characterize the approach of social movements in this new situation:

1 Their focus of action is often around specific issues rather than an elaborated programme, though these issues can change over time.
2 Movements arise from the failure of institutions to respond adequately to
  their interests and seek the satisfaction of their demands by institutions.
3 They creatively use a wide range of practices, strategies and tactics to
  achieve their goals, often shifting between protest, resistance and proposals.
4 Their power rests on their ability to mobilize and pressurize local governments, central government or powerful groups. (1999: 204–7)

It is clear therefore that Latin American social movements are not limited to the
social sphere but that they are also political, seeking change usually through
putting pressure on the state, though the issues they highlight are often ones
neglected by the state (such as the needs of the poor or gender issues). In this
way, they construct an intermediate sphere between civil society and the state
(Foweraker: 62).

Box 10.2 'Popular participation' or political control?

Philip Oxhorn has written that, historically, strong civil societies have been
constructed based on a wide understanding of what constitutes citizenship and
its rights (Oxhorn, 2001b: 33). With the advent of the neoliberal reformation and
under pressure from agencies like the World Bank and the Inter-American
Development Bank, Latin American states are expressing an interest in fostering
an active citizenship and designing mechanisms for greater popular participation
in public affairs. In this way they are redefining the meaning of citizenship and
helping channel its forms of expression.

   Despite the inclusive rhetoric, however, an examination of states' practice
reveals a narrowly conceived logic based, as Schild writes, 'on individual subjects
as bears of rights who must entrepreneurially fashion their overall development
through wider relations to the marketplace' (1998: 96). Within this view, active
citizenship entails promoting opportunities for individuals to access the market
and hold the state accountable. It entails an atomized conception of society and
a suspicion of collective social actors, whether they be political parties, trade
unions or social movements. This logic can be seen to operate through various
mechanisms of 'popular participation'.

   Examining the Bolivian experience (see Box 5.3), Oxhorn finds it based on a
very Western view of the rights of the individual citizen and he highlights the fact
that the Law of Popular Participation gives no recognition nor role to the
traditionally strong and militant Bolivian unions (both urban and rural). Instead
the new local democracy is based on giving legal recognition to territorial
indigenous and neighbourhood organizations. He concludes that what he calls
this top-down form of 'social engineering' is working well where such
organizations had helped foster a truly activist civil society that can hold local
government accountable. Yet in many parts of the country, a weak civil society is
not a strong enough counterweight to prevent co-option of local politics by the
political vested interests of central government (Oxhorn, 2001b).

Cunill Grau looks at mechanisms set up by various Latin American governments to permit citizens to examine the actions of government agencies and hold them accountable. She finds that what is missing are social actors with a strong sense of citizenship and with sufficient resources and access to information that would allow them to fulfil this role. She concludes that 'a way of opening up such conditions has hardly begun in Latin America' and she recommends strong social pressure on the state to achieve this (1997).

Under military dictatorships, Non-Governmental Organizations (NGOs) had emerged as powerful actors for fostering a more organized civil society through developing strong social movements. Under democratic governments, however, as foreign sources of funding are fast drying up, more and more NGOs have been forced to transform themselves into agencies that bid for government contracts to provide social services. As Cardelle puts it, 'NGOs are adapting to the new political agenda of aid, which emphasizes business cooperation, investment climates, and efficiency over concepts of solidarity and distribution', as they compete among one another for short-term government funding and cease the consciousness-raising and social mobilizing that played such a vital role in developing a strong civil society (2001: 198). Paradoxically, therefore, states are creating the conditions that often ensure a weak, dependent and compliant civil society.

In keeping with this, different spheres of social movements' action can be identified. The first is political democratization, including the defence and promotion of human rights, a sphere in which social movements were intensively active under military dictatorships. Since the return to democracy, social movements have been to the forefront in keeping up pressure to ensure the accountability of the armed forces for the crimes they committed. A second sphere of action has also opened up in this situation, focusing on the quality of citizenship achieved under the new democracies and emphasizing the extension of citizenship rights and the fostering of a more egalitarian and participative political culture. This is a central focus of the mobilization of indigenous peoples throughout Latin America (see next section) and of the women's movement. Under the military dictatorships, women emerged as key protagonists in struggling both on issues of economic survival (education, health care, basic services) and for democratization. While in some cases they did this through highlighting traditional gender roles (such as the Mothers of the Plaza de Mayo protesting against the disappearance of their partners and children by the Argentine military regime), their very mobilization and the gender solidarities it helped create also led them to question the unequal distribution of power within the household and the various ways in which they, as women, were being discriminated against. As Foweraker put it, their mobilization 'caused a sea-change in their lives, from passivity to combativeness' (p. 55). Since the return to democracy, Latin American women are active on a range of issues – 'from racism and black and indigenous women's struggles to women's growing impoverishment and to sexuality and reproductive rights' – though great differences are evident among them on strategies such as whether to work through government agencies or to maintain independence, and on whether to change laws and official programmes or to create a new public culture (Alvarez, 1998: 295). A third sphere of social movement action is the socio-economic, challenging the neoliberal restructuring of the region's economies and the growing social exclusion that results. This is prompting a wave of mobilization and protest in virtually every Latin American country (see Chapter 9), though one that is often 'dispersed, irregular and discontinuous' (López Maya, 1999: 7). An example of a social movement that has emerged as a major actor in contesting social exclusion is Brazil's Landless Movement (Movimento Sim Terra, MST). Founded in 1984 as a national movement by leaders of local land struggles with the support of sectors of the Catholic Church, it works with some of Brazil's 4.5 million landless workers, encouraging and supporting land occupations. In this way it is actively challenging the policy of successive Brazilian governments which promoted the industrialization of agriculture, resulting in greater concentration of land ownership and the marginalization of small agricultural producers. For example, in 1996 there were 398 land occupations throughout the country, involving 63,000 families, of which about half were carried out by MST members. Through its active mobilizations, it has transformed the issue of agrarian reform 'into one of the principal struggles of the Brazilian working class' and has emerged as one of the country's leading social movements (Fernandes, 1999: 108). Some authors see in movements like the MST 'the emergence of a new revolutionary Left in Latin America' (Petras, 1999: 13).

A more careful assessment of this widespread social activism, however, points to its limited achievements. Perhaps it is in the sphere of democracy and citizenship that most has been achieved, spheres that, for Oxhorn, unite all social movements since by and large the state is the focus of their demands and they are all 'trying to change what it means to be a citizen in their own countries' (2001a: 180). As is clear from the examples given in Boxes 10.1, 10.3 and 10.4, civil society is very active in reconstructing an active citizenry giving voice to a range of demands. They therefore can be said to have enhanced the quality of citizenship in the region's restricted democracies, through placing previously suppressed or marginalized demands on the political agenda, claiming rights to better state services and to land, and increasing popular participation in public life (Alvarez and Escobar: 327–8). Furthermore, beyond immediate gains, social movements are helping to erode authoritarian legacies and define a wider and more inclusive political culture. As Warren writes about Guatemala, the Pan-Maya movement 'has already contributed to a paradigm shift in the way ... many indigenous and Ladino Guatemalans think about the country' (quoted in Oxhorn, 2001a: 177). The impact of social movements is therefore best understood as being 'gradual and cumulative'; as they 'search for ways to express and represent popular demands ... the many small contests and conflicts can and do add up to a more comprehensive challenge to traditional political practices' (Foweraker: 112).

Yet, as Foweraker recognizes, social movements have two kinds of demands – one is for greater inclusion of the poor and marginalized in the existing system but the second is for changing the nature of the system (pp. 80–1).

States and ruling elites can satisfy the first, at least partially, though in doing so they may resort to clientelism and co-option, offering as favours what should be universal entitlements to all. Demands for more fundamental economic and social change are, however, actively resisted and social movements have had far less success in turning the tide of the neoliberal reformation. Alvarez and Escobar acknowledge this: 'We now know that social movements are unlikely to radically transform large structures of domination or dramatically expand elite democracies, certainly in the short run.' But they quickly add: 'Smaller transformations in power relations of daily life and in the practice of institutional politics, promoted by social movements, *are* in evidence today' (pp. 325–6; emphasis in original). It can be concluded therefore that social movements are more successful in helping the excluded survive neoliberalism than they are in challenging and changing it. As Scott put it:

> Social movements are agents of social change but not, as their theorists often suggest, necessarily or usually of total social transformation. Social movements typically bring about change, or attempt to bring it about, not by challenging society as a whole, though they may appear to do so, but by opposing specific forms of social closure and exclusion. (1990: 150)

The Emergence of Indigenous Peoples

'Indigenous peoples present perhaps the most striking challenge to the dominant cultural and social-economic models of *Latin* American societies,' write Alvarez and Escobar (1992: 328; emphasis in original). Three phases of their treatment over the 500 years since the European conquest can be identified. Firstly, there were the attempts at extermination, some instances of which can be found down to the twentieth century. For example, during the colonization of Patagonia from the 1850s onwards, the Tehuelche peoples were hunted and killed by the sheep ranchers of southern Chile who sought to use the land they roamed. The second phase appeared more benign as governments sought to assimilate their indigenous peoples through integrating them into the labour market and developing the areas where they lived. Known as 'indigenism', this was the dominant policy over the first half of the twentieth century and reflected the attempt to create national cultures which recognized indigenous elements but sought to integrate them into a *mestizo* or mixed culture. The third phase reflected the rise of the left whose militants sought to convince indigenous peoples of their primary 'class' identity as urban workers or, more often, rural *campesinos*. Once the left got to power, they were promised, their progress would be assured. All these ways of dealing with Latin America's original peoples were based on a failure to see anything positive in their cultures, languages or way of life. They were widely viewed as backward, primitive, even deficient, and racist treatment was rampant. In the eyes of the state, they were reduced to the status of the poor, while for many Latin Americans they had become invisible except for their use as 'native colour' in tourist brochures. Therefore, the 'emergence of the indigenous question' in the 1990s has taken governments and analysts by surprise. One reason is the leadership provided by well-educated, young indigenous, the beneficiaries of governments' integration policies, who both develop a new political agenda but also dedicate themselves to fostering and protecting their people's distinctive cultural traditions, languages and cosmovision. Among the structural causes is the undermining of the socialist paradigm with the end of the Cold War as this greatly weakened the appeal of a form of self-identification (as an oppressed class) that had exercised a great influence on many indigenous groups. Another is the neoliberal reformation as this undermined the capacity of the state to hold out to indigenous groups the promise that integration into national citizenship held benefits for them. However, globalization also features as a cause as the impact of global economic forces on local communities is, throughout the world, prompting the emergence of 'identity politics' where issues of racial, religious, linguistic and gender identities emerge as fundamental constituents of community struggle, what Manuel Castells calls 'the power of identity' (1997). The most forceful expression of this in Latin America is among indigenous peoples.

It is estimated that there are about 400 identifiable native peoples in Latin America who total altogether some 40 million people. These range from small groups of the Amazonian jungle to the Quechuas and Aymaras in the highlands of Peru and Bolivia who number some millions. Mexico, with about 10 million indigenous inhabitants, has the largest native population in Latin America but this constitutes only about 10–15 per cent of its population. In Bolivia and Guatemala, on the other hand, indigenous peoples constitute a majority of the population. In Ecuador and Peru they total about half the national population. Though in Brazil, the native peoples of the Amazonian jungle constitute only about 0.5 per cent of the population, they lobbied successfully to have their rights incorporated in the 1988 constitution (Stavenhagen, 1997: 62–3). Bengoa sees four stages in the emergence of indigenous peoples as important social actors. The first stage he dates to the 1980s when indigenous peoples in many countries began to recognize that beyond their struggles over land or other material resources lay struggles over ethnic identity and that both were inextricably linked. This new recognition also formed the basis for fostering links with other indigenous groups, out of which ethnic confederations began to be formed. The second stage came with the mobilization of indigenous peoples throughout Latin America to oppose the official celebrations in 1992 of the 500 years of the 'discovery' of the Americas. Calling their response '500 years of indigenous resistance', committees were formed in most countries of the region that organized counter-events. The award of the Nobel Peace Prize that year to the Guatemalan indigenous woman Rigoberta Menchú also gave important international recognition. 'It was a context in which new indigenous identities, new discourses over ethnicity, new organizations and new movements were able to emerge,' writes Bengoa (2000: 88). The third stage is marked by two major events: indigenous mobilization in Ecuador throughout the 1990s (see Box 10.3) and the Zapatista uprising in the southern Mexican state of Chiapas on 1 January 1994. 'The novelty of this movement,' writes Bengoa, 'is the active participation of tzeltales, tzotziles, tojolabales and other groups of indigenous who are fully aware of their ethnic identity' (p. 104).

Indeed, in some villages, the first public communiqué about the uprising was given in native languages. The fourth stage Bengoa sees as happening is the many ways in which Latin American states are responding to the demands being made by their indigenous peoples, including giving legal and constitutional recognition, often for the first time, to their distinctive identity. He sums up what has happened over these four stages as 'a "reinvention" of the indigenous question by indigenous leaders themselves. At the turn of the century, the actual situation of indigenous is no longer that of isolated communities studied as "folk societies" by anthropologists as happened for decades but an ever more complex combination of urban and rural relations, with international links and in permanent confrontation between their ethnocultural tradition and modernity' (pp. 20–1).

Box 10.3 Ecuador: Indigenous contest the state

'The massive marches, blockades, and protests that became known as the June 1990 uprising marked the dramatic reentrance of indigenous people onto the national stage of Ecuadorian politics,' writes Lucero (2001: 61). The economic crisis of the 1980s, with rising prices of foodstuffs and agricultural inputs, a halt to agrarian reform which had given land to *campesino* families, policies that favoured agroexports over production for the home market, and the scarcity of construction work in urban areas which put an end to the practice of temporary migration as a means of generating family income, had fuelled rural discontent. Alongside this another process was taking place as indigenous organizations began to create confederations, firstly the Confederation of Indigenous Nationalities of Ecuadorian Amazonia (CONFENIAE) in 1982 and the Confederation of Indigenous Nationalities of Ecuador (CONAIE) in 1986, thus uniting both the highland and Amazonian indigenous. This strengthened the tendency to channel rural discontent along ethnic lines, moving beyond land issues to contesting the nature of the state itself. But indigenous mobilization also attracted other social sectors such as trade unionists, non-indigenous *campesinos*, informal workers and ecologists, who found there a vehicle for pressing their own demands.

   Again and again since 1990, CONAIE has led mass protests and forced the state into negotiating. Celebrating 500 years of indigenous resistance in 1992 established it as Ecuador's most important social movement. In 1994 it mobilized to prevent passage of the Agrarian Law that sought to put a legal end to agrarian reform. In 1996, following extensive debate, CONAIE established an indigenous political party, the Pachakutik Plurinational Unity Movement (MUPP), named after an Inca leader. Winning 20 per cent of the national vote and 10 per cent of congressional seats, this has allowed indigenous representatives to press their demands through the political system. As a result, the 1998 reform of the constitution defines Ecuador as a multicultural and plurinational country, recognizes the collective rights of indigenous peoples, and declares respect for their ancestral medical and judicial practices. In 1997, CONAIE took part in the huge manifestations that led to the resignation of President Abdala Bucaram. In

1999 it led a march of 15,000 on Quito and in 10 hours of talks with President Jamil Mahuad forced him to retreat on price rises and to modify his handling of a major banking crisis. In January 2000, CONAIE responded to President Mahuad's announcement of dollarization by setting up 'popular parliaments' in every province and 'a parliament of the peoples' in Quito. With the help of junior army officers, the indigenous occupied Congress and a Junta of National Salvation was established including an army colonel, a former Supreme Court chief justice and the CONAIE president, Antonio Vargas. Following an ultimatum from military chiefs, President Mahuad resigned, though the same chiefs replaced him with vice-president Gustavo Noboa rather than recognize the Junta. President Noboa's neoliberal reforms led to another uprising in February 2001 that was initially met with a hardline military response. Leaders were arrested and protestors fired upon. However, intensive international pressure, mobilized through an internet campaign resembling that of the Zapatistas in Mexico, forced the government to negotiate with indigenous leaders, resulting in a pledge to 'forge a new kind of relationship between the state and indigenous peoples' (quoted in Lucero, 2001: 69).

In these ways, as Lucas puts it, the indigenous movement has shown itself to be 'the only one capable of paralyzing the country, and became a feature of politics in Ecuador that could no longer be ignored' (Lucas, 2000: 4). Its impact on the country has been summed up as follows: 'Through organizational and agitational activity, indigenous organizations like CONAIE succeeded in changing the political culture of Ecuador from one in which Indians literally had to ride in the back of buses to a pluricultural one in which Indians occupy public office at every level' (Lucero: 67).

This has given rise to numerous forms of struggle – such as mass mobilizations and marches, land occupations, and creative protests[1] – but indigenous peoples have also begun to engage with the state, winning seats in parliament, participating in constituent assemblies drawing up national constitutions, and taking part in consultations with multilateral bodies such as the UN Working Group on Indigenous Peoples and the Inter-American Commission of Human Rights. Rejecting development ideologies of right and left such as the promises held out by modernization or by social revolution, the new indigenous leadership articulates what Stavenhagen says is not an ideology but rather 'an indigenous cosmovision'. He identifies five elements in this: (1) that their self-definition as peoples be given legal recognition (a rejection of the practice of centuries when their status was defined for them by others, whether Christian missionaries or government bureaucrats); (2) that their communal landholding be given legal status, since they see this as essential for their way of life; (3) that their cultural identity be recognized and fostered through, for example, education in their own languages or other forms of active support; (4) that their forms of social organization and local juridical customs be given legal and administrative recognition; and (5) that they be given self-governing autonomy over ancestral regions (1997: 69–73). In furthering these demands, they have built alliances with other social groups, among them ecologists with whom they share a profound respect for the integrity of nature. Over the 1990s many Latin American states conceded some of their demands, at least in law if not always in practice. For example, the 1996 peace treaty between the Guatemalan state and the URNG guerrilla front, that put an end to decades of brutal ethnocide by the state, contained an agreement on the identity and rights of the country's Mayan peoples, including advanced clauses on cultural recognition, self-government at municipal level and communal landholding. However, the state has proved slow in implementing these. In Nicaragua, the Sandinista government conceded autonomy to the indigenous peoples of the Atlantic Coast. In Bolivia, the leader of the indigenous party, the Tupac Katari Liberation Movement (MRTKL), Victor Hugo Cardenas, became the country's vice-president from 1993 to 1997 when his party entered into an electoral alliance with the MNR. While the gesture has been criticized for being more symbolic than substantive, his period in office was marked by a constant reiteration of indigenous rights, and the country's constitution was changed to recognize the state as 'multiethnic and pluricultural'. Constitutional reform in Colombia in the early 1990s gave constitutional recognition to indigenous territorial rights and established seats in the Senate for indigenous representatives. The constitutions of Argentina, Brazil, Ecuador, Guatemala, Mexico, Nicaragua, Panama, Paraguay, Peru and Venezuela were also changed to recognize indigenous rights and identities.

However, two examples illustrate the limits of what states are currently willing to concede to their native peoples. In Mexico, as in Guatemala, indigenous rights formed a major element of the San Andres accords reached between the state and the Zapatistas (EZLN) but implementation remained stalled. When Vicente Fox assumed the presidency in December 2000, he pledged to undo centuries of humiliation for the country's indigenous peoples and to pass an indigenous law establishing their rights. In support of these moves, the Zapatistas' leader, Subcomandante Marcos, led a 3,000 km march of thousands of sympathizers from the Lacandon jungle in Chiapas to the capital, arriving to a tumultuous welcome on 11 March 2001. During their two weeks in the capital, the Zapatista leadership addressed the Mexican Congress, reminding legislators of their debt to the country's 57 indigenous nations. Following their return, however, and when the indigenous law was passed by Congress, the EZLN rejected it 'as not responding in the slightest to the demands of Mexico's indigenous peoples' (Ramonet, 2001: 7). They were concerned that the indigenous rights conceded by the constitutional reform were diluted and even negated by other constitutional clauses and laws, while no recognition was given to the municipal and regional autonomy already achieved by indigenous in Chiapas and confirmed in the San Andres accords. The second example concerns the struggles of the Mapuche peoples in the south of Chile. Following the end of the Pinochet dictatorship, they achieved legal recognition, a mechanism was established to give them land, and bilingual education was provided. But the state has been unwilling to support indigenous rights against the multimillion dollar Ralco hydroelectric plant which will flood the lands of 84 Pehuenche families, a subgroup of the Mapuches (Bengoa, 2000: 117–25). In an attempt to prevent the plant being built, indigenous leaders have resorted to militant tactics, including ambushing and burning the huge turbines as they were being transported to the site. As these examples illustrate, the requirements of economic progress or the fears of undermining national unity through conceding recognition to indigenous peoples as separate nations having rights to autonomy pose limits to how far states are willing to go. This may succeed in only further radicalizing indigenous groups.

'Globalization-from-Below'?

The networking of social movements across borders signifies another form of globalization, what some call the emergence of a 'global civil society'. For Jan Aart Scholte this is composed of social movements and civic associations that engage in some or all of the following:

1　Address issues that transcend borders such as AIDS, climate change or reform of international agencies such as the World Bank, the United Nations or the World Trade Organization;
2　Communicate and network globally through travel, the use of the internet and e-mail to collect and disseminate information across borders;
3　Organize across borders by having members in more than one country. Examples of such groups would be Amnesty International or the campaign for international debt reduction which draws on groups in more than one country;
4　Work based on the aspiration to transnational solidarity such as the campaign for the Tobin tax on international financial speculation or attempts to develop universal norms of child protection (Scholte, 2000: 178–82).

Richard Falk sees in the emergence of a global civil society the possibility of what he calls a 'globalization-from-below' which reacts against and may even counteract some of the detrimental impacts of 'globalization-from-above', namely 'the way in which transnational market forces dominate the policy scene, including the significant co-optation of state power' (1999: 130). Furthermore, he contrasts the homogeneity of globalization-from-above with the diversity, and even tension and contradiction, of globalization-from-below. 'This contrast highlights the fundamental difference between top-down hierarchical politics and bottom-up participatory politics. It is not a zero-sum rivalry, but rather one in which the transnational democratic goals are designed to reconcile global market operations with the well-being of peoples and with the carrying capacity of the earth. Whether such a reconciliation is possible is likely to be the most salient political challenge at the dawn of a new millennium' (pp. 135–6).

In the succession of major UN world summits, from the Rio summit on the environment in 1992 to the Istanbul summit on habitat in 1996, Falk identifies 'a flow of gatherings that acknowledged to varying degrees the emergent role of globalization-from-below' (p. 134). These summits mobilized social movements and NGOs from all over the world who gathered in NGO fora parallel to the intergovernmental meetings to contest the agenda of states, to influence the outcomes achieved, and to network among themselves, thus strengthening global civil society. The presence of groups from Latin America at these summits is an indicator of the extent to which the region is participating in this bottom-up participatory global politics, while the development in Latin America of a World Social Forum is another (see Box 10.4).

Box 10.4 World Social Forum: 'Another world is possible'

For six days in late January and early February 2001, some 12,000 people from 120 countries gathered in the southern Brazilian city of Porto Alegre for the first World Social Forum under the title 'Another World is Possible'. Held to coincide with the annual gathering of senior world politicians, financiers and multinational entrepreneurs at the Swiss resort of Davos where they discuss the state of the world economy, in Porto Alegre leading figures in the struggle against neoliberal globalization gathered, including Uruguayan writer Eduardo Galeano, Brazilian dramatist Augusto Boal, French farm leader José Bové, former French first lady Danielle Mitterrand, and Latin American political leaders such as Mexican PRD leader Cuauthemoc Cardenas, Uruguay FA leader Tabaré Vázquez, Brazilian PT leader Luis Ignacio 'Lula' da Silva and Porto Alegre and Sao Paulo mayors Tarso Genro and Marta Suplicy.

Discussion centred on two major themes: firstly, the formation, concentration and distribution of wealth (and as subthemes employment, environment and financial liberalization) and, secondly, 'limitations on the democracy of national states compared to the extensive liberty given financial capital and the power of organizations such as the International Monetary Fund' (Gabetta, 2001: 39). Four large conferences took place simultaneously every morning on (1) the production of wealth and social reproduction; (2) access to wealth and sustainability; (3) affirming civil society and public spaces; and (4) political power and ethics in the new society. In over 400 workshops, themes such as the following were discussed in further detail: how to implement the Tobin tax on speculative capital transactions; measures necessary to protect the environment and achieve sustainable and equitable development; how to abolish the international debt of the poorest countries and put an end to financial tax havens; eradicating poverty; respecting and broadening human rights; strengthening real democracy; promoting the defence of minorities and the liberation of women in tolerance and diversity; and applying the precautionary principle to genetic manipulation. In a television link-up with Davos, George Soros said that 'even though it would damage my interests as a financial speculator, I believe the Tobin tax would benefit humanity' (quoted in de la Fuente, 2001: 46).

A year later, the second World Social Forum brought to Porto Alegre some 70,000 people from 130 countries who participated in 900 workshops. 'From ecology to drugs, through themes such as gender, childhood, infancy and adolescence, and multiculturalism; from the Argentine crisis to world peace, through the Free Trade Area of the Americas, Afghanistan and Plan Colombia,

almost no issue was left which thousands of participants did not raise and
analyze, trying to fulfill the forum organizers' slogan – develop practical proposals
that can be studied, improved and applied in every country and at a world level'
(Gabetta, 2002: 4). Main speakers included US activist Noam Chomsky and
Portuguese Nobel Literature Prize winner José Saramago, while the Spanish
judge Baltasar Garzon, whose case against Chilean dictator Augusto Pinochet led
to his arrest in London, also attended. Given widespread publicity and coverage
by the world's media, Porto Alegre is providing a space for civil society to
promote its alternative globalization agenda.

Taking the summits at Rio, at Vienna in 1993 on human rights and at
Beijing in 1995 on women, Friedman et al. (2001) find that Latin American
NGOs and social movements participated actively in all three conferences,
dominating at Rio (since it was held in Latin America) but having a substantial presence in Vienna and Beijing as well. Latin American civil society
delegations to Beijing heeded the call for traditionally underrepresented
women to be included, such as the young and indigenous. In developing
links with governments, many of which tended to pay lip service to their
role, civil society groups showed a willingness to dialogue yet adopted positions critical of governments where warranted. For example, before Rio the
South American Ecological Action Alliance issued a statement noting Latin
American governments' failure to implement previous environmental agreements and announcing a strategy of strengthening alliances with other citizens' groups in Latin America and in other parts of the world while keeping
dialogue open with governments. Before Vienna, Latin American human
rights groups, which had a long experience of struggling to get their governments to accept their responsibilities on human rights, met the governmental
drafting committee and commented on their draft declaration. At Beijing,
civil society groups were critical of many of their governments' support for
the Vatican's attempts to sideline discussion of such issues as reproductive
rights, gays and lesbians, and abortion. In this situation, many Latin
American NGO delegates prioritized networking over lobbying their governments, while some organized imaginative protests against their governments'
stance. Finally, while Latin American governments tended to be reluctant to
cede any role to civil society groups in ongoing monitoring of the implementation of summit outcomes, such groups used the opportunity of the
gatherings to strengthen their participation in global networks, thereby
strengthening their position to advocate positions to their own governments
that remain contentious. Overall, Friedman et al. conclude that there was a
surprising amount of basic agreement between Latin American civil society
groups and their governments on issues of poverty and the environment, on
the universal nature of human rights and on neoliberal economics, though the
former voiced their critiques in language that was often 'stronger and more
targeted' (p. 27). They write: 'Latin Americans' involvement in global civil
society seems stronger than we anticipated. Latin Americans are participants
and not just followers in the reworking of global governance' (p. 32).

Serbin (2001) finds exogenous and endogenous influences on the creation of this regional civil society. Since funding for groups often comes from outside the region, such as from Northern NGOs or from such agencies as the World Bank, the Inter-American Development Bank and the Organization of American States, there is a danger that this might influence the agendas of Latin American groups, prioritizing global themes over local demands. Among the endogenous influences is the need for civil society groups to respond to the many forms of regionalization occurring in the Americas (see Chapter 6). For example, a Civil Society Forum of the Grand Caribbean has been created with links to the Association of Caribbean States, Caricom and the Central American Integration System (SICA). Various civil society networks monitor the negotiations for a Free Trade Area of the Americas (FTAA), and a Continental Social Alliance, funded by trade unions, organizes popular assemblies parallel to the Summits of the Americas 'questioning the development of free trade agreements, adjustment programmes and a form of regionalization conceived according to the dictates of the Washington Consensus' (Serbin: 81). In southern Mexico and Central America, hundreds of civil society groups and NGOs (including indigenous rights organizations, cooperatives, unions, and women's and environmental groups) are creating a broad network in opposition to Plan Puebla-Panama, demanding that they be informed and consulted about it, drawing attention to the fact that 82 per cent of its funding is for infrastructure and only 2.9 per cent for health or social development, and arguing that it will destroy local and rural economies and pose a grave risk to the region's rich biological and cultural diversity (Call, 2002). Despite these initiatives, Serbin writes that regional civil society groups still face major challenges such as the need to improve their capacity to elaborate policy proposals, putting in place mechanisms to better represent local, national and regional demands, and ensuring transparency and efficiency in decision-making and use of funds (p. 85).

Conclusions

Even though social movements have become an established part of all Latin American societies, their role and impact remains circumscribed by both state and market. The power of trade unions has been severely eroded in the liberalized economy and their very survival is under threat. The most militant new social movements, such as indigenous movements in Mexico and Ecuador, are actively contesting the powers of state and market, and their actions have had a major impact on their societies. At best, however, these movements exercise a certain veto over aspects of economic liberalization rather than offering an alternative to neoliberalism. Meanwhile, social movements and NGOs are being drawn into collaboration with states and, in some cases, even becoming successful players in the market (such as NGOs winning contracts to run public services against private-sector competition). Over the longer term, it is likely that the work and struggles of social movements are helping to foster a more democratic culture, in particular giving a voice and some modest power to groups that have been long excluded from an equitable share in power and resources, including poor urban and rural dwellers, women and indigenous peoples. However, at a time when growing levels of social polarization are fuelling a crisis of governability, social movements are failing to channel the energy and demands of civil society in a more constructive direction. Paradoxically, when a strong and active civil society is more than ever needed, states seem determined to constrain and rein-in the creative potential of social movements.

Note

[1] For example, on International Women's Day 2002, an indigenous Mapuche woman climbed on the stage during the Chilean government's official celebration in Santiago and in a dignified but insistent way began to ask the Minister for Women's Affairs why indigenous women were not being given a voice. The photographs of male security guards ejecting her as the Minister looked on dominated the coverage of the event in the media.

Section IV

Prospects

11

Latin America in the Twenty-First Century

P redicting the future is, even in the most stable situations, a hazardous undertaking. The history of the social sciences is littered with firm predictions which the complexity of historical change has quickly proven to be totally mistaken. Amid the uncertainties and volatility of a fast-globalizing world, it would be foolhardy to predict what lies in store for Latin America and the Caribbean. Yet, neither should the social scientist be content simply with analysing the past, since it is out of that past that the future emerges. The tools of social scientific analysis therefore provide instruments that help identify the structures and forces shaping the future and the complex interactions between them. While this knowledge can never capture the entire range of variables that configure outcomes in any particular historical place or moment, nor the role of accidents or agents in influencing those outcomes, it can help to delimit the principal structural features and social forces out of whose interactions the future will emerge. This should serve as a strong warning against attempting to predict the future but it does open possibilities for deepening our understanding of the prospects facing us. Acknowledging these possibilities places a responsibility on the social scientist to contribute to public debate and policy-making, being yet another actor, albeit a very modest one, in helping shape the future. Some social scientists, particularly neoclassical economists, play this role with such certainty that their contributions often serve to narrow the range of public awareness and the content of policy, which in some cases has contributed to disastrous consequences for hundreds of millions of men, women and children around the globe. For example, the economic and social analyses of the World Bank are often criticized by other social scientists for the ways in which they seek to impose a particular interpretation (of a country's economy or of a wider issue of public concern such as world poverty) as the only correct one, thus restricting the horizons of debate and of policy. To a large extent, this flows from the nature of economics as 'problem-solving theory' with its narrow focus on solving problems at the expense of an understanding of the historically constituted nature of the wider social structures in which these problems are embedded (see Chapter 1 for a discussion of this issue).

The approach used in this book, which in Chapter 1 was explained and entitled the international political economy of development (IPED), adopts a wider and more historical focus in attempting to identify 'the forces driving social change today, as well as the constraints or possibilities they produce'. As has been illustrated in the previous chapters, such an approach uses a variety of methods to capture the complex economic, political, social and cultural dimensions of social processes and their impact at regional, national, local and even personal levels. This results in a more multifaceted analysis in which a wider range of variables are identified, something that should induce in the social scientist a sense of humility when facing the task of outlining future prospects. Yet this very complexity offers what is perhaps the richest contribution to discussions of social change, since it refuses to reduce such change to the limited horizons of the problem-solving theorist, particularly the economist. The possibilities offered by the IPED approach in elucidating the parameters of future change was illustrated in Chapter 8's discussion of the prospects for Cuba's uncertain transition. In this chapter, the approach is used to discuss the prospects for Latin America and the Caribbean as it is integrated more and more into a globalized world. The first section offers a reading of the positive and negative features of the way the region has integrated itself into the international system, placing these in the context of the present era of globalization. Section two focuses on different countries and regions within Latin America and the Caribbean, identifying those best placed to benefit from globalization and those most likely to be more and more marginalized. The following section takes the discussion further, in seeking to distinguish the various forces shaping the region's future, both internal and external forces, and the prospects for a more developmental form of globalization to emerge. The final section argues that Latin America and the Caribbean is a laboratory for the nature of the future world order and that it offers evidence as to whether this globalized order can satisfy widespread aspirations for an equitable, sustainable and humane development for all peoples, especially the poorest.

Optimism or Pessimism?

Latin America is no newcomer to globalization. Some date the beginnings of globalization to the region's incorporation into a North Atlantic economy following the Spanish and Portuguese conquest in the sixteenth century. However, the emergence of a largely worldwide trading economy is usually dated to around 1870 with advances in steamships, railways and the telegraph all helping to draw hitherto distant parts of the world into a single trading network. Unlike most of Africa and much of Asia at the time, Latin America was deeply integrated into this first phase of globalization, which was to last until the disruption of the First World War, exporting unprocessed raw materials and foodstuffs and importing manufactured goods, from household appliances to railways (see Chapter 3). While this produced economic growth for the region, the benefits flowed largely to the land-owning and mining elites rather than to the majority of Latin Americans. The disruption of the First World War lasted through the Great Depression of 1929 and the rise of protectionism that followed, until a new phase of globalization opened after the

Second World War. This second phase lasted until the oil crisis of 1973 and was characterized by growing international trade in manufactured goods but strong national restrictions on capital and labour mobility, resulting in what is often called 'the golden age of welfare capitalism', especially in the industrialized countries of North America and Western Europe. Following inward-oriented industrialization policies during this period, Latin America saw a drastic reduction in its participation in world trade, from 9.3 per cent in 1950 to 3.9 per cent in 1973 (CEPAL, 2002: 32). However, as shown in Table 11.1, this was the period in which Latin America achieved its highest levels of economic growth in modern times which, with the exception of Japan, were the world's highest rates at the time; it also achieved substantial social advances over this period. A third phase of globalization opened from the mid 1970s onwards, gathering force gradually and by the 1990s generalizing itself throughout the world. This is characterized by an ever greater mobility of capital, by the considerable expansion of trade worldwide drawing regions like Latin America ever more deeply into international trade networks, by the increasing similarity or homogenization of development models in all parts of the world (the triumph of neoliberalism), by the growing global dominance of transnational corporations in the production of goods and services, and by continuing restrictions on labour mobility.

The third stage of globalization has opened new opportunities for Latin America to overcome some of the limitations that gradually undermined its protectionist, state-led development model in the 1970s. Among these limitations were the failure to find export markets for its manufactured products, the inefficiencies and high costs induced by protectionism and the very limited competition it fostered, and the lack of investment in technological and productive upgrading. Embracing these new opportunities enthusiastically, the region has registered one of the world's highest rates of growth in merchandise trade, both in volume and in value. Between 1990 and 2001, the export of goods from Latin America and the Caribbean has grown by an annual average rate of 8.4 per cent in volume and by 8.9 per cent in value. These rates were exceeded only by China and the most dynamic Asian countries. Furthermore, the nature of the goods being exported by the region has shown a marked change. The share of primary products and goods based on processing natural resources in the region's total exports has fallen from 73.5 per cent in 1985 to 44.3 per cent in 2000, while that of high-, intermediate- and low-technology manufactured goods has grown from 24.3 per cent in 1985 to 52.3 per cent in 2000. Foreign direct investment (FDI) grew more than five-fold, from an annual average of $18 billion in 1990–4 to a high of $103 billion in 1999, before falling back to $59 billion in 2001 under the impact of the US economic downturn. European investments grew notably over the period, and Spain emerged as the second largest source of foreign investment after the United States (CEPAL, 2002: 175–96). Inflation, which had reached over 1,000 per cent annually in some Latin American countries in the 1980s and early 1990s, was reduced from an average of 877 per cent for the region as a whole in 1993 to 7.5 per cent in 2001 (CEPAL, 2001c: Table A-7, p. 38). Apart from the strictly economic effects of globalization, the region's reintegration into the

TABLE 11.1 GDP GROWTH RATES BY REGION, 1820–1998 (AVERAGE ANNUAL INCREASES, %)

Region	1820–70	1870–1913	1913–50	1950–73	1973–98
Latin America and the Caribbean	1.37	3.48	3.43	5.33	3.02
USA, Australia, New Zealand and Canada	4.33	3.92	2.81	4.03	2.98
Western Europe	1.65	2.1	1.19	4.81	2.11
Japan	0.41	2.44	2.21	9.29	2.97
Asia (excluding Japan)	0.03	0.94	0.9	5.18	5.46
Eastern Europe and former USSR	1.52	2.37	1.84	4.84	-0.56
Africa	0.52	1.4	2.69	4.45	2.74
World	0.93	2.11	1.85	4.91	3.01

Source: CEPAL, 2002: Table 2.8, p. 52

international political system has helped strengthen its links with North America (through the Summits of the Americas) and Europe (through the Rio Group) (see Chapter 6), and reinforced the process of democratization throughout Latin America. The globalization of such values as respect for the rule of law and the accountability of state agents for their violations of human rights (as powerfully symbolized by the arrest of former Chilean dictator General Augusto Pinochet, in London in 1998) is also contributing to a changing political culture in the region. Finally, Latin America has made notable advances in the second half of the 1990s in internet connectivity, a central social component of the third phase of globalization, increasing the numbers connected between 1995 and 2000 from 0.2 to 5.6 per 1,000 people, the largest such increase among developing regions (CEPAL, 2002: 227–31).

While such advances point towards an optimistic reading of the opportunities opened by globalization for Latin America's development, an understanding of the fuller picture offers grounds for greater pessimism and a more negative assessment of globalization (see Box 11.1). For example, the region's dynamic export growth has been accompanied by an even higher growth of imports, reaching average annual increases of 11.7 per cent in volume and 11.6 per cent in value over the 1990–2001 period. This is leading to growing trade deficits which, together with service payments on the region's foreign debt and profit remittances by foreign companies, is resulting in a growing deterioration in the balance of payments. This grew steadily from the late 1980s until the mid 1990s when it stabilized at an average of 3 per cent of regional GDP. Furthermore, high levels of international trade and foreign investment are not translating into high levels of economic growth, which has only managed an average annual rate of 2.7 per cent between 1990 and 2001, equivalent to a third of the rate of increase in exports and a quarter of the rate of imports. As CEPAL put it in 2002:

> The contrast between strong export dynamism and the region's great capacity to attract foreign direct investment and, on the other hand, the weak dynamism of overall productive activity is, without doubt, one of the most significant facts of the regional situation over the past decade. In fact, despite the region's economic turnaround in the 1990s, its rhythms of economic growth continue being significantly inferior to those before the debt crisis. (2002: 178)

Four principal characteristics of Latin America's insertion into this third phase of globalization can be identified:

1 *Volatility.* Two types of volatility are evident. The first is volatility of economic growth which has gyrated like a rollercoaster over the 1990s with peaks of growth in 1994, 1997 and 2000, followed by troughs as short-term capital flowed out of the region in response to sudden changes in foreign investor confidence, often for reasons that have little to do with any real problems in the economy. This volatility of capital flows (short-term credit lines and portfolio flows) results in exchange rate volatility as inward capital flows tend to raise the value of a domestic Latin American currency

Box 11.1 'The sickness of the new millennium'

In an interview in the Miraflores presidential palace in Caracas in 2001, President Hugo Chavez of Venezuela offered his views on globalization:

Globalization has been built on the dogma of neoliberalism. It is nothing else than the effort to implement worldwide the neoliberal dogma, the false idea that, with the fall of the Berlin Wall and the Soviet Union, history itself has come to an end and that neoliberal capitalism has emerged victorious. This is dogma, a sort of fundamentalist religion. Many, blindly and uncritically, have been pushed to support a model that is being presented as if the end of history was the bridge to happiness.

We have to study well the position of the anti-globalization movement. It is not a homogenous movement, with one single position. We have to analyze what inspires it. Why has it emerged with such force? It is like water: when an attempt is made to dam it, it attacks with more fury. We must listen to the people, to workers, to students, to the indigenous peoples, to the peasants, to the middle classes, to the professionals, and from their standpoint rethink the world.

I believe that this world being constructed is not viable. No peaceful future is in store for the world by means of neoliberal globalization. Therefore it is a sickness. We are reconsidering this, rethinking it, and based on this, trying to contribute to a new way forward. (2001: 4–5)

(since demand to buy it is growing), which then drops precipitously when capital leaves (since the domestic currency is being sold). This tends to deepen recessions, and require painful economic adjustments.

2   *Asymmetry.* Latin America's reinsertion in the global economy in the 1990s has highlighted marked asymmetries between production in the most developed countries, characterized by high levels of technological innovation and specialization, and production in regions like Latin America which is concentrated in less dynamic sectors, such as primary products or assembly. The concentration of technological production in the industrialized countries has been growing with the liberalization of the world economy (as the privatization of state firms in regions like Latin America has weakened greatly indigenous capacity for technological innovation) and the tightening of intellectual property protection under World Trade Organization (WTO) rules. This structural hierarchy built into the nature of the world economy results in growing disparities between average incomes in developed and developing countries. The third phase of globalization has been found to be accentuating inequalities both within countries and between the developed and developing world (see CEPAL, 2002: 82–7).

3   *Vulnerability.* Heightened vulnerability to sharp swings in economic growth results from the volatility of capital flows. The liberalization of capital flows has weakened the ability of developed countries to adopt

policies to deal with this phenomenon, unlike industrialized countries which tend not to suffer from the same sharp inflows and outflows, and which possess a greater ability to manage financial instability due to the inherent strength of their currencies as media of international exchange (the dollar, the euro and the yen). Macroeconomic vulnerability translates into increased social vulnerability for the majority of Latin Americans through increasing unemployment and higher risks of poverty (see Chapter 7). CEPAL estimates that, apart from the 35 per cent of regional households in poverty, a further 25–30 per cent are at risk of falling into poverty, since they live just above the poverty line (2002: 335). In some countries, this includes middle-class sectors. Finally, environmental vulnerability is growing due both to the increased incidence of socio-natural disasters and to the greater social destruction they are causing (see Chapter 7).

4 *Dependence.* The third phase of globalization has increased Latin America's dependence on outside forces. This is true, for example, of various features of the region's productive economy resulting from the neoliberal reformation such as the linking of subsectors with others outside national economies rather than stimulating employment and production through developing linkages with domestic producers, or the fact that foreign firms are capturing ever larger shares of the Latin American market (see Chapter 4). To these must be added the region's loss of capacity for technological innovation. Finally, the failure to expand national savings over the course of the 1990s means that increases in investment over the decade depended on foreign investment.

Winners and Losers

As well as asymmetries between regions in the global economy, there are growing asymmetries within Latin America and the Caribbean. Depending on such 'given' features as geographical location, natural resources, demography, and the economic structures inherited from the past, as well as on policy choices, political leadership and regional or global opportunities, some countries have made major advances, while others have seen stagnation or even declines. Listing annual average changes in per capita incomes over the 1990s, as is done in Table 11.2, offers an initial identification of winners and losers, showing some dramatic success cases and some equally dramatic failures. However, since this only captures incomes at a particular moment in time it does not capture the full picture and may give a misleading impression of what are the more enduring success cases. For example, extending the period by even one year into 2001 would reduce Argentina's ranking, since the country was experiencing its worst economic crisis ever with negative growth over an extended period (see Box 11.4). Peru's positive performance must be seen against the backdrop of major declines in living standards in the 1980s (between 1986 and 1990, per capita income fell by 31 per cent (ECLAC, 1995: Table 1, p. 132)). Therefore, in the early 1990s it was largely returning to where it had been before the crisis of the 1980s rather than substantially

TABLE 11.2 GDP PER CAPITA (IN 1995 US$) AND
PERCENTAGE INCREASE, 1990–2000

Country	1990	2000	Change
Chile	3,425	5,309	35.4
Dominican Republic	1,370	2,035	32.6
Argentina	5,545	7,305	24
Peru	1,894	2,390	20.7
El Salvador	1,406	1,749	19.6
Uruguay	4,707	5,841	19.4
Mexico	3,925[a]	4,831	18.7
Costa Rica	2,994	3,672	18.4
Panama	2,700[b]	3,306	18.3
Bolivia	816[b]	951	14.1
Guatemala	1,347[b]	1,554	13.3
Brazil	3,859	4,337	11
Nicaragua	454	482	5.8
Colombia	2,158[a]	2,282	5.4
Honduras	686	709	3.2
Venezuela	3,030	3,097	2.1
Ecuador	1,472	1,417	−3.8
Paraguay	1,697	1,552	−9.3

[a]1989. [b]1991.

Source: Calculated from CEPAL, 2001a: Table 1,
pp. 181–2

improving its people's living standards. Indeed, its performance in the late 1990s has been far less impressive. On the other hand, Mexico's relatively poor performance reflects the impact on living standards of the country's 1994 financial crisis; since 1996 average incomes have shown significant increases. Finally, the appearance of the Dominican Republic very high on the list indicates that country's success in tourism and in attracting *maquiladoras* in textiles and clothing. However, this latter success against competition from other Caribbean countries is based on low-wage labour and attractive incentives for multinational companies.

To identify more accurately the enduring winners and losers, it is necessary therefore to examine a wider range of evidence. Table 11.3 shows the percentages of the total foreign direct investment going to Latin America and the Caribbean by the countries and subregions it goes to, in 1999, 2000 and 2001. Correlating this with population figures given in Chapter 1 reveals how some countries are much more integrated into transnational capital flows than are others. Brazil, as the largest country, would be expected to get the largest amount of FDI. However, it is revealing to compare Colombia with Argentina, both countries with similar populations, to compare Chile with Peru or Venezuela which are both substantially larger, or Uruguay with Paraguay as the latter has the larger population. Table 11.3 therefore allows us to identify countries, and indeed regions, that are succeeding in capturing some of the benefits of globalization and those whose relative marginalization from these benefits runs the risk of seeing them left further and

TABLE 11.3 FOREIGN DIRECT INVESTMENT IN LATIN AMERICA BY COUNTRY AND SUBREGION, 1999–2001 (% OF TOTAL FDI TO THE REGION)

Country	1999 (%)	2000 (%)	2001[a] (%)
Argentina	23	13.3	9
Bolivia	0.9	0.8	0.9
Brazil	27.4	37.5	29
Chile	8.8	4.2	7.4
Colombia	1.4	2.7	3.8
Ecuador	0.6	0.8	1
Mexico	11.4	15.2	21.4
Paraguay	0.08	0.09	0.13
Peru	2.2	0.7	1.2
Uruguay	0.2	0.3	0.4
Venezuela	3	4.7	1.8
Central America and the Caribbean	5	4.1	5

[a] Based on preliminary estimates.

Source: Calculations based on CEPAL, 2002: Table 6.5, p. 198

further behind. Correlating the evidence from Tables 11.2 and 11.3 gives a firmer basis for identifying winners and losers. Based on this, the Andean region emerges as being particularly marginalized, both in its integration into capital flows and in its performance on raising living standards, whereas Brazil, Mexico and the Southern Cone countries are succeeding better. However, high levels of inequality in countries like Brazil and Chile reminds us that they are failing to distribute well the benefits of this success. The performance of Central American and Caribbean countries is more differentiated and warrants further investigation.

A further means of identifying how well placed countries are to avail of globalization is through looking at their export profiles. This is particularly revealing for smaller countries which, due to the limitations of their domestic market, depend more for their economic success on exporting. One traditional measure of success is the extent to which countries have been able to move away from a dependence on exporting primary commodities and have moved into the export of manufactured goods, particularly those requiring more sophisticated technology since this builds up skill levels among the workforce, gives workers higher earning power, and makes countries more competitive in high value-added sectors. This also allows the region's principal exporting companies to be identified, showing the extent to which Latin American companies have become global players and whether their main activities are in primary commodity exports or in more sophisticated manufactured goods (see Box 11.2). Overall, primary product exports have fallen from 50 per cent of Latin America's total exports in 1985 to 27.3 per cent in 2000. However, for the Andean Community (Bolivia, Peru, Ecuador, Colombia and Venezuela) they have remained constant, at 59.8 per cent in 1985 and 59.5 per cent in 2000. While Venezuelan oil accounts for a significant proportion of this, in all the other countries, with the exception of Peru, primary

Box 11.2 Latin American companies go global

From the mid 1960s, Latin American transnational companies have featured on the *Fortune* list of the world's top 500 corporations (measured by their revenues). These were mostly state companies involved in the extraction and export of primary commodities, including the Mexican, Argentine, Brazilian, Venezuelan and Colombian state oil companies and the Chilean copper company, Codelco. In 1975, Latin American corporations constituted over 30 per cent of all Third World corporations on the *Fortune* list. However, with the emergence of the East Asian developmental states and other Third World economic success cases such as China and India, the number and percentage of Latin American corporations on the list fell from a high of eleven in 1985 to five in 2001 when they constituted 16 per cent of corporations with headquarters in Third World states. The still state-owned oil companies of Venezuela, Mexico and Brazil remained the largest Latin American corporations in 2001 (Sklair and Robbins, 2002).

Turning to the region's main export companies, listed by the value of their exports, the Venezuelan and Mexican oil companies head the list in 2000. Of Latin America's 20 top export companies, 11 were foreign-owned in that year and these were mostly in manufacturing such as the auto and computer industries. Among the nine companies owned by Latin American capital, four were state-owned (the Venezuelan, Mexican and Colombian oil companies and the Chilean copper company) and five privately owned, in tobacco, commerce, cement and mining. Only the Brazilian aerospace company, Embraer, was in a high-tech manufacturing sector (CEPAL, 2002: Table 6.8, p. 196).

commodities still constitute over half their exports (in Peru they constitute 42 per cent). At the other end of the spectrum, less than 1 per cent of the Andean Community's exports are made up of high-technology manufactured goods and a further 6.4 per cent of intermediate-technology goods. Mexico presents a very different profile, having reduced its primary commodity exports from 53 per cent of its total exports in 1985 to 12 per cent in 2000 while increasing its high-tech exports from 10 per cent to 25 per cent and its intermediate-tech exports from 18 to 39 per cent over the same period. This has been greatly helped by NAFTA and Mexico's integration into North American assembly circuits, including assembling of televisions, computers and telecommunication equipment. Brazil too, though less dependent on exports due to the large size of its domestic market, has reduced its primary commodity exports from 38 per cent to 27 per cent and steadily increased its intermediate- and high-tech manufactured exports (from 22 per cent to 33 per cent) over the period. At first glance, the Southern Cone region presents a profile closer to that of the Andean Community, with 46 per cent of its exports still being primary commodities, a decrease from 52 per cent in 1985. Indeed Chile, seen as one of the region's leading economic success cases, has almost the same percentage of primary commodity exports in 2000 (40.3 per cent) as in 1985 (41 per cent)

(CEPAL, 2002: Table 6.3, p. 184). However, with the exception of Paraguay, the Southern Cone countries have succeeded in breaking into what are called Non-Traditional Exports (NTEs) such as fruits, vegetables and fish for North American, European and, in Chile's case, Asian markets which require high quality control and do not suffer in the same way as do traditional commodities from a long-term decline in the prices they fetch on the international market. But having won markets for such products through entering them early, countries like Chile face ever more intense competition as more and more countries try to enter the same markets. An example is the emergence of Vietnam as a significant exporter of coffee (after oil, the most traded commodity and the largest source of export earnings for developing countries): in the early 1990s it decided to develop coffee as a 'non-traditional export' and by 2000 had displaced Colombia as the world's second largest coffee producer and exporter (Ramirez-Vallejo, 2002: 26). On the other hand, Argentina, Uruguay and, to a lesser extent, Chile have had some successes in exporting intermediate- and high-tech manufactured goods.

The two microregions of Central America and the Caribbean present a very diversified picture. Though overall figures for the Central American Common Market (Guatemala, El Salvador, Honduras, Nicaragua and Costa Rica) show a decline in primary commodity exports from 72 per cent in 1985 to 28 per cent in 2000, and an increase in high-tech manufactured exports from 3.7 per cent to 14.5 per cent over the same period, the latter figure is almost entirely due to Costa Rica's success in attracting high-tech manufacturing plants. Instead, the other four Central American countries depend on garment assembly for the US market, and have moved into such non-traditional exports as fruits, flowers, ornamental plants, winter vegetables and spices. An illustration of the region's new role in the globalized market place is its export of labour to the United States, Canada and places as far afield as New Zealand and Australia. As a result, remittances from its emigrants have become a major support for local economies, in 1997 constituting 15.6 per cent of El Salvador's GNP and 44.3 per cent of its export earnings, 7 per cent of Nicaragua's GNP and 17.3 per cent of its export earnings, and 3.9 per cent of Guatemala's GNP and 12.9 per cent of export earnings (Robinson, 2002: 241). Critics of Plan Puebla-Panama (see Chapter 6) argue that it is preparing the way for the region's deeper insertion into globalized trade and investment flows, which will 'open the region's natural resources to vast exploitation by multinationals, encourage rampant environmental destruction of its rich biodiversity, trample on the rights of indigenous peoples, and dislocate communities', while 'the only jobs created will be low-paying factory jobs vulnerable to flight to still more desperate populations' (Treat, 2002: 3). Finally, the Caribbean has found itself disadvantaged both by the outcome of the dispute between the United States and the European Union over the latter's preferential access for Caribbean banana exports (see Chapter 2) and by Mexico's accession to NAFTA which gives it more advantageous access for its manufactured goods to the US market. As a result, banana production has declined from 12 per cent of the Windward Islands' GDP in the early 1990s to 7 per cent in 1999 and the volume produced has fallen by 50 per cent, while manufacturing has been in decline in many of the region's countries. Caribbean countries have progressively reduced their participation in their main export markets (USA and Canada, Europe, the Andean Community and Mercosur). In this situation, tourism plays an ever greater role in the region's economies, contributing 35 per cent of external earnings and 18 per cent of GDP in 1999–2000 (CEPAL, 2002: 358). With relatively high unemployment in some countries, both intraregional and extra-regional migration has increased. Remittances from emigrants constitute 17 per cent of Haiti's GDP, 11 per cent of Jamaica's and are also significant in Granada and Saint Kitts and Nevis. Overall, therefore, most Central American and Caribbean countries are left highly vulnerable due to their integration into the third phase of globalization.

Change from Within or from Without?

Despite Latin America's success in reintegrating itself into the third phase of globalization, it is therefore far from clear that this has put it on a road to sustainable and equitable development for most of its people. Development was defined in Chapter 1 as a process leading to growing social inclusion through rising living standards, meaningful employment, active political and social participation and a satisfying cultural life extending to all sectors of society, thereby widening the life choices and possibilities for the great majority. Evidence given in Chapters 7, 9 and 10 indicates that the present form in which Latin America is integrated into the global economy is reducing rather than widening the life choices and possibilities for the majority of the region's people, while the first section of this chapter has summarized some principal structural features of this form of integration that are corroding the region's development prospects. In such a situation, the prospects for Latin America's development rest on major structural changes in the global economy and on the way in which the region is integrated into it, entailing changes both in national policies and in the nature of the world economic and political order, what CEPAL calls 'the development of a more solid globalization and a better insertion into it' (2002: 99) (see Box 11.3). This section outlines what these major structural changes might entail and the likelihood of achieving them.

Box 11.3 'An agenda for the global era'

In its study of globalization and development, prepared for the governments of Latin America and the Caribbean in 2002, CEPAL elaborates 'an agenda for the global era' (pp. 99–132). While it urges that Latin America and the Caribbean 'should adopt a positive agenda for the construction of a new international order and commit itself effectively to bringing it about', it recognizes that this requires major changes at both global and national levels. Its agenda for global change contains three objectives:

1   Guarantee an adequate supply of global public goods:[1] CEPAL stresses the contrast between the need for these and the weakness of the international structures that could provide them;

2   Correct the asymmetries in the global order through mechanisms to accelerate the transfer from developed to developing countries of such dynamic productive assets as technology, through actions by the international financial institutions to develop more adequate means to counter and manage financial instability, and through ensuring that labour mobility receives the same attention in the global agenda as capital mobility;

3   Construct an international social agenda based on recognizing all people as citizens of the world whose economic, social and cultural rights, as well as their civil and political rights, be assured at both national and global levels (pp. 100–2).

'Given the lack of adequate institutions, globalization is showing itself to be a disintegrative force,' writes CEPAL (p. 103), and it urges the development at both global and regional level of a network of institutions more adequate to ensuring the three objectives of its global agenda are adequately met. Such global action needs to be complemented by action at national and regional level, it argues. Individual states need to develop a more impartial and relatively efficient state bureaucracy to:

1   Implement a macroeconomic strategy designed to reduce vulnerability and facilitate productive investment;

2   Develop competitiveness through accumulating technological capability, fostering productive chains linking dynamic economic sectors, and providing quality infrastructure;

3   Put in place clear and coherent regulatory frameworks for environmental sustainability with adequate public resources;

4   Adopt active social policies, especially as regards education, employment and social protection (pp. 106–15).

Finally, CEPAL urges action at regional level to foster macroeconomic cooperation through, for example, regional and subregional financial institutions; to harmonize regulatory systems; to take common action to develop high-technology sectors; to harmonize infrastructure networks; to cooperate in sustainable development; to protect migrant workers and promote education; and to move towards deeper political integration (pp. 115–18).

The CEPAL agenda recognizes the weaknesses of the current third phase of globalization and promotes a form of globalization in which institutions, at global, regional and national levels, would curb the anarchy of market forces and provide the conditions to ensure that the benefits of globalization would be captured more equitably by developing countries and for the majority of the world's citizens. The strength of such an agenda is that it formulates the huge changes required if globalization is to effect equitable and sustainable development; its weakness is that its implementation rests on the goodwill of those economic and political powers who are benefiting from globalization as currently structured, and whose power has been greatly enhanced by it. Indeed, this agenda would entail a fundamental shift in power, from private economic actors (primarily global corporations) to public state and civil society actors, at global, regional and national levels. The lessons of history tell us that such major shifts in power happen through social and political struggles and therefore the prospects for realizing this agenda rest on the balance of forces between those who seek to deepen further the present form of globalization (essentially handing more and more power to market forces and reconfiguring public institutions so that they facilitate this) and those who seek to use public power to regulate market forces so that they serve equitable and sustainable social objectives.

While the balance of forces is heavily weighed towards global market forces in the present conjuncture, this balance is never set in stone and is always shifting. For example, the emergence of the so-called 'anti-globalization' movement since the late 1990s has dramatically undermined in the eyes of public opinion the credibility and legitimacy of some major forces supporting the present form of globalization (major corporations, and institutions like the World Bank, the International Monetary Fund and the World Trade Organization), thereby depriving them of some of their power and putting them on the defensive. In assessing the prospects for a new form of developmental globalization in Latin America, therefore, we need to identify the various forces ranged for and against it, and their respective power. Among these forces are structural features of the present form of globalization which configure power in particular ways, without ever predetermining outcomes. A number of these structural features have been identified in earlier chapters. For example, in Chapter 4 the international competitive advantages of Latin America and the Caribbean in the third phase of globalization were identified. For Brazil, the Southern Cone and some Andean countries, these are based on the processing of natural resources for export markets; for Mexico, Central America and some larger Caribbean islands, their advantage lies in assembling electrical goods, computers and clothes, in *maquiladoras*, principally for the US market. These tend to use low-wage and relatively unskilled labour, and involve little technological innovation. Being oriented towards external markets, they have emerged in response to market demand in the developed world (and to the advice of the World Bank) rather than emerging from internal efforts to develop competitive advantages through technological innovation and the fostering of industrial clusters. Their predominance attracts investment to further deepen and develop such activities, rather than to more innovative and high-technology activities. In using low-wage and insecure labour, they fail to develop the preconditions for strong market demand in their domestic economies, since few workers have high disposable incomes. These structural features therefore predispose the region towards supplying relatively low-wage and low-skill mass produced goods to the markets of more developed countries. To break out of this, as CEPAL recognizes, will take determined state

action at national and regional level. It will, in other words, involve a fundamental shift of orientation, away from simply responding to demand from
without and towards a new model conceived, incubated and nurtured from
within. It will need to create new competitive advantages through new structural features, such as happened with the development of import-substitution
industrialization in the mid-twentieth century, though on this occasion it will
have to be oriented towards winning export markets from its inception as well
as towards substituting for the high level of goods currently imported by the
region.

Changing structural features focuses attention on the principal actors that
have helped shape the present situation. Again, these are largely actors from
without, such as global corporations, which have emerged as major market
players in Latin America with significant political influence, the international
financial institutions whose liberalizing agenda has exercised such influence,
and the United States government, which, particularly in the wake of the
terrorist attacks of 11 September 2001, is more and more shaping its
agenda towards Latin America in security terms. As was shown in
Chapter 9, this is exercising ever more influence over its relations with
the Andean region but elements of Plan Puebla-Panama also seem oriented
to stem emigration from the region to the United States. As the history of
US–Latin American relations during the Cold War period showed only too
clearly, prioritizing security comes at the expense of equitable and sustainable development. Turning to internal actors, Latin America's insertion into
the third phase of globalization has tended to weaken some, such as political parties and the trade union movement, while fragmenting others, such
as the state, domestic business and social movements. As a result, some
sectors of the state, some domestic businesses and some social movements
may help foster stronger indigenous capacities, while others are strongly
bound to the interests of global economic forces. Tilting the balance of
forces towards a more developmental globalization will require that internal
actors emerge with greater strength and a distinct agenda to counter the
strong liberalizing forces from without. As is clear from Box 11.3, CEPAL is
increasingly providing that agenda but the social actors in most societies
remain at present too weak and fragmented to implement it with determina-
tion, in many cases more wary of sending negative signals to markets than
determined to lay the foundations of a more beneficial form of globalization.

However, in many ways the international balance of forces is moving in
favour of a more developmental globalization. Civil society action is developing among citizens and their leaders a new awareness of the economic and
social vulnerability being caused by the present form of globalization and the
threat this poses to more open societies and economies (as evidenced by the
political rise of the ultra-right in Europe). Concrete proposals are emerging for
a new financial architecture to regulate volatile capital flows and to reform the
large international institutions, making them more transparent and accountable. Consumers are becoming more conscious of workers' exploitation and
environmental damage and using their market power to demand reforms.

While all these are very fragile developments, they indicate a turning of the tide and the end of the 'born-again' zeal for the market that marked the 1980s and 1990s. Furthermore, the inherent contradictions of a world economic system that seeks to maximize growth and production while simultaneously undermining consumer markets as inequality grows and many workers lose buying power makes the present system ever more unsustainable. Amid the crisis of ungovernability that increasingly engulfs Latin American countries, the conditions are growing for a more determined shift in the direction indicated by CEPAL. Whether such a shift actually happens depends on how domestic actors use the new opportunities opening up to them.

In this situation, three alternative scenarios can be delineated:

1   *The conservative.* This essentially would mean a continuation of the present situation, in which Latin American countries remain caught in productive activities that fail to generate developmental benefits for the majority. This would be a recipe for growing social breakdown and political turmoil.
2   *The reformist.* This would see piecemeal reforms being implemented involving, for example, social programmes to help ease burdens on the poor, political changes that make politicians more accountable, and economic investments that seek to upgrade productive capacity and win new markets. While these might help defuse some of the more explosive social unrest, they are unlikely to lay the foundations for a more beneficial form of globalization.
3   *The radical.* This would involve more determined efforts to reform global and local economic and political institutions, shifting power back to public bodies and away from private market actors, and ensuring effective forms of social protection for the majority. While this seems the least likely scenario at the turn of the twenty-first century, the conditions may grow over time that make the need for it more obvious.

Outlining such scenarios offers a conceptual framework for understanding how things may develop; it does not attempt to second-guess history. Certainly, how history develops over the coming decades of the new millennium will be more messy and untidy than any conceptual framework can capture. But the framework may help make sense of the general trends emerging beneath the flux of historical events. The lessons of Latin American history over the past two centuries with its shifts from primary commodity exporting to import-substitution industrialization and then on to neoliberalism teach us that dominant models can persist for decades as conditions and social forces build up that eventually lead to a shift to a new model. The region's history also teaches that the most adequate responses come from within, open to wider currents of international thinking, but with Latin American academics, decision-makers, political parties, business groups and social movements fashioning creatively a road forward for their own countries. Watching how this happens over the coming decades will be fascinating.

A Laboratory for Tomorrow's World Order

Of all the major regions of the world, Latin America and the Caribbean is perhaps the clearest test case as to whether the market-led prescriptions of the international financial and development institutions hold out the prospect of equitable and sustainable development for most of the world's people. It is a region with long experience of integration into the world economy and, compared with many African and some of the poorer Asian states, it has well-developed institutions of state and civil society (such as universities and research institutes, political parties, and an experienced private business sector). In development terms, most of its countries fall into the middle-income category, indicating the extent of development already achieved but also the major challenges still facing them. Over the past half century, it has become a predominantly urbanized and industrialized region, offering a potential for advance that compares favourably with that for countries that are still predominantly rural and agricultural. The migration of many millions of its people into the cities over that period expresses their aspirations for greater social progress. More than any other region, its history over the past century and a half is marked by two very different and relatively coherent attempts to capture for itself the benefits of development, firstly through primary commodity exporting and secondly through import-substitution industrialization (ISI). As a result, its academics, policy-makers and politicians can draw on a rich legacy of lessons learnt from both successes and failures. Despite this and the major contributions to development thinking made by CEPAL over the decades, the region proved by and large unable to implement coherent, sustained and successful responses to the growing problems associated with ISI in the 1970s, with the result that it embraced liberalization in a situation of intense economic, political and social crisis.

This distinguishes it from the East Asian developmental states (especially South Korea, Taiwan, Singapore and Hong Kong, but also Malaysia, Thailand and Indonesia) that proved better able to manage and even benefit from the major changes in the world economy following the oil price rises in the 1970s and the Reagan and Thatcher 'counter-revolutions' of the 1980s. Crisis was to hit these societies in 1997 as a result of financial liberalization, but even in this regard it hit some more than others (Taiwan and Singapore were relatively unscathed) and South Korea and Malaysia appear to have recovered remarkably quickly. It can be concluded therefore that the indigenous developmental capacity built up by these states has left them better able to capture the benefits of a more globalized world order and to weather its storms, particularly due to their strong indigenous industrial base and the directive capacity of their states. For this reason, they are less useful as test cases of the third phase of globalization, since their ability to benefit from it derives from the success of the heterodox policies they followed in the past, policies very distinct from and even the opposite of those urged by the international financial institutions. Latin America and the Caribbean, on the other hand, despite the heterodox road the region travelled under ISI, have tried faithfully to implement the advice of the World Bank and the IMF, following

the free-market orthodoxy that dominated development and economic thinking after the end of the Cold War. It is therefore the closest we have to a
laboratory test case of the globalizing orthodoxy at the dawn of the new
millennium. A careful analysis of the impact of this orthodoxy on the region's
economies, politics and society holds many lessons about how this third phase
of globalization is reshaping all our societies, wherever they are located. An
analysis of particular national experiences (such as the dramatic Argentine
crisis, see Box 11.4) adds further detail to what can be learnt.

The experience of Latin America therefore tells us a lot about globalization
and what it holds in store. It provides a rich body of material for social
scientists to examine and offers the possibility for influencing the design of

---

Box 11.4 Argentina's crisis: Is globalization the culprit?

Argentina entered the new millennium suffering the worst economic crisis of its
history; indeed newspaper commentators were calling it the worst economic
crisis ever suffered by a country in peacetime. From being one of the world's
most prosperous countries a hundred years earlier and Latin America's most
developed country throughout the twentieth century, the country's economy had
been reduced in size from US$229 billion in 1998 to $156.5 billion by the end
of 2002, following four continuous years of negative growth. Incomes were only
half of what they had been four years earlier and over 50 per cent of the
population had fallen below the poverty line. 'We are the Ethiopia of Latin
America,' economist José Luis Espert said (Rodriguez, 2002: 28).

What is striking is the swift turnabout. Even in the late 1990s an informed
observer could write that, in the case of Argentina, 'global insertion and the new
political and economic internationalism ... are an undoubted success' (Lewis,
1999: 55). Is the globalization of the Argentine economy therefore a cause of its
woes? The answer lies more in the ways in which Argentine policy-makers
responded to the challenges of globalization. Three central features can be
identified. Firstly, more and more the country's exports have been based on raw
materials such as natural gas or such manufactured goods as vegetable oils, the
prices of which showed a tendency to fall during the 1990s. Secondly, the result
of fixing the peso to the dollar from 1991 until 2002 was to overvalue the
currency, making exports more expensive and imports cheaper. This was
compounded by the Brazilian devaluation in 1999, since two-thirds of Argentine
exports go to the Mercosur market dominated by Brazil. Overall, this policy
robbed Argentine policy-makers of the ability to adopt more flexible exchange
rate policies in response to changing needs. Finally, politicians misused income
generated during the boom years of the mid 1990s, building up a large foreign
debt which grew from $40 billion to $90 billion during the presidency of Carlos
Menem (1989–99). As Aldo Ferrer put it: 'The Menem government deepened
external vulnerability and has reduced to levels never before known in the
Argentine experience, the space for an autonomous economic policy' (1998:
91).

policies so that they can effectively address the need for directing markets and strengthening public power. In undertaking this task, Joseph Stiglitz reminds us that 'it is important to view problems in a dispassionate way, to put aside ideology and to look at the evidence before making a decision about what is the best course of action'. Unfortunately, during his time at the White House (as economic advisor to the Clinton administration) and at the World Bank, he says: 'I saw that decisions were often made because of ideology and politics. As a result many wrong-headed actions were taken, ones that did not solve the problem at hand but that fit with the interests or beliefs of the people in power' (Stiglitz, 2002: x). This draws the attention of social scientists to the need for a subtle dialectical interplay between theory and evidence, seeking always to ensure that the evidence is examined in as thorough and wide-ranging a way as possible and that the theory guiding the examination is adequate to the range and complexity of what is being examined. To undertake this task as well as possible, with an independence of mind, a distance from vested interests and ideology, close attention to the needs of those who suffer most from the way the world is currently structured, and a critical rigour, is the vital contribution the social scientist has to make to fashioning a better future for the world's peoples, especially the poor and marginalized.

Note

[1] As 'global public goods', CEPAL lists the following: the defence of democracy (including civil and political rights), peace, security (including combating terrorism), disarmament, international justice, the struggle against international delinquency and corruption, environmental sustainability, the mitigation and future eradication of pandemics, public health cooperation, the elimination of the world drugs problem, the accumulation of human knowledge, cultural diversity, the defence of common spaces, global macroeconomic and financial stability and, more generally, the development of public institutions that provide a framework for economic interdependence (2002: 100).

Useful Websites

The following websites will enable the reader to explore further many of the topics covered in this book, keeping in touch with developments and gaining an immediate knowledge of the positions and strategies of key actors.

This list should be regarded as a set of starting points for exploration. By no means does it exhaust the almost limitless range of possibilities provided by the internet for accessing further information, and readers are encouraged to use the many links provided at the sites listed to take them further. However, one word of caution is advisable when surfing the net: many sites encountered may provide unreliable and unsubstantiated information; indeed, there are those that provide little more than prejudiced opinions not based on fact. Seek to ensure therefore that the site is hosted by a responsible organization and develop the habit of treating information encountered on the internet with caution, always double-checking if there is any doubt about its veracity. If this is done, the internet is an invaluable tool for students, though always as an aid to rigorous analysis, never as a substitute.

Academic and Policy Analysis

Two major sites containing a wealth of academic information and analysis relating to Latin America with large numbers of links to other relevant sites are:

1   Internet Resources for Latin America, hosted by the New Mexico State University and available at:

    lib.nmsu.edu/subject/bord/laguia

2   The Latin American Network Information Center, LANIC, hosted by the University of Texas at Austin and available at:

    www.lanic.utexas.edu

FLACSO is the Latin American Faculty of Social Sciences with centres in a number of Central American and South American countries. Its site, in Spanish, is at:

www.flacso.org

The website of the Society for Latin American Studies, SLAS, provides links to all the major academic centres of Latin American studies in the UK and others in Western Europe:

www.slas.org.uk

The US-based Latin American Studies Association, LASA, is at:

lasa.international.pitt.edu

The Americas Program of the Interhemispheric Resource Center has available a range of documentation on US policy and major developments in Latin America, such as NAFTA. It is at:

www.americaspolicy.org/index.html

The Summit of the Americas Center includes up-to-date information and analysis on developments relating to the Free Trade Area of the Americas and other inter-American projects. It is at:

www.americasnet.net

Inter-American Dialogue also produces a range of valuable information on the Americas. It is at:

www.iadialog.org

Organizations

Many intergovernmental organizations also produce large amounts of high-quality academic and policy-oriented documentation and information. Among the leading ones are the following.

The UN Economic Commission for Latin America and the Caribbean, ECLAC, is probably the best source of information and data on the economies and societies of the region. Its website, containing a large amount of papers and reports for downloading, is at:

www.eclac.cl

The website of the Inter-American Development Bank is also a source of large amounts of reports and studies, available for downloading. It is at:

www.iadb.org

The United Nations Development Programme, UNDP, has country offices in most of the region's countries. Many of these publish reports on various aspects of development in their country. Access to these is available through the main UNDP website at:

www.undp.org

One principal activity of many national UNDP offices is to produce national or regional human development reports, applying to more local levels the analytical approach of the UNDP's annual Human Development Reports (HDR). There is a special website for the HDRs through which the text of many national and regional reports is also available for downloading. It is at:

hdr.undp.org

The International Labour Organization, ILO, has regional offices in Latin America and produces studies and reports on labour issues in the region. Its main website in English is at:

www.ilo.ch/public/english/index.htm

while access to ILO documentation on Latin America is at:

www.ilo.ch/public/english/support/lib/contact/americas.htm

The website of the Organization of American States, OAS, contains documentation on inter-American political relations. It is at:

www.oas.org

The websites of the two main regional integration models, Mercosur and NAFTA, are:

www.mercosur.org.uy
www.nafta-sec-alena.org

A comprehensive database of electoral results for countries of the region is available at the Political Database of the Americas. Its website is at:

www.georgetown.edu/pdba

Latinobarometro is a source of reliable region-wide opinion surveys and other information. It is at:

www.latinobarometro.org

Sources of information from perspectives more critical of the dominant neoliberal globalization are the World Social Forum and the Bretton Woods Project. Their websites are at:

www.forumsocialmundial.org.br/home.asp
www.brettonwoodsproject.org

News and Information Sources

Quality newspapers provide an excellent way of keeping in regular touch with developments in the region. A site containing links to large numbers of newspapers around the world, including throughout the Americas, is:

www.onlinenewspapers.com

A site providing a news service on the region is:

www.latinnews.com

Nacla publishes regular in-depth analyses of the region from a left-wing viewpoint. Its website, which provides access to the text of many of its publications, is at:

www.nacla.org

While it covers the world as a whole and not just the Americas, the liberal US magazine *Foreign Policy* has a website with valuable links which is an excellent source of information on the Americas. It is at:

www.foreignpolicy.com

One World is a website which, while covering development issues throughout the world, contains a wealth of up-to-date information and analyses on Latin America. It is at:

www.oneworld.net

Bibliography

Abel, Christopher and Lewis, Colin M. (eds) (1993) *Welfare, Poverty and Development in Latin America*. Basingstoke: Macmillan.

Acosta, Alberto (2001) *Breve Historia Económica del Ecuador*. Quito: Corporación Editora Nacional.

Acosta, Alberto (2002) 'Ecuador: Experiencias y lecciones de una economía dolarizada', unpublished paper. Quito: ILDIS.

Agüero, Felipe and Stark, Jeffrey (eds) (1998) *Fault Lines of Democracy in Post-Transition Latin America*. Miami: North-South Center Press.

Aguilo, Sergio (2002) 'Chile Entre Dos Derechas', public document, March.

Alvarez, Sonia E. (1998) 'Latin American Feminisms "Go Global": Trends of the 1990s and challenges for the new millennium', in Sonia E. Alvarez, Evelina Dagnino and Arturo Escobar (eds), *Cultures of Politics, Politics of Cultures: Re-visioning Latin American social movements*. Boulder, Colorado: Westview Press, pp. 293–324.

Alvarez, Sonia E. and Escobar, Arturo (1992) 'Conclusion: Theoretical and political horizons of change in contemporary Latin American social movements', in Arturo Escobar and Sonia E. Alvarez (eds), *The Making of Social Movements in Latin America: Identity, strategy, and democracy*. Boulder, Colorado: Westview Press, pp. 317–29.

Alvarez, Sonia E., Dagnino, Evelina and Escobar, Arturo (1998a) 'Introduction: The cultural and the political in Latin American social movements', in Sonia E. Alvarez, Evelina Dagnino and Arturo Escobar (eds), *Cultures of Politics, Politics of Cultures: Re-visioning Latin American social movements*. Boulder, Colorado: Westview Press, pp. 1–29.

Alvarez, Sonia E., Dagnino, Evelina and Escobar, Arturo (eds) (1998b) *Cultures of Politics, Politics of Cultures: Re-visioning Latin American social movements*. Boulder, Colorado: Westview Press.

Alvear, Maria Soledad (2002) '19 Países con una Sola Voz', *La Tercera*, 15 January: 7.

APDH del Ecuador (2002) *Bandera Blanca*, 1, junio. Quito: APDH.

Aravena Bolivar, Pamela (2002) 'El Fin de la Tercera Via', *El Mercurio*, 24 March 2002: D10–D11.

Arnson, Cynthia J. (ed.) (1999) *Comparative Peace Processes in Latin America*. Stanford: Stanford University Press.

Arruda, Marcos (2000) *External Debt: Brazil and the international financial crisis*. London: Pluto Press.

Azpiazu, Daniel and Vispo, Adolfo (1994) 'Some Lessons of the Argentine Privatization Process', *Revista de la Cepal*, 54: 129–47.

Bakewell, Peter (1997) *A History of Latin America: Empires and sequels 1450–1930.* Oxford: Blackwell.

Banega, Cyro, Hettne, Björn and Söderbaum, Fredrik (2001) 'The New Regionalism in South America', in Michael Schulz, Fredrik Söderbaum and Joakim Öjendal (eds), *Regionalization in a Globalizing World: A comparative perspective on forms, actors and processes.* London: Zed Books, pp. 234–49.

Barton, Jonathan R. (1997) *A Political Geography of Latin America.* London: Routledge.

Bauer, Arnold J. (2001) *Goods, Power, History: Latin America's material culture.* Cambridge: Cambridge University Press.

Beezley, William H. and MacLachlan, Colin M. (2000) *Latin America: The peoples and their history.* Fort Worth, Texas: Harcourt Brace College Publishers.

Benavente, Andrés and Jaraquemada, Jorge (2002) 'América Latina: Rebeldía social y crisis política', *La Tercera*, 16 April: 7.

Bengoa, José (2000) *La Emergencia Indígena en América Latina.* Santiago: Fondo de Cultura Economica.

Bethell, Leslie (ed.) (1984–95) *The Cambridge History of Latin America.* 11 volumes. Cambridge: Cambridge University Press.

Biehl, John (2002) 'La Soledad de Colombia', *La Tercera*, 10 March: 20.

Biekart, Kees (2001) 'The Double Defeat of the Revolutionary Left in Central America', in J. Demmers, A.E. Fernández Jilberto and B. Hogenboom (eds), *Miraculous Metamorphoses: The neoliberalization of Latin American populism.* London: Zed Books, pp. 182–200.

Bobes, Velia Cecilia (2000) *Los Laberintos de la Imaginación: Repertorio simbólico, identidades y actores del cambio social en Cuba.* Mexico City: El Colegio de Mexico.

Bonicelli, Carlos Otero (2001) *Perú: Gestión del Estado en el período 1990–2000.* Santiago: CEPAL.

Bonilla, Adrián (2001) 'Colombia, Estados Unidos y Seguridad Nacional en los Países Andinos', *Iconos*, 11: 17–28.

Bresser Pereira, Luiz Carlos (1996) *Economic Crisis and State Reform in Brazil: Toward a new interpretation of Latin America.* Boulder, Colorado: Lynne Rienner.

Bresser Pereira, Luiz Carlos (1998) 'La Reconstrucción del Estado en América Latina', *Revista de la Cepal*, numero extraordinario, October 1998: 105–10.

Brockett, Charles D. (1998) *Land, Power and Poverty: Agrarian transformations and political conflict in rural Central America.* 2nd edn. Boulder, Colorado: Westview Press.

Browitt, Jeff (2001) 'Capital Punishment: The fragmentation of Colombia and the crisis of the nation-state', *Third World Quarterly*, 22 (6): 1063–78.

Buitelaar, Ruud and van Dijek, Pitou (eds) (1996) *Latin America's New Insertion in the World Economy: Towards systemic competitiveness in small economies.* Basingstoke: Macmillan.

Bull, Benedicte (1999) 'Multilateral Development Banks and Governance Reforms: A proposed approach', Working Paper 1999: 4, Centre for Development and the Environment (SUM), University of Oslo.

Bull, Benedicte (2000) 'The Quest for De-politicizing Telecommunications in Central America: Does privatization matter?', Working Paper 2000: 2, Centre for Development and the Environment (SUM), University of Oslo.

Bulmer-Thomas, Victor (1987) *The Political Economy of Central America since 1920*. Cambridge: Cambridge University Press.

Bulmer-Thomas, Victor (1994) *The Economic History of Latin America since Independence*. Cambridge: Cambridge University Press.

Bulmer-Thomas, Victor (ed.) (1996) *The New Economic Model in Latin America and Its Impact on Income Distribution and Poverty*. Basingstoke: Macmillan.

Bulmer-Thomas, Victor and Dunkerley, James (eds) (1999) *The United States and Latin America: The new agenda*. London: Institute of Latin American Studies.

Burgos-Debray, Elisabeth (ed.) (1984) *I, Rigoberta Menchú*. London: Verso.

Burki, Shahid Javed and Perry, Guillermo E. (1998) *Beyond the Washington Consensus: Institutions matter*. Washington DC: The World Bank.

Bushnell, David and Macauley, Neill (1994) *The Emergence of Latin America in the Nineteenth Century*. 2nd edn. Oxford: Oxford University Press.

Buxton, Julia and Phillips, Nicola (eds) (1999a) *Case Studies in Latin American Political Economy*. Manchester: Manchester University Press.

Call, Wendy (2002) 'Resisting the Plan Puebla-Panama', Americas Program. Silver City, New Mexico: Interhemispheric Resource Center (available at: www.americaspolicy.org).

Caponi, Orietta (2001) 'La Nueva Doctrina', in Aurora Morales (ed.), *Cuadernos Bolivarianos: Materiales para el estudio N. 1*. Caracas: MVR, pp. 31–7.

Cardelle, Alberto (2001) 'Democratization, Health Care Reform, and NGO-Government Collaboration in the 1990s: Catalyst or constraint?', in Jeffrey Stark (ed.), *The Challenge of Change in Latin America and the Caribbean*. Miami: North-South Center Press, pp. 185–215.

Cárdenas, Miguel Eduardo (2001) 'Colombia: La persistente búsqueda de alternativas', *Nueva Sociedad*, 175: 20–7.

Cardoso, Eliana and Helwege, Ann (1995) *Latin America's Economy: Diversity, trends, and conflicts*. Cambridge, Massachusetts: The MIT Press.

Cardoso, Fernando Henrique and Faletto, Enzo (1979) *Dependency and Development in Latin America*. Berkeley: University of California Press.

Carranza, Mario Esteban (2000) *South American Free Trade Area or Free Trade Area of the Americas? Open regionalism and the future of regional economic integration in South America*. Aldershot: Ashgate.

Castañeda, Jorge G. (1993) *Utopia Unarmed: The Latin American Left after the Cold War*. New York: Knopf.

Castells, Manuel (1997) *The Power of Identity*. Oxford: Blackwell.

Castells, Manuel (1998) *End of Millennium*. Oxford: Blackwell.

Centeno, Miguel Angel (1997) 'Cuba's Search for Alternatives', in Miguel Angel Centeno and Mauricio Font (eds), *Toward a New Cuba? Legacies of a revolution*. Boulder, Colorado: Lynne Rienner, pp. 9–24.

CEPAL (2000) *Un Tema de Desarrollo: La reducción de la vulnerabilidad frente a los desastres*. Mexico City: CEPAL.

CEPAL (2001a) *Panorama Social de América Latina 2000–2001*. Santiago: CEPAL.

CEPAL (2001b) *México: Evolución económica durante 2000*. Mexico City: CEPAL.

CEPAL (2001c) *Situación y Perspectivas: Estudio económico de América Latina y el Caribe, 2000–2001*. Santiago: CEPAL.

CEPAL (2001d) *Estudio Económico de América Latina y el Caribe*. Santiago: CEPAL.

CEPAL (2001e) *Una Década de Luces y Sombras: América Latina y el Caribe en los años noventa*. Santiago: CEPAL.

CEPAL (2002) *Globalización y Desarrollo*. Santiago: CEPAL.

Chalmers, Douglas A., Vilas, Carlos M., Hite, Katherine, Martin, Scott B., Piester, Kerianne and Segarra, Monique (eds) (1997) *The New Politics of Inequality in Latin America: Rethinking participation and representation*. Oxford: Oxford University Press.

Chavez, Hugo (2001) 'Globalización: La enfermedad del nuevo milenio', *Foreign Affairs en Español*, 1 (3): 3–28.

Chen, Shaohua and Ravallion, Martin (2000) 'How Did the World's Poorest Fare in the 1990s?', Policy Research Working Paper 2409, The World Bank Development Research Group.

Collier, Simon, Skidmore, Thomas E. and Blakemore, Harold (1992) *The Cambridge Encyclopedia of Latin America and the Caribbean*. Cambridge: Cambridge University Press.

Conniff, Michael L. (ed.) (1999) *Populism in Latin America*. Tuscaloosa, Alabama: University of Alabama Press.

Coronil, Fernando (1997) *The Magical State: Nature, money, and modernity in Venezuela*. Chicago: University of Chicago Press.

Cotler, Julio and Grompone, Romeo (2000) *El Fujimorismo: Ascenso y caída de un regimen autoritario*. Lima: Instituto de Estudios Peruanos.

Cox, Robert W. (1995) 'Critical Political Economy', in Björn Hettne (ed.), *International Political Economy: Understanding global disorder*. London: Zed Books, pp. 31–45.

Cox, Robert W. (1999) 'Civil Society at the Turn of the Millennium: Prospects for an alternative world order', *Review of International Studies*, 25 (1): 3–28.

Crabtree, John (1999) 'Peru', in Julia Buxton and Nicola Phillips (eds), *Case Studies in Latin American Political Economy*. Manchester: Manchester University Press, pp. 107–21.

Crawley, Andrew (2000) 'Toward a Biregional Agenda for the Twenty-first Century', *Journal of Interamerican Studies and World Affairs*, 42 (2): 9–34.

Cunill Grau, Nuria (1997) *Repensando lo Público a Través de la Sociedad: Nuevas formas de gestión y representación social*. Caracas: Nueva Sociedad.

Davis, Harold Eugene (1972) *Latin American Thought: A historical introduction*. New York: The Free Press.

de la Fuente, Alejandro and Glasco, Laurence (1997) 'Are Blacks "Getting Out of Control"? Racial attitudes, revolution, and political transition in Cuba', in Miguel Angel Centeno and Mauricio Font (eds), *Toward a New Cuba? Legacies of a revolution*. Boulder, Colorado: Lynne Rienner, pp. 53–71.

de la Fuente, Victor Hugo (2001) 'La Sociedad Civil en Marcha', in *Otro Mundo es Posible*. Santiago: Le Monde Diplomatique, pp. 45–7.

de Ramón, Armando, Couyoumdjian, Ricardo and Vial, Samuel (1993) *Historia de America II: Ruptura del viejo orden hispanoamericano*. Santiago: Editorial Andres Bello.

de Ramón, Armando, Couyoumdjian, Ricardo and Vial, Samuel (2001a) *Historia de America I: La gestación del mundo hispanoamericano*. 3rd edn. Santiago: Editorial Andres Bello.

de Ramón, Armando, Couyoumdjian, Ricardo and Vial, Samuel (2001b) *Historia de America III: América Latina. En búsqueda de un nuevo orden (1870–1990)*. Santiago: Editorial Andres Bello.

del Olmo, Rosa (2000) 'Ciudades Duras y Violencia Urbana', *Nueva Socied*, 167: 74–86.

Demmers, Jolle, Fernández Jilberto, Alex E. and Hogenboom, Barbara (eds) (2001) *Miraculous Metamorphoses: The neoliberalization of Latin American populism.* London: Zed Books.

Dilla Alfonso, Haroldo and González Núñez, Gerardo (1997) 'Participation and Development in Cuban Municipalities', in Michael Kaufman and Haroldo Dilla Alfonso (eds), *Community Power and Grassroots Democracy: The transformation of social life.* London: Zed Books, pp. 55–83.

Dilla Alfonso, Haroldo and Oxhorn, Philip (2001) 'Virtudes e Infortunios de la Sociedad Civil en Cuba', *Nueva Sociedad*, 171: 157–75.

Dollar, David and Kraay, Aart (2000) 'Growth *Is* Good for the Poor', Development Research Group. Washington DC: The World Bank.

Domínguez, Jorge I. (2001) 'Cuban Foreign Policy and the International System', in Joseph S. Tulchin and Ralph H. Espach (eds), *Latin America in the New International System.* Boulder, Colorado: Lynne Rienner, pp. 183–206.

Dornbusch, Rudiger and Edwards, Sebastian (1991) *The Macroeconomics of Populism in Latin America.* Chicago: The University of Chicago Press.

Draibe, Sonia M. (1994) 'Neoliberalismo y Politicias Sociales: Reflexiones a partir de las experiencias latinoamericanas', *Desarrollo Económico*, 34 (134): 181–96.

Dresser, Denise (2002) 'The Making of El Presidente', *Foreign Policy*, January/February 2002, pp. 84–6.

Dunning, John H. (2000) 'Globalization and the New Geography of Foreign Direct Investment', in Ngaire Woods (ed.), *The Political Economy of Globalization.* Basingstoke: Macmillan, pp. 20–53.

ECLAC (1995) *Social Panorama of Latin America.* Santiago: ECLAC.

ECLAC (1999) *Social Panorama of Latin America 1998.* Santiago: ECLAC.

ECLAC (2000a) *Equity, Development and Citizenship.* Santiago: ECLAC.

ECLAC (2000b) *Social Panorama of Latin America 1999–2000.* Santiago: ECLAC.

ECLAC (2001a) *Social Panorama of Latin America 2000–01.* Santiago: ECLAC.

ECLAC (2001b) *A Territorial Perspective: Towards the consolidation of human settlements in Latin America and the Caribbean.* Santiago: ECLAC.

Edwards, Sebastian (1995) *Crisis and Reform in Latin America: From despair to hope.* New York: Oxford University Press for the World Bank.

Ellner, Steve (1998) 'Izquierda y Política en la Agenda Neoliberal Venezolana', *Nueva Sociedad*, 157: 125–36.

Erisman, H. Michael (2002) 'The Cuban Revolution's Evolving Identity', *Latin American Politics and Society*, 44 (1): 145–53.

Escobar, Arturo and Alvarez, Sonia E. (1992) 'Introduction: Theory and protest in Latin America today', in Arturo Escobar and Sonia E. Alvarez (eds), *The Making of Social Movements in Latin America: Identity, strategy, and democracy.* Boulder, Colorado: Westview Press, pp. 1–15.

Evans, Peter (1979) *Dependent Development: The alliance of multinational, state and local capital in Brazil.* Princeton: Princeton University Press.

Evans, Peter (1995) *Embedded Autonomy: States and industrial transformation.* Princeton: Princeton University Press.

Fajnzylber, Fernando (1994) 'ECLAC and Neoliberalism', *Revista de la Cepal*, 52: 205–8.

Falk, Richard (1999) *Predatory Globalization: A critique.* Cambridge: Polity Press.

Fernandes, Bernardo Mancano (1999) 'La Territorialización del Movimiento de los Trabajadores Sin Tierra en Brasil (MST)', in Margarita López Maya (ed.), *Lucha Popular, Democracia, Neoliberalismo: Protesta popular en América Latina en los años de ajuste.* Caracas: Nueva Sociedad, pp. 73–110.

Ferrer, Aldo (1998) *El Capitalismo Argentino*. Buenos Aires: Fondo de Cultura Económica.

Ferrer, Aldo (1999) *De Cristóbal Colón a Internet: América Latina y la globalización*. Buenos Aires: Fondo de Cultura Económica.

Foweraker, Joe (1995) *Theorizing Social Movements*. London: Pluto Press.

Franco, Rolando (1996) 'Social Policy Paradigms in Latin America', *Revista de la Cepal*, 58: 9–23.

Frank, André Gunder (1967) *Capitalism and Underdevelopment in Latin America: Historical studies of Chile and Brazil*. New York: Monthly Review Press.

Frieden, Jeffry A. (1991) *Debt, Development, and Democracy: Modern political economy and Latin America, 1965–1985*. Princeton, New Jersey: Princeton University Press.

Frieden, Jeffry, Pastor Jr, Manuel and Tomz, Michael (eds) (2000) *Modern Political Economy and Latin America: Theory and policy*. Boulder, Colorado: Westview Press.

Friedman, Elisabeth Jay, Hochstetler, Kathryn and Clark, Ann Marie (2001) 'Sovereign Limits and Regional Opportunities for Global Civil Society in Latin America', *Latin American Research Review*, 36 (3): 7–35.

Furtado, Celso (1976) *Economic Development of Latin America: Historical background and contemporary problems*. Cambridge: Cambridge University Press.

Furtado, Celso (1999) *El Capitalismo Global*. Mexico City: Fondo de Cultura Económica.

Gabetta, Carlos (2001) 'Porto Alegre: Activismo y propuestas para un future distinto', in *Otro Mundo es Posible*. Santiago: Le Monde Diplomatique, pp. 35–40.

Gabetta, Carlos (2002) 'Laboratorio por una Mundialización para el Hombre', *Le Monde Diplomatique*, Chilean edition, No. 17, March: 4–5.

Giddens, Anthony (1998) *The Third Way: The renewal of social democracy*. Cambridge: Polity Press.

Giddens, Anthony (1999) *Runaway World: How globalisation is reshaping our lives*. London: Profile Books.

Giddens, Anthony (2000) *The Third Way and Its Critics*. Cambridge: Polity Press.

Gill, Lesley (2000) *Teetering on the Rim: Global restructuring, daily life, and the armed retreat of the Bolivian state*. New York: Columbia University Press.

Gómez, José Javier (2001) 'Vulnerabilidad y Medio Ambiente'. Unpublished paper. Santiago: CEPAL.

Gonzalez, Guadalupe (2001) 'Foreign Policy Strategies in a Globalized World: The case of Mexico', in Joseph S. Tulchin and Ralph H. Espach (eds), *Latin America in the New International System*. Boulder, Colorado: Lynne Rienner, pp. 141–81.

Gordon, Lincoln (2001) *Brazil's Second Chance: En route toward the First World*. Washington DC: Brookings Institution Press.

Gott, Richard (2000) *In the Shadow of the Liberator: Hugo Chavez and the transformation of Venezuela*. London: Verso.

Green, Duncan (1995) *Silent Revolution: The rise of market economics in Latin America*. London: Cassell and LAB.

Green, Duncan (1999) 'A Trip to the Market: The impact of neoliberalism in Latin America', in Julia Buxton and Nicola Phillips (eds), *Developments in Latin American Political Economy: States, markets and actors*. Manchester: Manchester University Press, pp. 13–32.

Griffith-Jones, Stephany (2000) *International Capital Flows to Latin America*. Serie Reformas Economicas No. 55. Santiago: ECLAC.

Grindle, Merilee S. (2000a) *Audacious Reforms: Institutional invention and democracy in Latin America.* Baltimore: Johns Hopkins University Press.

Grindle, Merilee S. (2000b) 'The Social Agenda and the Politics of Reform in Latin America', in Joseph S. Tulchin and Allison M. Garland (eds), *Social Development in Latin America: The politics of reform.* Boulder, Colorado: Lynne Rienner, pp. 17–52.

Grugel, Jean (1996) 'Latin America and the Remaking of the Americas', in Andrew Gamble and Anthony Payne (eds), *Regionalism and World Order.* Basingstoke: Macmillan, pp. 131–67.

Guedes da Costa, Thomaz (2001) 'Strategies for Global Insertion: Brazil and its regional partners', in Joseph S. Tulchin and Ralph H. Espach (eds), *Latin America in the New International System.* Boulder, Colorado: Lynne Rienner, pp. 91–115.

Guerrero Barón, Javier (2001) 'Is the War Ending? Premises and hypotheses with which to view the conflict in Colombia', *Latin American Perspectives*, 28 (1): 12–30.

Guillén Romo, Hector (1997) *La Contrarevolución Neoliberal en México.* Mexico City: Ediciones Era.

Guimaraes, Roberto P. (1997) 'The Environment, Population, and Urbanization', in Richard R. Hillman (ed.), *Understanding Contemporary Latin America.* Boulder, Colorado: Lynne Rienner, pp. 177–207.

Gwynne, Robert N. (1999) 'Globalization, Neoliberalism and Economic Change in South America and Mexico', in Robert N. Gwynne and Cristóbal Kay (eds), *Latin America Transformed: Globalization and modernity.* London: Arnold, pp. 68–97.

Gwynne, Robert N. and Kay, Cristóbal (eds) (1999) *Latin America Transformed: Globalization and modernity.* London: Arnold.

Halebsky, Sandor and Harris, Richard L. (eds) (1995) *Capital, Power, and Inequality in Latin America.* Boulder, Colorado: Westview Press.

Hardy, Clarisa (2002) 'Redefinición de las Políticas Sociales', in Luciano Tomassini (ed.), *La Modernización del Estado en América Latina: Experiencias y desafíos.* Santiago: LOM.

Hartlyn, Jonathan (2002) 'Democracy and Consolidation in Contemporary Latin America: Current thinking and future challenges', in Joseph S. Tulchin (ed.), *Democratic Governance and Social Inequality.* Boulder, Colorado: Lynne Rienner, pp. 103–30.

Held, David, McGrew, Anthony, Goldblatt, David and Perraton, Jonathan (1999) *Global Transformations: Politics, economics and culture.* Cambridge: Polity Press.

Hellinger, Daniel (1999) 'Electoral and Party Politics', in Julia Buxton and Nicola Phillips (eds), *Developments in Latin American Political Economy: States, markets and actors.* Manchester: Manchester University Press, pp. 49–71.

Hettne, Björn (1995) *Development Theory and the Three Worlds.* Harlow: Longman.

Hillman, Richard S. (ed.) (1996) *Understanding Contemporary Latin America.* Boulder, Colorado: Lynne Rienner.

Hofman, André A. (2000) *Economic Growth and Performance in Latin America.* Santiago: ECLAC.

Hoskin, Gary and Murillo, Gabriel (2001) 'Colombia's Perpetual Quest for Peace', *Journal of Democracy*, 12 (2): 32–45.

Huneeus, Carlos (2001) 'La Nueva Desigualdad: El dinero en las campañas', *La Tercera*, 15 December: 11.

Hunter, Wendy (1998) 'Civil-Military Relations in Argentina, Brazil, and Chile: Present trends, future prospects', in Felipe Agüero and Jeffrey Stark (eds), *Fault Lines of Democracy in Post-Transition Latin America*. Miami: North-South Center Press, pp. 299–322.

Huntington, Samuel (1968) *Political Order in Changing Societies*. New Haven: Yale University Press.

Huntington, Samuel (1991) *The Third Wave: Democratization in the late 20th century*. Norman: University of Oklahoma Press.

IADB (1998) *Facing Up to Inequality in Latin America: 1998–99 report on economic and social progress*. Washington DC: IADB.

IADB (2000) *Development Beyond Economics: Report on economic and social progress in Latin America 2000*. Washington DC: IADB.

IADB (2001) *Latin American Economic Policies*, 14 (Second Quarter). Washington DC: IADB

Ibarra, David and Mattar, Jorge (1998) 'La Economía de Cuba', *Revista de la Cepal*, 66: 29–37.

IESOP (2002) 'Informe Confidencial, Avance No. 140'. Quito: IESOP.

ILO (2001) *2001 Labour Overview: Latin America and the Caribbean*. Lima: ILO.

Insunza, Andrea and Urrutia, Pamela (2002) 'Las Desconocidas Campañas de la UDI en América Latina', *La Tercera*, 15 April: 4.

Joyce, Elizabeth (1997) *Latin America and the Multinational Drug Trade*. Basingstoke: Macmillan.

Kanbur, Ravi and Squire, Lyn (1999) *The Evolution of Thinking about Poverty: Exploring the interactions*. Washington DC: The World Bank.

Katz, Jorge and Stumpo, Giovanni (2001) 'Regímenes Sectoriales, Productividad y Competitividad Internacional', *Revista de la Cepal*, 75: 137–59.

Kaufman, Michael and Dilla Alfonso, Haroldo (eds) (1997) *Community Power and Grassroots Democracy: The transformation of social life*. London: Zed Books.

Kay, Cristóbal (1989) *Latin American Theories of Development and Underdevelopment*. London: Routledge.

Keen, Benjamin (ed.) (1996) *Latin American Civilization: History and society, 1492 to the present*. Boulder, Colorado: Westview Press.

Keen, Benjamin and Haynes, Keith (2000) *A History of Latin America*. 6th edn. Boston: Houghton Mifflin Company.

Kirby, Peadar (1997) *Poverty Amid Plenty: World and Irish development reconsidered*. Dublin: Trócaire and Gill & Macmillan.

Kirby, Peadar (2002) 'The World Bank or Polanyi: Markets, poverty and social well-being in Latin America', *New Political Economy*, 7 (2): 199–219.

Klein, Emilio and Tokman, Victor (2000) 'Social Stratification under Tension in a Globalized Era', *Cepal Review*, 72: 7–29.

Kliksberg, Bernardo (1999) 'Social Capital and Culture: Master keys to development', *Cepal Review*, 69: 83–102.

Korzeniewicz, Roberto Patricio and Smith, William C. (eds) (1996) *Latin America in the World Economy*. Westport, Connecticut: Greenwood Press.

Korzeniewicz, Roberto Patricio and Smith, William C. (2000) 'Poverty, Inequality and Growth in Latin America: Searching for the high road to globalization', *Latin American Research Review*, 35 (3): 7–54.

Kumar, Chetan (2000) 'Transnational Networks and Campaigns for Democracy', in Ann M. Florini (ed.), *The Third Force: The rise of transnational civil society*. Washington DC: Carnegie Endowment for International Peace, pp. 115–42.

Lander, Luis E. and López Maya, Margarita (2002) 'Venezuela, Golpe y Petróleo', unpublished article.

LaRosa, Michael and Mora, Frank O. (eds) (1999) *Neighborly Adversaries: Readings in US-Latin American relations*. Lanham, Maryland: Rowman and Littlefield.

Latin American Newsletters (2001) 'The War in Colombia: Peace or escalation?', Special Report June 2001. London: LAN.

Latinobarometro (2001), available at www.latinobarometro.org.

Leiva, Fernando I. (2001) '"Participation" and Social Control Under Chile's *Concertación* Governments', paper delivered at the Latin American Studies Association, Washington DC, September 2001.

LeoGrande, William M. (2000a) 'Cuba: The shape of things to come', in Susan Kaufman Purcell and David Rothkopf (eds), *Cuba: The contours of change*. Boulder, Colorado: Lynne Rienner, pp. 1–12.

LeoGrande, William M. (2000b) 'Conclusion: Cuba's dilemma, and ours', in Susan Kaufman Purcell and David Rothkopf (eds), *Cuba: The contours of change*. Boulder, Colorado: Lynne Rienner, pp. 127–31.

Lewis, Colin M. (1999) 'Argentina', in Julia Buxton and Nicola Phillips (eds), *Case Studies in Latin American Political Economy*. Manchester: Manchester University Press, pp. 33–61.

Lievesley, Geraldine (1999) *Democracy in Latin America: Mobilization, power and the search for a new politics*. Manchester: Manchester University Press.

Lloyd-Sherlock, Peter (1998) 'Inverted Targeting: Why public social spending in Latin America fails the neediest', Employment Studies Paper 21, University of Hertfordshire.

Londoño, Juan Luis and Székely, Miguel (1997) 'Sorpresas Distributivas Después de una Década de Reformas: América Latina en los noventas', Serie de Documentos de Trabajo 352. Washington DC: Inter-American Development Bank.

López Maya, Margarita (ed.) (1999) *Lucha Popular, Democracia, Neoliberalismo: Protesta popular en América Latina en los años de ajuste*. Caracas: Nueva Sociedad.

Lucas, Kintto (2000) *We Will Not Dance on Our Grandparents' Tombs: Indigenous uprisings in Ecuador*. London: CIIR.

Lucero, José Antonio (2001) 'Crisis and Contention in Eduador', *Journal of Democracy*, 12 (2): 59–73.

Lustig, Nora (ed.) (1995) *Coping with Austerity: Poverty and inequality in Latin America*. Washington DC: Brookings Institution.

Mainwaring, Scott P. (1999) *Rethinking Party Systems in the Third Wave of Democratization: The case of Brazil*. Stanford: Stanford University Press.

Mainwaring, Scott and Scully, Timothy (1995) *Building Democratic Institutions: Party systems in Latin America*. Stanford: Stanford University Press.

Mainwaring, Scott, O'Donnell, Guillermo and Valenzuela, J. Samuel (eds) (1992) *Issues in Democratic Consolidation: The New South American democracies in comparative perspective*. Notre Dame: University of Notre Dame Press.

Malloy, James M. and Seligson, Mitchell A. (eds) (1987) *Authoritarians and Democrats: Regime transition in Latin America*. Pittsburgh: University of Pittsburgh Press.

Manzetti, Luigi (ed.) (2000) *Regulatory Policy in Latin America: Post-privatization realities*. Miami: North-South Center Press.

Manzetti, Luigi and dell'Aquila, Marco (2000) 'Conclusions', in Luigi Manzetti (ed.), *Regulatory Policy in Latin America: Post-privatization realities*. Miami: North-South Center Press, pp. 281–4.

Marchand, Marianne H. (2001) 'North American Regionalisms and Regionalization in the 1990s', in Michael Schulz, Fredrik Söderbaum and Joakim Öjendal (eds), *Regionalization in a Globalizing World: A comparative perspective on forms, actors and processes*. London: Zed Books, pp. 198–210.

Mayorga, René Antonio (1995) *Antipolitica y Neopopulismo*. La Paz: Cebem.

Medina, Medófilo (2001) 'Chavez y la Globalización', *Revista Venezolana de Economia y Ciencias Sociales*, 7 (2): 115–28.

Miller, Eden (2002) 'Designing Freedom, Regulating a Nation: Socialist cybernetics in Allende's Chile', STS Working Paper No. 35, MIT Program in Science, Technology and Society. Boston: Massachusetts Institute of Technology.

Moguillansky, Graciela and Bielschowsky, Ricardo (2001) *Investment and Economic Reforms in Latin America*. Santiago: ECLAC.

Morales, Aurora (ed.) (2001) *Cuadernos Bolivarianos: Materiales para el estudio N. 1*. Caracas: MVR.

Morales, Mauricio and Bugueño, Rodrigo (2001) 'La UDI, Como Expression de la Nueva Derecha en Chile', *Estudios Sociales*, 107 (1): 215–48.

Morton, Adam David (2002) '"La Resurrección del Maíz": Globalisation, resistance and the Zapatistas', *Millennium*, 31 (1): 27–54.

Moulian, Tomás (1997) *Chile Actual: Anatomía de un mito*. Santiago: LOM.

Muñoz, Heraldo (2001) 'Good-bye U.S.A.?', in Joseph S. Tulchin and Ralph H. Espach (eds), *Latin America in the New International System*. Boulder Colorado: Lynne Rienner, pp. 73–90.

Muñoz, Heraldo and Tulchin, Joseph S. (eds) (1996) *Latin American Nations in World Politics*. 2nd edn. Boulder, Colorado: Westview Press.

Muñoz Gomá, Oscar (2001) *Estrategias de Desarrollo en Economías Emergentes: Lecciones de la experiencia Latinoamericana*. Santiago: FLACSO.

Narayan, Deepa, Chambers, Robert, Shah, Meera K. and Petesch, Patti (2000) *Crying Out for Change*. Oxford: Oxford University Press.

Nederveen Pieterse, Jan (2001) *Development Theory: Deconstructions/reconstructions*. London: Sage Publications.

Negrón, Marco (2000) 'La Catástrofe del Estado Vargas', *Nueva Sociedad*, 167: 37–46.

North, Douglass C. (1990) *Institutions, Institutional Change and Economic Performance*. New York: Cambridge University Press.

Ocampo, José Antonio (1998) 'Beyond the Washington Consensus: An ECLAC perspective', *Revista de la Cepal*, 66: 7–28.

O'Donnell, Guillermo, Schmitter, Philippe C. and Whitehead, Laurence (eds) (1986) *Transitions from Authoritarian Rule: Prospects for democracy*. Baltimore: Johns Hopkins University Press.

Ospina, Pablo (2000) 'Reflexiones Sobre el Transformismo: Movilización indígena y regimen politico en el Ecuador (1990–1998)', in Julie Massal and Marcelo Bonilla (eds), *Los Movimientos Sociales en las Democracias Andinas*. Quito: FLACSO, pp. 125–46.

Oxhorn, Philip (2001a) 'From Human Rights to Citizenship Rights? Recent trends in the study of Latin American social movements', *Latin American Research Review*, 36 (3): 163–82.

Oxhorn, Philip (2001b) 'La Construcción del Estado por la Sociedad Civil: La Ley de Participación Popular de Bolivia y el desafío de la democracia local',

Working Document, INDES. Washington DC: Inter-American Development Bank.

Parsons, Talcott (1951) *The Social System*. New York: The Free Press.

Pastor, Manuel Jr. (2000) 'After the Deluge? Cuba's potential as a market economy', in Susan Kaufman Purcell and David Rothkopf (eds), *Cuba: The contours of change*. Boulder, Colorado: Lynne Rienner, pp. 31–55.

Pastor, Robert A. (2000) 'Exiting the Labyrinth', *Journal of Democracy*, 11 (4): 20–4.

Pérez-Stable, Marifeli (1999) *The Cuban Revolution: Origins, course, and legacy*. 2nd edn. New York: Oxford University Press.

Petras, James (1999) *The Left Strikes Back: Class conflict in Latin America in the age of neoliberalism*. Boulder, Colorado: Westview Press.

Phillips, Lynne (ed.) (1998) *The Third Wave of Modernization in Latin America: Cultural perspectives on neoliberalism*. Wilmington, Delaware: Scholarly Resources.

Phillips, Nicola (1999) 'Global and Regional Linkages', in Julia Buxton and Nicola Phillips (eds), *Developments in Latin American Political Economy: States, markets and actors*. Manchester: Manchester University Press, pp. 72–90.

Pizarro Leongómez, Eduardo (1999) 'Colombia: En el ojo del huracán', *Nueva Sociedad* 163: 4–13.

PNUD (1998) *Desarrollo Humano en Chile 1998: Las paradojas de la modernizacion*. Santiago: PNUD.

PNUD (2000) *Desarrollo Humano en Chile 2000: Más sociedad para gobernar el futuro*. Santiago: PNUD.

Polanyi, Karl (1957) *The Great Transformation: The political and economic origins of our time*. Boston: Beacon Press. (Original edn, 1944.)

Power, Timothy J. (2001–2) 'Blairism Brazilian Style? Cardoso and the "Third Way" in Brazil', *Political Science Quarterly*, 116 (4): 611–36.

Purcell, Susan Kaufman (2000) 'Why the Cuban Embargo Makes Sense in a Post-Cold War World', in Susan Kaufman Purcell and David Rothkopf (eds), *Cuba: The Contours of Change*. Boulder, Colorado: Lynne Rienner, pp. 81–103.

Raczynski, Dagmar (ed.) (1995) *Strategies to Combat Poverty in Latin America*. Baltimore: Johns Hopkins Press.

Raczynski, Dagmar (2000) 'Overcoming Poverty in Chile', in Joseph S. Tulchin and Allison M. Garland (eds), *Social Development in Latin America: The politics of reform*. Boulder, Colorado: Lynne Rienner, pp. 119–48.

Radcliffe, Sarah A. (1999) 'Civil Society, Social Difference and Politics: Issues of identity and representation', in Robert N. Gwynne and Cristóbal Kay (eds), *Latin America Transformed: Globalization and modernity*. London: Arnold, pp. 203–23.

Radcliffe, Sarah A. and Westwood, Sallie (1996) *Remaking the Nation: Place, identity and politics in Latin America*. London: Routledge.

Ramirez-Vallejo, Jorge (2002) 'A Break for Coffee', *Foreign Policy*, September/October: 26–7.

Ramonet, Ignacio (2001) *Marcos: La dignidad rebelde*. Santiago: Le Monde Diplomatique.

Ribeiro, Darcy (1990) 'The Latin American People', in Leonardo Boff and Virgil Elizondo (eds), *1492–1992: The voice of the victims*. London: SCM Press.

Roberts, Kenneth M. (1998) *Deepening Democracy? The modern left and social movements in Chile and Peru*. Stanford: Stanford University Press.

Roberts, Paul Craig and Araujo, Karen LaFollette (1997) *The Capitalist Revolution in Latin America*. New York: Oxford University Press.

Robinson, William I. (2002) 'Globalisation as a Macro-Structural-Historical Framework of Analysis: The case of Central America', *New Political Economy*, 7 (2): 221–50.

Rodriguez, Mauricio (2002) 'Crisis Argentina es Peor que el Crash Chileno del '82 y de la UP', *La Tercera*, 28 April: 28–9.

Roett, Riordan (ed.) (1999) *Mercosur: Regional integration, world markets*. Boulder, Colorado: Lynne Rienner.

Rosenbluth, Guillermo (1994) 'The Informal Sector and Poverty in Latin America', *Cepal Review*, 52: 155–75.

Rostow, W.W. (1960) *The Stages of Economic Growth*. Cambridge: Cambridge University Press.

Rozenwurcel, Guillermo (2001) *Los Países del Mercosur Buscan su Lugar en el Mundo: El ALCA y la nueva agenda de negociaciones internacionales*. Buenos Aires: Friedrich Ebert Stiftung.

Sachs, Jeffrey and Larrain, Felipe (1999) 'Why Dollarization is More Straitjacket than Salvation', *Foreign Policy*, fall: 80–92.

Safford, Frank and Palacios, Marco (2002) *Colombia: Fragmented land, divided society*. New York: Oxford University Press.

Salazar, Gabriel and Pinto, Julio (1999) *Historia Contemporánea de Chile I: Estado, legitimidad, ciudadanía*. Santiago: LOM.

Sánchez, Gonzalo and Avilés, William (2001) 'Introduction', *Latin American Perspectives*, 28 (1): 5–11.

Schedler, Andreas (2000) 'The Democratic Revelation', *Journal of Democracy*, 11 (4): 5–19.

Schild, Veronica (1998) 'New Subjects of Rights? Women's movements and the construction of citizenship in the "new democracies"', in Sonia E. Alvarez, Evelina Dagnino and Arturo Escobar (eds), *Cultures of Politics, Politics of Cultures: Re-visioning Latin American social movements*. Boulder, Colorado: Westview Press, pp. 93–117.

Scholte, Jan Aart (2000) 'Global Civil Society', in Ngaire Woods (ed.), *The Political Economy of Globalization*. Basingstoke: Macmillan, pp. 173–201.

Schulz, Michael, Söderbaum, Fredrik and Öjendal, Joakim (eds) (2001) *Regionalization in a Globalizing World: A comparative perspective on forms, actors and processes*. London: Zed Books.

Schuurman, Frans J. (ed.) (2001) *Globalization and Development Studies: Challenges for the 21st century*. London: Sage.

Scott, Alan (1990) *Ideology and the New Social Movements*. London: Routledge.

Sen, Amartya (1999) *Development as Freedom*. Oxford: Oxford University Press.

Serbin, Andrés (1998) *Sunset over the Islands: The Caribbean in an age of global and regional challenges*. Basingstoke: Macmillan.

Serbin, Andrés (2001) 'Globalifóbicos vs. Globalitarios: Fortalezas y debilidades de una sociedad civil regional emergente', *Nueva Sociedad*, 176: 67–86.

Sheahan, John (1987) *Patterns of Development in Latin America: Poverty, repression and economic strategy*. Princeton: Princeton University Press.

Sheahan, John (1998) 'Changing Social Programs and Economic Strategies: Implications for poverty and inequality', *Latin American Research Review*, 33 (2): 185–96.

Shirk, David A. (2000) 'Vicente Fox and the Rise of the PAN', *Journal of Democracy*, 11 (4): 25–32.

Silva, Patricio (1999) 'The New Political Order in Latin America: Towards technocratic democracies?', in Robert N. Gwynne and Cristóbal Kay (eds), *Latin America Transformed: Globalization and modernity*. London: Arnold, pp. 51–65.

Skidmore, Thomas E. (1999) *Brazil: Five centuries of change*. New York: Oxford University Press.

Skidmore, Thomas E. and Smith, Peter H. (1997) *Modern Latin America*. 4th edn. Oxford: Oxford University Press.

Sklair, Leslie and Robbins, Peter T. (2002) 'Global Capitalism and Major Corporations from the Third World', *Third World Quarterly*, 23 (1): 81–100.

Smarth, Luc (1997) 'Popular Organizations and the Transition to Democracy in Haiti', in Michael Kaufman and Haroldo Dilla Alfonso (eds), *Community Power and Grassroots Democracy: The transformation of social life*. London: Zed Books, pp. 102–25.

Smith, Peter H. (1996) *Talons of the Eagle: Dynamics of US-Latin American relations*. Oxford: Oxford University Press.

Smith, Peter H. (2001) 'Strategic Options for Latin America', in Joseph S. Tulchin and Ralph H. Espach (eds), *Latin America in the New International System*. Boulder, Colorado: Lynne Rienner, pp. 35–72.

Smith, William C. and Korzeniewicz, Roberto Patricio (eds) (1997) *Politics, Social Change and Economic Restructuring in Latin America*. Miami: North-South Center Press.

Snyder, Richard (1999) 'After Neoliberalism: The politics of reregulation in Mexico', *World Politics*, 51: 173–204.

Spoor, Max (2000) *Two Decades of Adjustment and Agricultural Development in Latin America and the Caribbean*. Santiago: ECLAC.

Stallings, Barbara and Peres, Wilson (2000) *Growth, Employment, and Equity: The impact of the economic reforms in Latin America and the Caribbean*. Washington DC: Brookings Institution.

Stark, Jeffrey (1998) 'Globalization and Democracy in Latin America', in Felipe Agüero and Jeffrey Stark (eds), *Fault Lines of Democracy in Post-Transition Latin America*. Miami: North-South Center Press, pp. 67–96.

Stark, Jeffrey (ed.) (2001) *The Challenge of Change in Latin America and the Caribbean*. Miami: North-South Center Press.

Stavenhagen, Rodolfo (1997) 'Las Organizaciones Indígenas: Actores emergentes en América Latina', *Revista de la Cepal*, 62: 61–73.

Stein, Stanley J. and Stein, Barbara H. (1970) *The Colonial Heritage of Latin America: Essays on economic dependence in perspective*. Oxford: Oxford University Press.

Stiglitz, Joseph (1998) *More Instruments and Broader Goals: Moving towards the Post-Washington Consensus*. Helsinki: WIDER.

Stiglitz, Joseph (2001) 'The Role of the IMF in the Impending Global Slowdown', Los Angeles Times Syndicate International syndicated article, 19 November 2001.

Stiglitz, Joseph (2002) *Globalization and Its Discontents*. London: Allen Lane.

Stokes, Susan C. (1991) 'Politics and Latin America's Urban Poor: Reflections from a Lima shantytown', *Latin American Research Review*, 26 (2): 75–101.

Suchlicki, Jaime (2000) 'Castro's Cuba: Continuity instead of change', in Susan Kaufman Purcell and David Rothkopf (eds), *Cuba: The contours of change*. Boulder, Colorado: Lynne Rienner, pp. 57–79.

Suchlicki, Jaime (2001) *Mexico: From Montezuma to the fall of the PRI*. 2nd edn. Washington DC: Brassey's.

Sunkel, Osvaldo and Zuleta, Gustavo (1990) 'Neo-structuralism versus Neo-liberalism in the 1990s', *Cepal Review*, 42: 35–51.

Tardanico, Richard and Larín, Rafael Menjívar (eds) (1997) *Global Restructuring, Employment, and Social Inequality in Urban Latin America*. Miami: North-South Center Press.

Tedesco, Laura (1999) 'NGOs and the Retreat of the State: The hidden dangers', in Julia Buxton and Nicola Phillips (eds), *Developments in Latin American Political Economy: States, markets and actors*. Manchester: Manchester University Press, pp. 131–45.

Teichman, Judith (2002) 'Private Sector Power and Market Reform: Exploring the domestic origins of Argentina's meltdown and Mexico's policy failures', *Third World Quarterly*, 23 (3): 491–512.

Tendler, Judith (2000) 'Safety Nets and Service Delivery: What are social funds really telling us?', in Joseph S. Tulchin and Allison M. Garland (eds), *Social Development in Latin America: The politics of reform*. Boulder, Colorado: Lynne Rienner, pp. 87–115.

Thorp, Rosemary (1986) 'Latin America and the International Economy from the First World War to the World Depression', in Leslie Bethell (ed.), *Cambridge History of Latin America*, vol. IV. Cambridge: Cambridge University Press, pp. 57–81.

Thorp, Rosemary (1998) *Progress, Poverty and Exclusion: An economic history of Latin America in the 20th century*. Washington DC: Inter-American Development Bank.

Tokatlian, Juan Gabriel (2001) 'El Plan Colombia: De la Guerra interna a la intervención internacional?', in *Anuario Social y Político de América Latina y El Caribe*. Caracas: FLACSO and Nueva Sociedad, pp. 77–85.

Tomassini, Luciano (ed.) (2002) *La Modernización del Estado en América Latina: Experiencias y desafíos*. Santiago: LOM.

Topik, Steven (2001) 'Karl Polanyi and the Creation of the "Market Society"', in Miguel Angel Centeno and Fernando López-Alves (eds), *The Other Mirror: Grand theory through the lens of Latin America*. Princeton: Princeton University Press, pp. 81–104.

Torres Torres, Felipe and Gasca Zamora, José (2001) *Ingreso y Alimentación de la Población en el México del Siglo XX*. Mexico City: Instituto de Investigaciones Económicas, UNAM.

Treat, Jonathan (2002) 'Plan Puebla-Panama's Merida Summit', Americas Program. Silver City, New Mexico: Interhemispheric Resource Center (available at: www.americaspolicy.org).

Tulchin, Joseph S. and Espach, Ralph H. (eds) (2001) *Latin America in the New International System*. Boulder, Colorado: Lynne Rienner.

Tulchin, Joseph S. and Garland, Allison M. (eds) (2000) *Social Development in Latin America: The politics of reform*. Boulder, Colorado: Lynne Rienner.

Tulchin, Joseph S., with Romero, Bernice (eds) (1995) *The Consolidation of Democracy in Latin America*. Boulder, Colorado: Lynne Rienner.

UNDP (1999) *Human Development Report 1999*. New York: Oxford University Press.

UNDP (2000) *Human Development Report 2000*. New York: Oxford University Press.

UNDP (2001) *Human Development Report 2001*. New York: Oxford University Press.

UNICEF (2001) *Profiting from Abuse*. New York: UNICEF.

Utzig, José Eduardo (1998) 'La Izquierda en el Gobierno: Notas sobre el PT en Porto Alegre', *Nueva Sociedad*, 157: 107–24.

Vellinga, Menno (1998) 'The Changing Role of the State in Latin America', in Menno Vellinga (ed.), *The Changing Role of the State in Latin America*. Boulder, Colorado: Westview Press, pp. 1–25.

Veltmeyer, Henry, Petras, James and Vieux, Steve (1997) *Neoliberalism and Class Conflict in Latin America: A comparative perspective on the political economy of structural adjustment*. Basingstoke: Macmillan.

Vilas, Carlos M. (1998) 'La Izquierda Latinoamericana: Búsquedas y desafíos', *Nueva Sociedad*, 157: 64–74.

Ward, John (1997) *Latin America: Development and conflict since 1945*. London: Routledge.

Weaver, Frederick Stirton (2000) *Latin America in the World Economy: Mercantile colonialism to global capitalism*. Boulder, Colorado: Westview Press.

Weyland, Kurt (1999) 'Populism in the Age of Neoliberalism', in Michael L. Conniff (ed.), *Populism in Latin America*. Tuscaloosa: University of Alabama Press, pp. 172–90.

Wiarda, Howard J. and Kline, Harvey F. (1996) *Latin American Politics and Development*, 4th edn. Boulder, Colorado: Westview Press.

Williams, David and Young, Tom (1994) 'Governance, the World Bank and Liberal Theory', *Political Studies*, XLII: 84–100.

Williamson, Edwin (1992) *The Penguin History of Latin America*. London: Penguin.

Williamson, John (1993) 'Democracy and the "Washington Consensus"', *World Development*, 21 (8): 1329–36.

Willis, Eliza, Garman, Christopher da C.B. and Haggard, Stephan (1999) 'The Politics of Decentralization in Latin America', *Latin American Research Review*, 34 (1): 7–56.

Wise, Carol (ed.) (1998) *The Post-NAFTA Political Economy: Mexico and the Western Hemisphere*. Pennsylvania: The Pennsylvania State University Press.

Woods, Ngaire (ed.) (2000) *The Political Economy of Globalization*. Basingstoke: Macmillan.

Woodward, Ralph Lee (1999) *Central America: A nation divided*. 3rd edn. Oxford: Oxford University Press.

World Bank (1993) *Latin America and the Caribbean: A decade after the debt crisis*. New York: World Bank.

World Bank (2000) *World Development Report 2000/01: Attacking poverty*. New York: Oxford University Press.

World Bank (2001) *World Development Report 2002: Building institutions for markets*. New York: Oxford University Press.

Yelvington, Kevin A. (1997) 'Patterns of Ethnicity, Class, and Nationalism', in Richard R. Hillman (ed.), *Understanding Contemporary Latin America*. Boulder, Colorado: Lynne Rienner, pp. 209–36.

Zapata, Francisco (2001) 'Los Sindicatos Latinoamericanos Frente a la Apertura Económica', unpublished paper. Mexico City: Colegio de Mexico.

Zimbalist, Andrew (2000) 'Whither the Cuban Economy?', in Susan Kaufman Purcell and David Rothkopf (eds), *Cuba: The contours of change*. Boulder, Colorado: Lynne Rienner, pp. 13–29.

Index

This index is in alphabetical, word–by–word order. It does not cover the contents list or preface. Location references are to page number, e.g.:

academic analysis 2–4

indicates that information relating to this aspect can be found starting on page 2 and finishing on page 4

Argentina, economic crisis 202(Box 11.4)

indicates that information relating this aspect can be found in Box 11.4 which is on page 202, (similarly Table).

Abbreviations: GDP = gross domestic product; Tab = Table